The Windsor Diaries

The Windsor Diaries

1940–45

ALATHEA FITZALAN HOWARD

Foreword by Isabella Naylor-Leyland

Edited by Celestria Noel

HODDER &
STOUGHTON

First published in Great Britain in 2020 by Hodder & Stoughton
An Hachette UK company

2

Copyright in the Foreword and Diaries © Isabella Naylor-Leyland 2020

Map illustration on endpapers © Florence Houston

A CIP catalogue record for this title is available from the British Library

Hardback ISBN 978 1 529 32808 0
Trade Paperback ISBN 978 1 529 32809 7
eBook ISBN 978 1 529 32811 0

Typeset in Simoncini Garamond by Palimpsest Book Production Ltd,
Falkirk, Stirlingshire

Printed and bound in Great Britain by
Clays Ltd, Elcograf S.p.A.

Hodder & Stoughton policy is to use papers that are natural, renewable
and recyclable products and made from wood grown in sustainable forests.
The logging and manufacturing processes are expected to conform
to the environmental regulations of the country of origin.

Hodder & Stoughton Ltd
Carmelite House
50 Victoria Embankment
London EC4Y 0DZ

www.hodder.co.uk

In memory of Alathea

Contents

Foreword

Alathea came into my life in 1975, when I met my husband, Philip. I was seventeen, and she was his maternal aunt, aged forty-two. She was married to the Hon. Edward Ward, younger brother of the Earl of Dudley. To me they seemed, and indeed were, a very old-fashioned couple.

She wasn't physically attractive and had an odd gait, but I liked her immediately, and over time found her beautiful. She was cool and composed, dispassionate, quaint, undemonstrative, generous, quite forthright and loved to laugh, though she wasn't always quite sure how to go about it. She was also kind, impractical and funny, though she didn't always mean to be. I came to adore her. When she died in 2001 she left me her diaries of which there are sixty-four (one per year) and in her words 'not <u>one</u> day's exception from 1940!'*

It was only when I started to read them that I discovered what sadness she had felt during her life.

Alathea Alys Gwendolen Mary Fitzalan Howard was the elder daughter of the second and last Viscount Fitzalan of Derwent, and of Joyce Langdale, who later became Countess Fitzwilliam. She was born at Norfolk House, Sheffield, on 24 November 1923. Had she been a boy she would have succeeded as Duke of Norfolk, since her father's first cousin Bernard, the

---

* The process of editing the diaries for publication means that not all of the entries are reproduced.

16th duke, had only daughters. Alathea's mother could not have anticipated at the time the full poignancy of her telegram to her maternal grandparents: 'Alas, no tassel'.

In the event, the title went sideways to her third cousin, Baron Howard of Glossop. In 1956, Alathea writes: 'Anne, Miles's wife, produced a son yesterday, which has caused great excitement in the family, as he will one day be the Duke of Norfolk.' And then she adds: 'I do wish I'd been a boy!' She would have been Earl Marshal and, as such, played a major role in state occasions after 1975, when he died. Indeed years later in Lausanne, where she eventually lived, watching the State Opening of Parliament, she writes: 'How busy I'd have been.'

Her mother sprang from the closely linked world of old Catholic families, such as the Stourtons, premier barons of England. In this she took an intense, though muted pride. Joyce was a woman of style, taste and wit, but had little interest in children and took not the faintest pleasure in their company. She was separated from her husband and moved between Houghton, her family home in Yorkshire, and London.

It wasn't always the case that the diaries would come my way. The only inkling I ever had of Alathea's intention was once when I found her writing in what looked like a journal. When I asked her what she was doing, she replied, 'You know perfectly well – and you'll just have to wait!'

In 1962 she left them in her will to a friend, writing, 'I trust her one day to do what she thinks fit with them.' Then in 1972 she writes: 'Sometimes I see them stretching along a long shelf at Arundel* and perhaps this is what I should

---

* Arundel Castle is the principal seat of the Fitzalan Howard family.

one day arrange.' In 1987 she repeats: 'I plan one day to leave all my diaries in the archives at Arundel, to be read perhaps by someone 100 years hence out of curiosity.' And then in 1990: 'Philip and Isabella are interested – or curious – but that's a bit near and one can't rely on Tom and Violet!'* So, I felt a little triumphant that they ended up in this house so are now stretching along a long shelf at Milton. In 1974 she considered leaving her jewellery to The Queen, but later had another change of heart. I was quite pleased about that too!

At the beginning of the war Alathea was sent to live with her rather staid, old-fashioned paternal grandfather and maiden aunt Magdalen at Cumberland Lodge in Windsor Park, her mother visiting rarely. Alathea's father, known as Boydey, had been wounded in the First World War and one gets the feeling was very fond of his daughter, but his marriage was troubled and he was ill equipped to deal with a teenager. He spent most of his time in London and came to Cumberland Lodge at weekends. Alathea had one adored younger sister, Elizabeth Anne, whom she seldom saw.

Old Lord Fitzalan, a widower – his wife had died in 1938 – was a distinguished elder statesman and leading Roman Catholic layman. Cumberland Lodge had been loaned to him for his lifetime as a grace-and-favour house by King George V in 1924. Lord Fitzalan had been the last Viceroy of Ireland, from 1921 until 1922, the first Catholic since the Reformation to hold the post. His family home, Derwent Hall, in Derbyshire, was compulsorily purchased in 1939 and drowned for the creation of Ladybower reservoir, serving Sheffield. He brought many fixtures and fittings from

---

* My two eldest children.

Derwent to Cumberland Lodge, which remain there to this day.

In Helen Hudson's *Cumberland Lodge* she writes:

The two great passions of Lord Fitzalan were his Church and his politics; in both spheres he wielded influence and his advice was sought by princes and leaders of both Church and state. Rosary was recited each evening at six thirty. Any member of the household could come but the family were expected, even if they were not all as devout as Lord Fitzalan, who said prayers aloud when driving his car.

She also tells this story:

When Lady Fitzalan died, her body awaiting burial was laid in the chapel surrounded by candles, while two nuns kept prayerful watch. It so happens that a burglar chose this night to break into the lodge. Creeping upstairs he saw a dim light through a slightly open door, peeped in and was aghast at the sight that met his eyes; the nuns were hidden from view, and hearing a low voice saying, 'Come in,' he thought the dead had spoken and took to his heels in fright.

Cumberland Lodge had played its part in the Abdication Crisis. Stanley Baldwin, the then prime minister and a friend of Lord Fitzalan, held a meeting there, with the King's private secretary Alexander Hardinge, among others. The purpose was to impress upon all the extent of the King's infatuation with Wallis Simpson. All the signatures of those present during the crisis talks are in the visitors' book, dated from 16 to 19 October. A month later the King invited Baldwin to Buckingham Palace to express his desire to marry Wallis.

After Lord Fitzalan died in 1947, Alathea wrote: 'I am to have the visitors' book, which I'm delighted about as it combines many famous people with all my own friends.' The first and last signatures in it are those of the King and Queen. In her will she asked for it to be returned to the Lodge. It felt quite an emotional journey for Philip and me to be able to return the book to where it had been all those years ago. The house is now in the hands of St Catharine's, an educational foundation.

Alathea spent a great deal of time whirling up and down the Long Walk in Windsor Great Park on her bicycle, past the statue of the Copper Horse to the Castle. In April 1942, the diarist James Lees-Milne, a family friend, during one of his visits to Cumberland Lodge, described her as 'the Fitzalans' pretty granddaughter aged 18, frail and freckled'. How pleased she would have been to read that.

Seen through the eyes of a teenager, it was a gloomy household, and because it was wartime, food was often sparse. In his *Ancestral Voices*, Lees-Milne mentions one luncheon as consisting only of soup padded out with potato. He describes Alathea's father as a 'tiny rather wizened insignificant man with a wooden leg', which I find puzzling as no one else ever mentions this. Of Magdalen, he says, 'sad as ever, with heavy folds of tumbling wispy hair, parted in the middle of her head and looped behind somehow'. His bedroom was stuffy and old-fashioned, and Mass the following day seemed quite eccentric.

The chapel floor and the prie-dieu were covered with red plush carpet. Alathea came in late, snatched a black veil and adjusted it as she knelt. The ceremony, the ladies in veils, was served by the eighty-seven-year-old Lord Fitzalan. The priest was crippled with arthritis and could 'barely move with a stick. He crawls at a snail's pace and he and Lord F support each other from falling over.' Yet Lees-Milne found the scene impressive and enjoyed it. He visited once when Lord Fitzalan was ill in bed. Lees-Milne said: 'I believe, Sir, that you just go to bed whenever you hear I'm coming to stay', to which Fitzalan replied, 'It is you who keep away when you hear that I am up and about.' He also remembered some children remarking that Lord Fitzalan looked so old that he should never have been allowed out, and that Magdalen looked like a fish with a red neck.

This is the world in which we find Alathea as the diaries start.

Her only real solace was the friendship she had with Princess Elizabeth and Princess Margaret, who had been brought to Windsor for safety during the war. The war was never very far away, as the Park itself came under attack and people were killed there. In *Our Princesses at Home,* a book of photographs published in 1940 to show the princesses' daily lives, Lisa Sheridan wrote: 'Queen Elizabeth most desired for her children to be surrounded by affection and happiness.' I think that Alathea, living next door and already a friend, was an incidental beneficiary of this, and it shaped her life during the war.

In the diaries, there is a great deal about Alathea's time with the young princesses, and, though clearly very fond of them, she is not averse to recording things as she sees them. For instance she describes Prince Philip as 'not my type'. It is quite something to think that Princess Elizabeth was fourteen when she first mentioned him to Alathea.

In her diary entry for 25 June 1947 Alathea writes: 'Sonia told me that Princess E's engagement is imminent and that the wedding is fixed for the autumn. This is a dead secret and I couldn't ask her more, but I suppose she heard this through the Wernhers. She says he has kissed her and the ring is already bought.'

Despite the six-year age gap between them, Alathea adored Princess Margaret. In *Ma'am Darling*, Craig Brown includes Princess Margaret's Christmas List from 1936 and it is virtually identical to Alathea's. I wondered if one copied the other.

The diaries date from New Year's Eve 1939 to January 2001, when Alathea became too ill to write. Feeling quite daunted by the thought of ploughing through them, I nevertheless felt it an honour and a responsibility. I began to read them slowly. Suddenly I was hooked and proceeded to read them voraciously without stopping until I felt my life entwined with hers. I read around seven before it occurred to me to make notes. I then started to annotate them and eventually reread the first seven to complete this task. I became so engrossed in Alathea's life that I found myself going into Ferragamo, the shoe shop, which I would never normally frequent, just to imagine Alathea there, slipping her elegant feet into their rather expensive shoes.

Having dipped into various other biographies and diaries to see if I could glean any relevant information, I thought I might as well look up Princess Margaret on Wikipedia, just in case I found anything new about the war years. I'd long been told that Wikipedia is not to be relied on for accurate information, but in this case I found the surprisingly accurate and illuminating 'Princess Margaret spent much of her childhood with her parents and sister.'

What became very obvious as I read was Alathea's hope that some day the diaries would be recognised in some way or other. Nonetheless they weren't written with this in mind and there is nothing self-conscious about them. She felt that at the very least they were 'a portrait of an age no longer existing'.

As early as March 1940 and again in 1941 she writes of her wish to have them published.

In 1962 she writes:

I am seriously worried over what would happen to my diaries should I die, as Eddie says he would burn them because they are such nonsense and that to me would be even worse than [his] reading them! After all the hours of my life I have spent writing them, all the anguish and all the joy I have poured into them, I could not bear that, as I still think one day, they may be interesting to a future generation as a complete record of a way of life. I must take some steps to protect them.

In 1968:

I wonder if anyone will ever read my diaries . . . will unearth them and be interested to read how a person lived and thought and loved and laughed every day.'

In 1972:

'I know I don't lead a very interesting life . . . but perhaps what we think and read and eat might be of greater interest. But the problem is what to do with them with no descendants?

And in 1990:

I wrote to Ronald Blythe concerning my diaries – what arrangements to make for their preservation and possible publication after my death . . . he advises me to ask Philip to leave them to some library or record office and if possible to get someone to read them now, or some of them, to get an idea when and by whom they might be published. But who? I am convinced they will be of interest to someone in the future, a picture of social life over more than half a century and of a human life with all its dramas and sorrows and hopes and ambitions.

In 2000, a year before her death, she writes: 'My diaries must be preserved and published.' She considered ending the record just once, in 1953, when she was thirty: 'I have often thought lately of giving it up but I can't – so much of my life for so many years has gone into it & it is sometimes the only comfort I have.'

The quality of writing is good, in some parts beautiful, and the minutiae of everyday life is absorbing. At times, reading it made me think of Siegfried Sassoon's journals in 1921: 'Lunched alone; does that matter? (Grilled turbot and apple pudding, if you want full details.)'

The diaries fall into three parts: the war, her marriage, her widowhood. When I talked this through with my good friend Celestria Noel, who knew Alathea and was her distant cousin, she thought that the war years at Windsor were the best place to start, and this is where you will first find Alathea, soon after the outbreak of the Second World War.

A lonely, unhappy childhood with her grandfather and aunt Magdalen, whom she occasionally refers to as 'The Tigress', saddened and frustrated Alathea. She was unable to comprehend the apparent lack of parental love and understanding she experienced. In later life she once said to me, without a shred of self-pity: 'My dear, if I'd come from a different background I'd have been taken into care.' Her obsession with the eighteenth century, and the belief that she might have been Marie Antoinette in a former life, was perhaps a form of escapism brought on by unhappiness.

Alathea's mother undermined her confidence by comparing her to her friends: 'Mummy thought I had a vague puffy look, not "on the spot" like Brita, who is gay and knows her stuff, typical expressions of Mummy – a terrible wave of depression came over me.' It is hardly surprising that Alathea was so ill equipped to cope with the outside world that when she failed her nursing exams she 'collapsed into uncontrolled sobs'. She hated being called Howard (nurses were then addressed by their surnames) and being told she would never make a nurse: 'I began crying again and had to bathe my eyes thoroughly with rose water.'

Many years later, Alathea reread her diary from this time: 'I have to say that I don't really find myself *sympathique* – I made such a fuss about my work. I suppose we were a lot of spoiled girls (!) doing unaccustomed drudgery and my attitude towards the Royal Family was like that of Louis XIV's courtiers at Marly.' She regretted not being kinder to her admirer Miles Marriott and felt she was wrong in being 'so unfriendly and cold'.

The diaries were Alathea's greatest friend. She confided in them completely and I think they made her a little more aware of what was happening to her in trying to make sense of her life. She wrote down all her hopes, fears and frustrations. She could tell her diary what no one else knew, use it as a security, a perfect confidant. Perhaps one of the most touching comments is written in 1998 when she is rereading her entries about the last weeks of her sister's life, and the tragic days of her death and funeral. 'What a companion my diary has been to me for more than half a century! Not one day unrecorded in all that time!'

In later life, despite a lack of any formal education, she became an excellent linguist, speaking French, German, Spanish and Russian. It was said she spoke with ease and elegance but with an aristocratic carelessness over accent. In the diaries, she used her languages when she wanted to ensure complete secrecy, particularly Russian! Also in later life her impracticality showed in her Red Cross charity work, in which she sorted bags and bags of out-of-date pills on her bathroom floor. As one might imagine there were very stringent rules and requirements, which she found difficult to adhere to. I remember her saying to me 'I find it quite impossible to understand which pills are which and which go into which container . . .'

In 1994 Alathea met royal biographer Sarah Bradford. 'I was able to tell her all about my childhood with the princesses and stress what happy cheerful places Buckingham Palace and Windsor were, contrary to what the press now try to make out.'

The Queen kept up their friendship, even though Alathea lived abroad, and occasionally they would lunch together. She was always far too discreet to reveal the details of any conversation that passed between them, but gave my family and me a brief outline of the lunch, leaving anything more interesting to the diaries. Alathea was quite frugal but would take a taxi to Buckingham Palace, so that she could safely wear some of her jewellery. Afterwards she would put it into a battered carrier bag and take the tube home. When you read the diaries, you will discover that she loved clothes. Years ago, she was thrilled to be upgraded on a flight and said to me: 'I think they chose me because I looked rather smart.'

A few months before she died, she went to a ball at Windsor Castle and was pleased to be one of the few to be placed on The Queen's table. She had a wonderful evening: 'The Queen Mother was so sweet remembering the old days.'

In 2000 Alathea spent Christmas with my family and me. During that time it became clear she was not at all well, and by the New Year she had been diagnosed with an advanced malignant brain tumour. The doctors recommended she did not travel back to Lausanne but received treatment in England so we looked after her during her final months.

While she was with us I felt it would be nice to surround her with plants and flowers, and when she went into the hospital nearby for treatment, they went with her. A few years later, on reading her diaries about an earlier visit to Milton, I came across: 'My only criticism in the house is that Isabella puts too <u>many</u> pots of flowers all over the place.'

During one of her spells in hospital she had two bunches of flowers delivered and I couldn't resist looking at the cards to find out who had sent them. One was from Jools Holland, the other The Queen.

Alathea's faith never left her despite (or because of) the rigours of her religious upbringing. She went to Lourdes every year to help the sick and was made a Dame of the Order of Malta, of which she was very proud.

When she was nearing the end, we were lucky to have a wonderful constant in Anthony Freemantle, an old family friend, with a slight penchant for the bottle. When Philip and I were away with two of our children in the school holidays, he came to Milton and took over the supervision of care. He was ably assisted by some superb nurses, our daughter Violet, and by the staff, including the butler and housekeeper, whom Anthony referred to as David I and David II. Anthony would write us daily reports of her progress, or lack of. During that time David I took a call. He told me that he recognised the woman's incredibly familiar voice but couldn't put a name to it. She asked to speak to Mrs Ward. 'Who can I say is calling?' he enquired.

'Just say it's a friend,' said the familiar voice.

As he put the call through it suddenly dawned on him that it was The Queen. He couldn't resist afterwards asking Anthony if this was indeed the case. Anthony gave a knowing smile . . .

Anthony wrote a lovely obituary but sadly it was never published: the Grim Reaper and hence the obituarists were particularly busy that March. Among other jewels he wrote: 'Gentle and undaunted, she was always equal to her circumstances.' Also, as her health deteriorated and she completely lost her appetite, Alathea would firmly decline even the smallest sip of soup with a simple 'Shan't.'

Over that time Anthony, in his seventies, and my elder daughter Violet, who was seventeen, became very close. She reminded me the other day that they had had dinner in the small dining room at Milton every night, then sat up, chatted and visited Alathea together. 'He was very nice to be with while you were away, despite getting blind drunk most nights. We helped her write her last diary entry.'

I sincerely hope that nothing in these diaries will offend the Royal Family, as that is the last thing Alathea would have wanted. I like to think the childish comments that often appear are just that and nothing more. I do regret not writing to The Queen Mother to say that the kindness she showed to Alathea in the war years at Cumberland Lodge clearly made all the difference. I feel the inclusion in their family life and their warmth made Alathea's life more bearable. They showed her real imaginative kindness.

I also hope that the reader will understand Alathea's mindset during the war. Despite the dropping of bombs, which naturally terrified her, the loss of friends, and many nights spent in the cellar, the preoccupations of a teenager loomed large. I feel she dealt with her war by thinking and writing of happy things to pass the time and get through.

Alathea died at Milton, in what had always been her room, on 5 March 2001.

Thank you, Alathea, for entrusting me with your dearest possession. I only hope that I have honoured your wish in the way you would have wanted.

Isabella Naylor-Leyland
Milton
2020

1940

EGHAM 76

THE ROYAL LODGE,
THE GREAT PARK,
WINDSOR,
BERKS.

22nd April
1940.

Dear Alathea,

Just a line to thank you for the very useful book you gave me for my birthday. Now I shall know all the books I have read and the ones I want to read.

I hope you liked the film on Saturday. I think the whale looked very frightening!

I do hope the noisy old sheep do not disturb Lord FitzAlan or you.

Thanking you again.
With love from
Lilibet

A thank-you letter from Princess Elizabeth.

Rossley, Gloucestershire

Monday, 1 January

I'm staying here with Sonia.* It's a small country club. S and I sleep together. In morning we went for walk with grown-ups over the hills. Still snowy and very slippery.

Haverland, Norfolk

Tuesday, 9 January

I arrived at Brita's† by train. We went for long ride in the morning. I rode Topsy, a sweet Dartmoor pony. We had a melancholy conversation about life in general and both felt very sad. It is as if a light has gone out of both our lives. In afternoon we just messed about outside and rode ponies in from the field bareback. Played bezique after tea.

---

* Sonia Graham-Hodgson was the daughter of Dr H. K. (later Sir Harold) Graham Hodgson, an eminent radiologist. She came to know Princess Elizabeth through playing in the gardens at Hamilton Place, in London, where the young princesses played before they moved to Buckingham Palace. By 1940 she had become a friend of Alathea and was living with her family near Chertsey, which is just within cycling distance of Cumberland Lodge.
† Brita Cederstrom was the daughter of Baron Rolf Cederstrom. The Cederstroms lived in Norfolk in 1940, then moved near Newmarket.

Friday, 12 January

Felt <u>very</u> happy, then a tragedy occurred. I had a wire from Mummy at lunch to say how cross she was I hadn't written. When we went out Brita told me that Baroness C* was very annoyed with me and that she thought me perfectly half-witted. I cannot endure being thought stupid and was <u>miserable</u> but I enjoyed the last part of the afternoon as someone lent me some skates so we skated on the lake. Baroness C very nice in evening. I've forgiven her, as I know she calls everyone stupid.

Cumberland Lodge, Windsor Great Park

Friday, 19 January

Quite pleased to be back really. Elizabeth Anne and Ming-Ming† here.

Sunday, 21 January

Lilibet rang up to ask me to skate. She, Margaret and the King picked me up in the car and we drove to the lake in front of the house. Swept it first.‡ Queen came down and watched. Played hockey with about six other people – policemen and chauffeurs etc from Royal Lodge. <u>Great </u>fun. Lilibet is <u>so</u> much nicer by herself than at Guides.

---

* Brita's mother, Baroness Cederstrom.
† Ming-Ming, real name Miss Smith, nanny to Elizabeth Anne.
‡ They swept the loose snow away to make a smoother surface.

Tuesday, 23 January

Princesses picked me up in car and took me to skate on lake at Frogmore. <u>Lovely</u> lake for skating, as islands and bridges to go under.

Wednesday, 24 January

Yesterday and today the princesses wore kilts and short green coats and their hoods. They picked me up by the drive gates and we skated like yesterday at Frogmore. Great fun skating. I can go backwards a bit now.

Thursday, 25 January

I changed after lessons and Ming-Ming, EA and I walked over to Royal Lodge to tea. Crawfie* there. Princesses showed EA and Ming-Ming over the Little House† before tea, which we all had downstairs, and Ming-Ming had hers in nursery. Played various games after till about six thirty, when we left. Walked home in dark.

Saturday, 26 January

<u>Elizabeth Anne's sixth birthday.</u>

---

* Marion Crawford, known as 'Crawfie', was the Scottish governess to the princesses and had been since 1936, when they were still living in London. She stayed with them until 1947. She was tricked into writing a memoir, *The Little Princesses*, which was ghosted by a romantic novelist called Dorothy Black.
† Playhouse in the garden of Royal Lodge given to the princesses by the people of Wales.

Saturday, 3 February

Went to Winifred Hardinge's* Guides at the York Hall. About fourteen altogether. Lilibet came and Crawfie watched.

Saturday, 10 February

I went to Guides at two thirty. Third patrol made, of which PE is the leader. Very stuffy. I think we ought to go outside, so does Crawfie. My patrol is going to be called Blue Tits.

Thursday, 15 February

The princesses came to tea. Monty† came with them as Crawfie in London. Played games in the hall – blind man's buff, charades, etc. Miss Dunham‡ and Monty <u>so</u> funny together doing their charade! Then detective came for them and they walked back in the dark.

Friday, 16 February

It is <u>too</u> awful – EA has worn her green corduroy trousers to go out in today. How <u>can </u>anyone wear trousers to go out, here too above all, as it's not typically country.

---

* Winifred Hardinge, daughter of Sir Alexander Hardinge. He was private secretary to King George VI, having served Edward VIII. In 1940 they lived in Winchester Tower, Windsor Castle. Win was slightly older than Alathea, and had a younger sister, Libby.

† Mrs Montaudon-Smith, known as 'Monty' was second governess to the princesses. She was French and a Catholic. She sometimes went to mass with Alathea, whose governess she had been for a time in London before the war.

‡ Dulcibel Dunham was governess to Alathea in London and for her first year at Cumberland Lodge.

Friday, 23 February

Miss D infuriated me in lessons. Just because I got muddled up with how many pints there are in a quart, she said that a duchess – even the Queen – knows that, so if the Queen knows it, perhaps I would consent to learn it! Stupid idiot. How can I remember all these tables? Then in the afternoon she said why didn't I come up and tell her it was raining? If she can't see for herself out of the window whether it's raining or not, I'm sorry for her! Very dull walk in afternoon round Copper Horse. I do like Miss D, but she does annoy me sometimes and like all clever people she's extraordinarily stupid!

Monday, 26 February

EA and Ming-Ming went away in morning. I felt quite sad and lonely when they'd first gone.

Tuesday, 27 February

Mass eight thirty. I biked to the Hardinges for lunch. I looked at their photos of the princesses in Scotland and one of Lilibet in shorts!

Friday, 8 March

I've got a funny feeling in my tummy. I think it means I'll start 'it' soon. I hope it does, as all my friends have. I had to go for a walk with Grandpa in the afternoon in spite of my efforts to escape at lunch. As a matter of fact, it wasn't too dull as I kept him talking about wild animals in India, but I can't go on doing that.

Tuesday, 12 March

Peace treaty between the Finns and the Russians signed. Everyone very upset about it. A man shot dead at a meeting in London by an Indian.

Wednesday, 13 March

I changed and walked over to Royal Lodge. <u>Pouring,</u> so I had to go all in mackintosh etc. Had tea. We played charades. <u>Great</u> fun. Monty there, of course. Princesses wore navy kilts and navy jerseys.

Saturday, 16 March

I biked into Windsor. Bought some hair ribbon and biked back. I got nearly to the top of the Long Walk when I saw the King in the distance going for a walk. I tactfully went on without looking back but when I was pushing my bike over the grass, I saw him again, so I curtsied and went on. Crawfie told me at Guides in the afternoon that he'd seen me and waved to me but I didn't wave back! I'm rather cross I didn't see him wave! I had to take over the Guides this time and I got on very well. Both Lilibet and Crawfie were <u>sweet</u> to me. Crawfie said she expected the princesses would be seeing a lot of me over Easter and she asked me significantly when I was going to Yorkshire. Awful girl came to give us physical jerks and we had to take our shoes off!

Wednesday, 20 March

I secretly hoped, but hardly dared to believe, that I would go to Royal Lodge to tea! So imagine my delight when Monty rang up to ask me! We all dragged an old garden cart down to the rubbish heap below the vicarage and filled it with old iron etc and dragged it back to the garden (the detective helping)! Then we played charades indoors. Margaret's rather silly but she's very sweet. Lilibet's stopped wearing socks. Crawfie kissed me goodbye! Heavenly day.

Friday, 29 March

Annabel Newman* came just before tea. She doesn't really look more grown-up except that she had a fur coat and a <u>little</u> lipstick. We talked and had baths till dinner. I like Annabel <u>awfully</u>.

Saturday, 30 March

We walked <u>miles</u> right round by Virginia Water and we asked for a drink of water at a cottage on Smith's Lawn on the way back. We went to Guides at two thirty. Annabel was very keen to go which made it nicer. Diana Bowes-Lyon† is staying at Royal Lodge for a fortnight. She is lucky being their cousin. Lilibet took the meeting today and did it <u>quite</u> well. We did a bird competition, which was rather dull, but Lilibet loves birds. We did those <u>awful</u> physical jerks again!

---

* Annabel Newman was the elder daughter of Sir Cecil Newman. Her family was large and happy and they lived in great comfort at Burloes in Hertfordshire.

† Diana Bowes-Lyon was a first cousin of Princess Elizabeth. She was the daughter of Queen Elizabeth's brother John, second son of the Earl of Strathmore.

Monday, 1 April

I had to do lessons till twelve but Annabel sat in the school-room and read, and at twelve we went out. Went for a short walk in afternoon too but cold and windy so came in. Wanted to ring up someone for fun so we rang up Barbadee* to say I'd left my handkerchief there (quite untrue!) and to my delight I spoke to her mother! We couldn't stop laughing! After dinner we went straight up to bed as usual as it's more fun and put on our gas masks, which make lovely noises! Undressed together as usual and went to our own rooms.

Tuesday, 2 April

Daddy and I taxied to King's Cross. Lunch on train. Got to Houghton and Grandpa† and Mummy there. House very uncomfortable, of course, after Cumberland Lodge and that's not over comfortable! But I'm quite prepared to enjoy myself.

Houghton, Yorkshire

Wednesday, 3 April

Horrible weather. After tea EA and I played horses in garden till six o'clock when I bathed her.

---

* Barbadee Knight, whose parents lived just outside Windsor.

† Colonel Philip Langdale was Alathea's maternal grandfather. A widower, he lived at Houghton in the East Riding of Yorkshire. He was descended from the old Catholic nobility, and the father of three daughters. He left the estate to Joyce, the eldest, Alathea's mother.

Thursday, 4 April

Mummy loves telling me how well EA fits in in the country! It has ceased to annoy me, EA and Mummy wearing trousers in the winter. As long as they don't make <u>me</u> wear them. I can hold my peace. I have learned it is always best to be tactful with Mummy.

Tuesday, 9 April

Great commotion because the Germans have invaded Norway and Denmark. Listened to the news service several times during the day. We all went out for walk in the morning and as usual poor Daddy was ten yards behind. They wouldn't wait for him.

Wednesday, 17 April

EA and I went for a last walk together in the morning by the lake. I'm sorry I'm leaving as I shan't see her again for months and she'll have changed again by then. She's the only one of my relations that I could ever miss for company's sake.

Thursday, 18 April

Got back to Cumberland Lodge about six. Rang up Sonia and she's going to Lilibet's party on Saturday. I hadn't long to wait, however, before Lilibet herself rang to ask <u>me</u>!

Friday, 19 April

Went to the Token House to get a present for Lilibet. I got a book in which to write lists of books you've read and want to read. Quite nicely bound – white with bird and nest on cover.

Saturday, 20 April

Princess Elizabeth's fourteenth birthday tomorrow. Changed into my green skirt and striped blouse. Went in car to Windsor Castle. All waited in a corridor until King, Queen and princesses arrived. There were: Barclay family,* two Hardinges, Diana Legh,† Sonia, two Morsheads,‡ King and Q both charming. Tea four thirty. No proper birthday cake. After, we saw a film. Our presents have been kept for tomorrow, so I might get a letter! Everyone looked either awful or not suited to the occasion, except the princesses, Sonia and me. The princesses had lovely pale blue dresses (cloth skirts and silk tops). M's was frilly and L's was plainer. Margaret Elphinstone§ is staying there. King asked me if I'd been bicycling down the Long Walk lately! I sat next to Margaret (Rose) at tea. The whole family are really charming.

---

* The Reverend Humphrey Barclay was vicar of Windsor Park. The Royal Chapel of All Saints, a 'Royal Peculiar', was next to Royal Lodge, and the Royal Family could attend unmolested.
† Diana Legh was the daughter of Sir Piers (Joey) Legh, Master of the Household from 1941.
‡ Sir Owen Morshead was the Royal Librarian, who lived at Windsor with his wife, Paquita, and their two daughters, one of whom, Mary, was a friend and contemporary of Princess Elizabeth.
§ Margaret Elphinstone was the daughter of Lady Mary Bowes-Lyon (a sister of Queen Elizabeth), and therefore a first cousin to the princesses. She later became well known as Margaret Rhodes.

Tuesday, 23 April

Letter came 'by hand' from Lilibet. Very nice one signed 'with love from Lilibet'.

Friday, 26 April

I spent a lovely morning sitting on a clump of thyme in the poor old paved garden writing to Sonia. Sun boiling. I cannot believe that it's exactly two years since this garden's been all neglected and yet what a lot has happened since then! I went to meet Anne* and Zelda† on my bike on the main road (to Windsor). It poured before we got back. Played paper games in the hall before and after tea. They are very nice and I'm very glad I've made two more nice friends. I've always known them, of course, but somehow we'd fallen apart a bit.

Saturday, 27 April

I changed for Guides. Lilibet, Crawfie and Margaret Elphinstone there. We played in Royal Lodge most of time. Crawfie and the princesses are the one spark of youth and vitality here for me among all these middle-aged people! They are friends now, which they never could have been really but for the war. So, the war has done something for me, which I shall always look upon with gratitude.

---

* Anne Crichton was the daughter of Colonel the Hon. Sir George Crichton, Comptroller of the Lord Chamberlain's Department.
† Zelda Loyd was the daughter of Major Robert Loyd of the Life Guards.

Sunday, 5 May

A lot of soldiers have come to the stables* to guard the King, I <u>think</u>, and their commanding officer Captain Villiers† comes here for meals, which is rather amusing. I feel very happy. I'm reading a book about reincarnation. It intrigues me to think I've been born before. I think it's very probable and if so I <u>know</u> it was in the eighteenth century.

Monday, 6 May

Crawfie rang up early to say could the princesses come to tea today, as tomorrow doesn't suit. Nasty damp day but we went out and played in the garden till about six, then came in and did two charades, which were <u>great</u> fun. They wore the same as they did when they came last February, which I thought unnecessary (bricky coats and skirts and striped jerseys). They always seem to wear their nicest clothes at home. They were charming (I mean them, not the clothes).

Tuesday, 7 May

Walked over to Royal Lodge and we went to the Hardinges‡ (by car). The princesses wore blue coats and skirts and shrimp jerseys. Sat on roof garden till tea (which was very good) and then messed about indoors and out. Winifred rather Guidy! Lilibet said in car that she was nearly rude to her over the fuss about not being able to have Guides on Friday evening.

---

* The stables were near Cumberland and Royal Lodges.
† The Hon. William Villiers, a younger son of the Earl of Clarendon.
‡ The Hardinges lived in Winchester Tower, part of Windsor Castle.

Friday, 10 May

Hitler invaded Holland and Belgium at three a.m.! We all listened to the news at one o'clock. All Whitsun holidays cancelled. Miss Dunham and I went to Smith's Lawn in the afternoon to see the guns there.

Sunday, 12 May

I sat writing romantic little sketches! I <u>know</u> I shall write books one day as I <u>love</u> writing. In the evening I had a lovely talk with Sonia, which comforted me, as I'm really very lonely at times surrounded by all these people ranging in age from fifty upwards.

Tuesday, 14 May

Lovely day but spoilt by Winifred telling me that the princesses have moved to Windsor* for greater safety. I'm glad for them, of course, I mean that they're safe, but somehow it <u>does</u> feel lonely to know they're not next door.

Thursday, 16 May

Great battles going on in Belgium. (Holland surrendered yesterday.)

Sunday, 19 May

The princesses met me on their bikes and we went to Frogmore, where we went in the punt with Crawfie. Got out and looked at the pigs. Had tea sitting on bank. Lilibet,

---

* They had moved into the Castle from Royal Lodge.

Margaret and I biked about a bit and we said goodbye at Castle and I rode home (through the grounds). I've got to go there Thursday to paint but I <u>can't</u> paint!

Thursday, 23 May

I started off on my bike at quarter to two for Windsor. It <u>poured</u> with rain but I had my mac. I was very early so I sheltered under a tree in Home Park for a bit. Lilibet waiting for me at Castle. I went up to schoolroom (old nursery) and drew with Margaret. Mrs Cox* taught us. I got on surprisingly well. I drew a picture of a girl against a tree. Lilibet was doing German, then they changed over. At quarter to five we had tea in another schoolroom downstairs. Margaret took me to her room to wash and was sweet. Crawfie and Monty both there and after tea Monty, the princesses and I went for bike ride round Home Park.

Sunday, 26 May

Mass nine o'clock. Communion as it is the Sunday of national prayer for the war. Sonia arrived and as it was raining we stayed inside. She was <u>perfect</u> and I shan't have such fun again for <u>ages</u>. I've no idea when I shall see her again as now her school's been evacuated to Wales she can't come home.

Tuesday, 28 May

King Leopold of the Belgians capitulated early today and is consequently in disgrace! Silly fool!

---

* Mrs Cox was art teacher to the princesses.

Thursday, 30 May

I went off to painting like last Thursday. Lovely day but I can't think why the princesses still had coats and skirts and jerseys on. They usually get into cotton frocks earlier than other people. I suppose it's because it's the first year they've ever had coats and skirts and they're so pleased with them. Brought Lilibet's paint box home to finish my picture with. Margaret was <u>so</u> funny at tea.

Friday, 31 May

Winifred and I went for a short walk with the dogs in the Home Park and, <u>of course,</u> had to get tangled up with the princesses and their dogs! I could see they were rather cross at the disturbance (of dogs).

Saturday, 1 June

Grandpa's eighty-fifth birthday. Guides in afternoon. It was <u>awful</u> – my skirt started coming down!

Wednesday, 5 June

The Grenadier* is awfully funny – he teases Miss D the whole time about her spy mania and up to today she took it perfectly seriously! (She had lunch with us as we're a footman short.)

---

* Early in the war different officers were sent to Cumberland Lodge for their meals.

Thursday, 6 June

It was so hot that I left myself three-quarters of an hour to get to the castle for painting. Lilibet <u>has</u> grown – she was waiting for me at the door and I thought she was a grown-up person. Lilibet and I both drew the corner of the castle including Henry VIII's gateway. After tea we went for bike ride down by the river like last week.

Friday, 7 June

I changed (into my pinafore dress) and biked to the Castle again. Lilibet and Margaret and Crawfie met me at the door and we walked down to the guardroom for tea with some officers. <u>Enormous</u> tea, we thought the supply of food was never coming to an end – cakes galore, ices, cherries, with which we had competitions. Once Lilibet and I looked at each other and nearly laughed. Most wonderful drawing and carvings on the walls and Lilibet and Margaret wrote their names in pencil above the fireplace. Lilibet and Margaret for the first time (that I've seen) weren't dressed alike.

Saturday, 8 June

I sat in the garden in the shade by the corner of the house drawing all the morning, as I have to begin a picture for next week. In afternoon I had Guides, which was very hot and I had hay fever so badly. Sneezing is just <u>so</u> ignominious! After dinner we <u>all</u> went out towards Copper Horse to hear the bugle (calling the cavalry in). Coming back the sentry asked for the password, which was Savill! Because Mr

Savill* is the talk of the park today because he and the Duke of Beaufort† had a row because Mr Savill was furious that he'd been challenged! The Duke said that he'd tell his troopers to do exactly the same next time!

Monday, 10 June

Cooler and very dark and stormy-looking. On the six o'clock news I heard that Italy has come into the war (against us). The Duke of Beaufort then took us to see all the horses.

Saturday, 15 June

Zelda Loyd rang up and asked me to go there and play tennis so I decided to take a holiday from Guides. Billy‡ washed my hair and I sat in the garden all morning drying it. Biked to Zelda's. Anne Crichton and another nice girl of eighteen were there. Played tennis till tea, which was in the nursery and a lovely friendly nursery meal. All laughed a lot.

Monday, 17 June

Heard that France has given in, so now we are left to face Germany alone. Oh, God, what will become of us? Naturally if we are beaten we must all hope for death as our only release. But God in his mercy will grant us victory! After lessons I cried but controlled myself to go out. The unhappy fate of England is today reflected in a million hearts in a million minor ways.

---

*   Later, Sir Eric Savill was the Windsor Park ranger.
†   The 10th Duke of Beaufort was always called Master, including by his wife, as since boyhood he had been a Master of Hounds.
‡   Billy was a maid at Cumberland Lodge.

Wednesday, 19 June

I played hide and seek with Elizabeth Anne in the garden after tea. Ming-Ming told me that Miss D told her that she doesn't think the princesses have improved me a bit, not that they're like that but I've got grand ideas through going there so much.

Monday, 24 June

Very near to tears all during lessons – the war is bound to have an effect on everyone. The Germans have occupied all the northern and a strip of western France. What <u>will</u> come of all this?

Tuesday, 25 June

<u>Air-raid warning</u> woke us up at one thirty! I groped about in pitch dark and put on a cardigan and my Jaeger coat over my nightdress and we all trooped down to the cellar, which is very comfortable considering. E, Mabel* and I sat on a bench. Everyone there in various degrees of nudity, except Miss D, who marched down last of all dressed up in a coat and skirt and blouse and a bag with stockings in! Silly fool, we all laughed at her afterwards. Felt very sleepy in the morning but the air raid seems to have cleared the air a bit! Played with Elizabeth Anne in garden after tea. Siren woke me up, eleven thirty. I went and woke Aunt Magdalen up as she hadn't heard it, then dressed quickly – that is to say I put a cardigan on and my winter dressing gown, which is simply <u>perfect</u> for an air raid, and my slippers. We were all

---

* Mabel was housekeeper at Hans Place in London and occasionally came to Cumberland Lodge to help.

much more comfortable down there this time, as we'd brought rugs and cushions. Most of us slept as best we could as the garden chairs are very hard. We were there three and a half hours – till three a.m. Then we went up but the all-clear didn't go till three twenty.

Wednesday, 26 June

Robert Cecil* new officer here. He is too <u>sweet.</u>

Thursday, 27 June

Biked to drawing. Poor Dookie† had to be put to sleep last Sunday. Lilibet and Margaret great fun and we all laughed a great deal. They told me all about the air raid. Played Kan-U-Go [a card game] with Monty after tea. Margaret is sweet and makes one die of laughter.

Saturday, 29 June

I stayed up to dinner, as usual on Saturday nights, and afterwards I played backgammon till after ten with Robert Cecil. I really adore him. He has a great sense of humour and we laughed a lot over the game. He was awfully funny. Of course, I am writing to tell Sonia all about him.

---

*   Robert Gascoyne-Cecil, later 6th Marquess of Salisbury, served in the Grenadiers during the Second World War so was stationed at Windsor. He was from a powerful political dynasty dating back to Tudor times and went on to become an MP.
†   A royal corgi.

Sunday, 30 June

Very hot day. We sat out in the garden and read all morning. Played backgammon with Daddy and then with Robert again (in garden). I stayed up to dinner again and sat next to Robert and played backgammon with him again after. I don't for a moment believe I will marry him (though I'd love to) as one never does marry the person one first falls in love with.

Tuesday, 2 July

Miss D very stupid at lunch and Robert ragged her though she was quite oblivious to it! I went to the York Hall for a rehearsal of the concert on Saturday. The princesses came and Lilibet will tap dance in 'An Apple for the Teacher' (she's the teacher). Margaret is in it too. They both play the piano on the stage and then Margaret is the Dormouse in the Mad Hatter's Tea Party. We all come on in the finale. I'm a waitress and Lilibet plays the piano and 'God Save The King'. It's very good, but everyone I've met says it's making them much too cheap. They really shouldn't do it. They ought to get up little plays of their own with their friends but not dance <u>with</u> all the evacuees like this.

Wednesday, 3 July

Robert came up for tea, then we had to say goodbye to him, as he's been relieved. I am very sorry. He said he would come up and see us sometime but he probably won't. He is so sweet.

Saturday, 6 July

I went to York Hall and sold programmes ahead of the performance. All the family came. The King and Queen came at five and they both shook hands with me. Of course old Mrs Tannar* monopolised the honour of giving them their programmes! (Specially painted ones.) I had hoped to! Grandpa and Elizabeth Anne sat in the front row with the K and Q, who shook hands and spoke to EA, which I hoped they would, as it'll be so nice for her to look back upon in years to come, as I expect she'll move into quite a different set.

Saturday, 13 July

Spent most of the morning indoors starching my hair and curling EA's but we went out for an hour before lunch in the garden. Went to Castle by car. Very glad to get the car. Crawfie was in a bad mood. I think she's rather cross because I borrowed her purse last week for the programme money and now can't remember what I have done with it but I shall buy her another one if I can't find it. The princesses were rather cross too, because Lilibet played the piano badly and the curtain fell on Margaret's head!

Sunday, 21 July

Played with Elizabeth Anne in garden, went for a nice walk and read. After tea, we went down to wait for Mummy and

---

* The wife of Hubert Tannar, headmaster of the Royal School, Windsor Great Park, quite near to Cumberland Lodge.

Aunt Alathea.* I have come to rather an interesting conclusion about Mummy. Though I cannot <u>like</u> her I admire her outward exterior. After the dowdy atmosphere here it is wonderful to see someone who in every detail is a fashionable lady of society. In the eighteenth century she would have been the traditional mother. It's only hard experience that's made her practical and domesticated now. Perhaps when I'm forty I shall have ceased to build castles in the air! In proper circumstances I <u>know</u> no one would be so exacting in her standard of living as her. I would far rather have her as she is now, than have a dowdy homely mother, however kind. Also, although I know <u>quite</u> well that she knows nothing about children's clothes, I know I cannot do better than take her advice when I come out. I can condemn her trousers and her ideas of going without stockings and gloves and also of not wearing hats in the sun, because I know hundreds of grown-ups who would agree with me, but I cannot pretend I am in a position to criticise her ordinary clothes. She <u>always</u> dresses better than Aunt Alathea.

Monday, 22 July

Mummy's encouraging me to fall in love with the officers here! I told her about RC.

Monday, 29 July

Last day of lessons. Mummy left. It's funny – I've had that same feeling of sadness that I've had for several years on the last day of the summer term.

---

* Alathea, Lady Manton (née Langdale) was Alathea's aunt and had married Lord Manton. They divorced in 1936. During the war she and Joyce, Alathea's mother, shared various flats. She was a great beauty.

Tuesday, 30 July

I started off to meet Sonia just after ten (on my bike, of course) and we met just beyond Virginia Water station. Went back to Englefield Green slowly, talking all the way. I had my hair cut and she had a manicure.

Thursday, 1 August

Biked to drawing. Great fun. After tea we went down to the little stream to fish. Monty with us. Had two rods and we took it in turns. It wasn't very successful because Ching* ate nearly all the bait (which was dough and cotton wool), then Lilibet got her line caught in a holly bush and Monty had to wade into the middle of the stream to get it out! Then when we were coming back, we realised that if we had got any fish we should have had nowhere to put them as we'd forgotten to bring a BUCKET!

Saturday, 3 August

After tea EA and I played in the garden, then Daddy came so we went for a short walk with him. Duchess of Beaufort† came after tea for the weekend. She is sweet and very amusing. We all played Old Maid [a card game] for fun after dinner and laughed a lot.

---

* Ching was the King's dog.
† Born Lady Mary Cambridge, her father was 1st Marquess of Cambridge and had been Prince of Teck before the Anglicisation of royal titles in 1917. She married the Duke of Beaufort. Her aunt was Queen Mary, who lived with the Beauforts at Badminton during the Second World War.

Monday, 5 August

Walked down to the bottom of the garden and back with her and the duchess and her two dogs, one of which is an enchanting white woolly poodle. The princesses came to tea at four thirty with Monty. They wore their yellow dresses. After tea we had a swing and then walked over to Royal Lodge. Aunt Magdalen and EA came too and watched. We undressed in Royal Lodge (I went into Lilibet's room) and we bathed in the pool (just us three). <u>Great</u> fun. Lovely pool. They had their Bath Club bathing dresses on, which are black and plain – awful things. They swim and dive very well. I dived off the top step but jumped in a lot. Dressed again and looked at their garden and weeded it a bit, then they left (by car) and we walked home. Great fun. Lovely day.

Tuesday, 6 August

Now the duchess has gone, as always on these occasions that awful feeling of loneliness swept over me. Tonight feels very flat without her. I'd never seen her before and yet I love her. I instinctively see in her a mother who would have given me that love and affection that I have never known.

Friday, 9 August

I changed after lunch (into my pinafore dress) and biked to the Hardinges for tea. The princesses were there, Anne Crichton and three boys. We had an obstacle race all over the house and then a Wall's ice cream man came up and we all had one, though the princesses didn't fall in with it at all and hated theirs!

Tuesday, 13 August

I got ready to go to the Guide thing at the Castle but at a quarter to five I heard an air-raid warning so I had to put off going. All listened and looked but all-clear went at five o'clock. I went and had some cake in the kitchen, then Ming-Ming and I went for walk to the Copper Horse. We learned afterwards that a Messerschmitt had flown at four thousand feet over this house at five o'clock!

Thursday, 15 August

After lunch, I biked to drawing. Margaret Elphinstone is staying there and wore a dress of exactly the same stuff as my all coloured yellowy one, only in blue, which wasn't nearly as nice as mine. We all drew outside. Afterwards, I tidied as usual in Lilibet's room and she told me her silk stockings cost eight and six. Typical!

Friday, 16 August

Lavinia* had another daughter yesterday. Everyone very disappointed it is not a boy.

Tuesday, 20 August

Lilibet rang up early to ask us to tea tomorrow for Margaret's birthday. I biked into Windsor to the Token House to get M a present. I got a little blue painted tray, with wild flowers painted on it. Went up to the Hardinges for tea and then we all went to the Castle for the Guide thing. Lilibet forgot about it and turned up very late!

---

* Duchess of Norfolk.

Wednesday, 21 August

We went for walk round the Obelisk Pond in morning. Wrapped up Margaret's tray after lunch and got ready. I wore my spotted shantung and E her white muslin with the red spots. We went in the car with Ming-Ming to the Castle at four. Very cold and windy. We were taken out to the garden, where we said how do you do to everyone. Then we played kick the tin. The Hardinges wore awful coats and skirts and the princesses had their yellow cotton frocks on, so we were rather over-dressed but it's a fault on the right side. We had a lovely tea, then a cinema. EA and I sat in the front row. After that we had ices. The King and Queen were there, of course, and the Queen talked to EA and me quite a lot. Ming-Ming was upstairs with Bobo* all the time. Going to Margaret's birthday is a treat I never anticipated and it means all the more to me since I went to Lilibet's tenth birthday over four years ago at Royal Lodge. How different she was from what M is now – so much more serious and grown-up and yet not nearly so sweet and attractive.

Thursday, 22 August

Biked to drawing. It was the last lesson and I felt rather sad, but I am sure I shall be able to go again next term. The Queen came and looked at our drawings. I drew Lilibet. I felt sad saying goodbye to Lilibet because I'm really very fond of her and although I shall still see them

---

* Margaret (Bobo) MacDonald, the daughter of a Scottish farmer, was nursery-maid and later dresser to Princess Elizabeth and remained in service to her for her whole life. Her sister Ruby, also a nursery-maid at Windsor in 1940, stayed on with Princess Margaret.

every Tuesday at the Guides it's not the same thing but perhaps I shall see something of them during the holidays.

Saturday, 24 August

We all had to go down to the cellar at midnight for an hour and a half because bombs were dropping. I got up again to look out of my window at two and saw about twenty searchlights trained on one plane, which was German.

Sunday, 25 August

A quiet but very pleasant day. I went to bed about ten and was in the middle of praying that we would have a peaceful night when three terrible explosions shook my windows and bed. I lay paralysed for some minutes, then we all went down to the cellar amid more bombs and guns.

Tuesday, 27 August

Brita arrived. Gossiped till lunch and then biked to the Castle with all the hike things in our baskets. B was thrilled at going there and thought Lilibet very nice and very pretty. We were all divided into two groups with Lilibet and me in charge of each one. We made a fire and cooked sausages on sticks. This was only a practice hike. Next week we will be tested. Made delicious things in a frying-pan, with cheese in between fried bread.

Wednesday, 28 August

We had to go down to the cellar at nine fifteen. We've got sofas there now. B and I shared one. <u>Terrific</u> explosion very near. We were <u>frantic</u> with rage and tiredness.

Thursday, 29 August

In the morning Brita and I went with Ming-Ming and Elizabeth Anne down to the field by the lake to see the crater where the bomb exploded last night. Not very big. We picked up a bit of shrapnel. We spent several hours in the cellar again! I cannot endure this cellar business every night. <u>No one</u> else goes down (I mean in other houses). It is so unnecessary.

Saturday, 31 August

Brita and I went into the Rock Garden in the morning and sewed. Took Taffy, the new corgi, with us. We had air-raid warnings all day long only we take no notice of them in the daytime. All the same it does make the war seem curiously near to us now. For that reason we weren't allowed to go and bathe. I must say Grandpa <u>is</u> quite right though Brita simply can't see that. It's extraordinary how we get on together as we're the opposite in almost everything. Brita, EA and I looked at the horses and talked to Mr Hay (officer) sitting on the fence. Brita has fallen in love with him. He is too sweet but not as nice as Robert. Brita and her mother think I'm hideous. Isn't it awful? But I think Brita is ugly too and no one else thinks I am. We gossiped in bed till a quarter to eleven as we had a feeling we wouldn't go down to the cellar but we did at one.

Monday, 2 September

B and I biked into Windsor. Brita got an awful dress at Marks & Spencer and while we were there the siren went and we went down into the fitting room of the '50-shilling tailor'!* All-clear went ten minutes later so we came out. I got some pale mauve ribbon to put on my chiffon nightgown. Wandered round and came home very pleased with ourselves. Dragged down to the cellar at twelve and came up at two. It is ruining my nerves. I just could not bear it and I burst into tears and was in an awful state. Even when I got into bed, I just sobbed uncontrollably. How terrible this war is.

Tuesday, 3 September

Brita wanted to bathe so I said I'd come down with her and look on. I enjoyed sitting on the bank (of the Obelisk Pond) in the heavenly green haze of this beautiful morning. To think it's a whole year since that fateful day when war was declared. I am happier today than I was then, but it is a fleeting uncertain happiness, with a future far different from the one I expected looming ahead. B and I biked to the Castle at three for the hike. I had difficulty in persuading B to wear stockings. She wouldn't see that because Lilibet always does she ought to there. B says that I'm very much the princesses' type and also I'm in a younger, more childish set than her. We almost quarrelled over the stockings in the evening.

---

* A chain of shops selling men's clothes.

Wednesday, 4 September

B and I were in a very good humour again! She had to leave directly after tea. I felt very sorry B's gone, as we are very good friends really, and I miss her.

Sunday, 8 September

Mass nine o'clock. Colder. Watched Ming-Ming pack, then Elizabeth Anne and I went with the others across to Royal Lodge to watch the King inspect the Home Guard outside the church. Queen and princesses there and they all came and talked to us after. We had Taffy, so Lilibet fetched Coral* to meet him. They had grey coats and lovely pink linen hats shaped rather grown-uply. King talked to Taffy, and the Queen said it was nice to see me for just these few minutes. They were all charming. Had quite a difficulty to prevent Taffy from following them into the house.

Tuesday, 10 September

Taffy slept in my room, as we cannot leave him up in the nursery on account of the air raids. Went up to tea with the Hardinges and on to Guides after. Sat out on the terrace doing maps. King played golf and he stopped and talked to us, Deborah† showing off abominably to him; she was very bright and breezy, never called him Sir and was familiar to Lilibet in front of him.

---

* A royal dog.
† Deborah Green Wilkinson was one of a large family of a local vicar. A year or two older than Alathea, she could drive. She was a leading light in the Girl Guides and later the ATS.

Tuesday, 17 September

I sat indoors knitting and reading all afternoon and then went to Guides. I waited alone in the schoolroom till the others came and Lilibet came later still, as she'd forgotten again (she's obviously not very keen!).

Monday, 23 September

Lilibet rang up early to ask me to go there to help them pick damsons and stay to tea, so of course I felt very happy. Monty and the Hardinges came too and we all biked to the kitchen garden (miles away!) and proceeded to pick damsons (for jam). We picked <u>hundreds</u>! We biked back to the Castle for tea (in the schoolroom). We all listened to the King's speech on the wireless in the nursery and knitted (I borrowed some). I left about quarter to seven, having enjoyed this unexpected treat awfully.

Tuesday, 24 September

Went to the Hardinges for tea. Libby and I alone. She is very silly but quite nice. I looked at their albums again, which amuses me, as there are so many unorthodox photos of them with the princesses in Scotland! As I was biking home past Frogmore, I met the King walking with the dogs, so I got off, curtsied and we talked for a few minutes, then I came home feeling very happy.

Wednesday, 25 September

Schoolroom life began again! I was quite glad really as holidays are all very well when one is away or seeing friends all the time but here the last fortnight has been dull, though pleasant enough. Miss Dunham and I had our breakfast downstairs at eight and did lessons as usual from nine to twelve thirty.

Saturday, 28 September

The duchess [of Beaufort] arrived for lunch. I had Guides in the afternoon and I was told that Renee Kott's (one of the Guides) parents had both been killed by a bomb and I'm beginning to realise now that this war has a greater, a deeper meaning of terror that one would ever guess looking at the surface of things. Had great fun at dinner and after, playing racing demon, laughing and talking. The duchess said, 'Good night, dear Alathea,' to me. She likes me.

Sunday, 29 September

The duke and duchess went to church in the morning, but Daddy and I went out for quite a long walk round by the Copper Horse. The duke is almost as sweet as his wife. They adore each other, and I know it is a great sorrow to them that they have no children. I think that is why she likes me because I'm just about the age her daughter would be if she had one.

Monday, 30 September

I said goodbye to the duchess – that gentle woman with the loving heart. It was in her own room and I put both my arms round her neck and she put her arms round me and

I kissed her more warmly that I ever kiss anyone now, except Elizabeth Anne. Again, with the exception of this little sister, never does anyone now put their arms round me, nor am I <u>ever</u> tempted to put mine round <u>anyone's</u> neck, least of all my mother's. She told me last night to call her Mary but, of course, I shan't take advantage of it immediately.

Went to bed and slept well until twelve thirty, when a <u>shattering</u> explosion shook the house like a pack of cards. We all had to go down to the cellar after that, as there was still a time bomb unlocated. After hours of wakeful discomfort most of us returned to bed, only to be woken up at five thirty by another explosion. In my bed, I lay and shook with a wild terror I have never known before. This was on the morning of 1 October but I'm writing it as it belongs to this one never-to-be-forgotten night. Dear God!

Tuesday, 1 October

I woke up late and at nine o'clock the time bomb went off. I lay in speechless horror watching my walls <u>rock</u> violently from side to side. At breakfast we were told that the first bomb had been in our wood behind Smith's Lawn and the time bomb was right in the middle of Smith's Lawn. There are also lots of other time bombs in the Long Walk and near Bishop's Gate. Yesterday a Messerschmitt was brought down near Queen Anne's Gate. Went with Grandpa and the Grenadier officer to look at the craters. The one in our wood is <u>vast</u> and uprooted a large beech tree. Came back and did an hour's German reading and then I took Miss Dunham to the crater. After tea I wrote my diary and I'm so depressed, so miserably depressed. It seems as if all around me there is sorrow, suffering and bloodshed and I know now that people in the future will read about this war and will look upon it in horror as comparable only to the French or Russian Revolution and they will pity the generation whose youth was wasted by it.

Sunday, 13 October

We listened to <u>Lilibet speaking</u> on the <u>wireless.</u> She was <u>very</u> good and my heart went out to her.[*]

Wednesday, 16 October

The duchess is staying again. She did what no one else has <u>thought</u> of doing – not that I want them to – sat with me till the men came out of dinner – just her and me – what bliss! I had taken the precaution of doing my hair nicely and even of powdering my nose but I was doubly glad of this because when the men passed the duchess called out: 'Master, come and look at Alathea,' and not only he, but the <u>two officers</u> walked in too!!! One was Mr Waterhouse[†] who notices things! I was glad that I happened to have on my chiffon nightgown, and I hoped I made a good impression with the pale pinky-mauve frilled ribbon resting elegantly on my white bosom (unfortunately my bare shoulders had to be covered by my blue angora cardigan), my hair brushed loosely out almost on to my shoulders and my

[*] Princess Elizabeth made her first ever public speech by wireless to the children of Britain – it was to children across the world separated from their families. At the end she got Princess Margaret to join her and say, 'Goodnight, children.'
[†] Major Charles Waterhouse, later married to Lady Caroline Spencer Churchill, daughter of the Duke of Marlborough.

pink silk eiderdown over me. The eiderdown is really much too hot, but it is becoming so I put up with it.

Friday, 18 October

We were all playing a talking game after tea when Lilibet rang up and asked me to <u>dancing class</u> every Saturday at ten thirty!!! I could hardly believe my good fortune and my heart was in a flutter the whole evening. I wondered why God has seen fit to grant my dearest wish.

Thursday, 24 October

It cannot be good for anyone, whether they believe in atmospheres, as I do, or not, to live in an atmosphere of hate, or even dislike. But it has been my fate never to know an atmosphere of love among my own family. My father, mother and I have all been equally unlucky in our mothers, none of us three, or Elizabeth Anne, has ever known a mother's love. God help me to profit from this bitter knowledge and not let my own children suffer from it.

Friday, 25 October

It was strange because last night I was thinking very much of Nannie Davis (old family nannie) wondering if anything could have happened to her as she never answered my letter in July and this morning, I got a letter from her! Time and time again this has happened to me though I do not pretend this is unique. I do like to feel that I am more affected that way than some other people. My greatest wish is to develop this psychic quality, and perhaps one day I shall visit the

Trianon and see Marie-Antoinette, as some others have done. And why not? I have a secret feeling sometimes that in my last life I <u>was</u> Marie-Antoinette. Perhaps time will either prove or disprove this, but this I swear, that I knew and loved this unfortunate queen.

Saturday, 26 October

Went by car to the Castle. My dancing shoes hadn't arrived but the princesses wore beige strap shoes, as they haven't got any either. I am glad, though, that I've ordered mine, as they'll make me look both younger and shorter, which I want to do there. Libby, Anne, the Morsheads, two awful children who shouldn't be there at all, and a few small children came. Kent children[*] there. The princesses had blue and pink shantung dresses, which I didn't like. Miss Vacani[†] and several assistants came and the class went off very well. Anne, Libby, Margaret, Lilibet and I stood in the front row. Everything was very royal and I loved it all. That class is simply my idea of heaven but most modern girls, especially of my age, would <u>loathe</u> it.

Tuesday, 29 October

I walked up to the Hardinges, where Deborah and Anne joined us and we all went to the Castle. With Lilibet and

---

[*] The Duke of Kent was a younger brother of King George VI and married to Princess Marina of Greece. The Kent children were Prince Edward and Princess Alexandra.

[†] Miss Marguerite Vacani was the most fashionable dancing teacher of the era and had taught the princesses before the war. She came once a week to Windsor throughout the war to continue with the princesses in a class mainly made up of courtiers' children. She was assisted by her niece, Betty.

Crawfie we went down to the housekeeper's little kitchen and cooked – potatoes, cabbage, apples and fried eggs, for the cook's badge. Rather fun. Next week we make jam puffs and stay to tea to eat them.

Wednesday, 30 October

Letter from Mummy saying next term she wants me to go to some finishing school, as she thinks that if I stay here I shall get odd! <u>Somehow</u>, I must get out of it. The only reason I want to stay here is the dancing class and, of course, Lilibet. All the morning I had that awful restless worried feeling I nearly always get when Mummy's letters arrive. Went to Windsor Forest with Aunt M where there was a 'drag hunt'.* Saw lots of our officers and all walked about. I met Mr Profumo† and another officer in his car with the duchess inside, so I got in too, and we walked and drove about after the hounds for the rest of the afternoon. Mr Profumo would make the perfect 'gallant lover' and in bed I made up a lovely story: how I become Empress of Austria in a few years' time, and he comes to a court ball at Vienna and I ask him to dance with me, then suddenly a fanatic hurls a brick at me (misses, of course) and shouts that I'm giving Austria an heir and they don't want one, and down with the monarchy etc. The Emperor, my husband, who is enchanting, comes and, joining Philip's (Mr P's) and my hands says, 'Take her and sit down,' so we sit on a sofa and I talk to him sentimentally about old times, etc., and at last I am overcome and upset by everything and I leave with the Emperor.

---

* In a drag hunt, hounds hunt an artificial scent trail laid in advance.
† Philip Profumo was a Grenadier officer, a cousin of the more famous John.

Friday, 1 November

Mass at eight thirty and I nearly fainted so had to come out before the Communion. I went down and started breakfast alone with Profumo. I think he knows about my faint of which I'm pleased as I think it's romantic to faint. My dancing shoes arrived at long last – just the <u>one</u> colour I didn't want – bronze, so back they'll have to go. I'll go without any if I can't find what I want, but I <u>won't</u> have bronze – they're so ordinary.

Monday, 4 November

Grandpa, Aunt M and I went to see the cavalry off. Tears were not far from my eyes as I watched the dear horses ride away and realized that it was perhaps the last I shall see of them, for now they are to be mechanised. One by one everything that has character is disappearing. We shall no longer have our nice cavalry officer, and not even two Grenadiers as thought. The nice Grenadiers up here are so very few and far between and I have had such fun with them but everything passes.

Tuesday, 5 November

Crawfie and Lilibet came to CL, and we cooked soup, jam puffs and drop scones and they stayed to tea to eat them, which was great fun. I wore my new wine jersey and cardigan with my green coat and skirt with a wine velvet bow in my hair.

Wednesday, 6 November

At about ten thirty at night, when I was in bed, I suddenly heard two ghastly whistles through the air. I crouched down in bed knowing my last moment <u>might</u> be near. Nearer, nearer came that fearful inhuman noise until it seemed it must hit the house, then a heartrending crash and I knew that we at least were safe but the tragedy caused by this weapon of Hell we were to know the next day. After this we decided to go down to the cellar and there we slept fairly well until six fifteen the next morning, when we came up to a cold but comfortable bed. Later in the morning we heard that the Pearces' house (one of the new lodges at Royal Lodge) had been hit and one of the sons killed. Oh! The horror of the tragedy that has befallen this poor family. Oh! Dear God preserve us from this terrible fate, which surely we cannot have deserved.

Thursday, 7 November

Grandpa brought back my dancing shoes. I was mad with joy. They are silver ones, from Harrods, 17/6d, very expensive, but who cares, as long as I've got them?

Saturday, 9 November

Changed for dancing after breakfast and wore my silver shoes. Lilibet rang up to ask me to stay the weekend! I could hardly believe my ears – like that other time two and a half years ago! In great confusion I told Billy what to pack and rushed off. After dancing I played a French game in schoolroom with L and M and Monty, then I changed (into my green skirt and wine jersey) and we all had lunch with the

K and Q and household. Then L and M, Crawfie and I went out in the rain and messed about till the Queen joined us, when we gave some scarves to some soldiers, then unblocked a stream. Q sweet and held my hand to balance me on a stepping-stone. M pushed me into some barbed wire tearing my good stocking! Us three had tea with the K and Q and afterwards played Racing Demon with the Queen. At seven L and I went to our baths. My room was on the floor above theirs, a little way along the passage from the nurseries they had the last time I stayed. My bathroom was on the floor above that, the same one as I had last time, near my old room, and also Crawfie's and Monty's rooms. L and I had supper in our night things in the nursery. At about eight, L and I and Bobo walked down to their shelter, <u>miles</u> away, which was the greatest fun I've ever known. L and M sleep on two bunks on top of each other (M on top) and Mrs Knight* on a bed in the same room. I was put in an adjoining room but as my light didn't work, I sat on Mrs K's bed and wrote my diary on a piece of paper. M made us laugh a lot and except for when Mrs K came down for few minutes we were alone down there. The K and Q looked in on me to say good night. I would never have believed I could be so fortunate.

Sunday, 10 November

We came up from the shelter at a quarter to eight and dressed. I wore my pink skirt and blue jersey. Breakfast at eight in nursery. Did jigsaw puzzle after breakfast. L and M had to get ready for church early as they went in Guide

---

* Mrs Clara Knight, known as 'Allah', was nanny to the princesses.

uniform for a parade. I got ready and walked to mass with Monty (in Windsor). Horribly long service. Got back and played backgammon with Monty in schoolroom, as the others weren't back. Lunch one fifteen. Two Eton boys came, the Spencer boy* and another. L and I had to make conversation to them! Afterwards we all went round several rooms, looking at things, and then L, M and I went for a long walk in the Home Park with the K and Q and ran into the Archbishop of Canterbury. Tea with them and cards with the Q again after. She was very chatty to me. I simply love her. Bath then supper. K and Q were in nursery. It is lucky I have a respectable dressing-gown! Marched down to the shelter again complete with apples, clocks, books, etc! I stayed in my own bed as my light had come but left the door open to talk and I went into their room twice to get something and they came into mine when the light went out and an emergency one came on in my room. M made me die with laughter by asking me if I thought L and her and myself were pretty! She is an angel, that child. I am so very fond of them both, as well as the K and Q, and Crawfie and Mrs K, etc. In time of trouble I should never desert them and whatever may happen in the dim future I shall openly stand by them. The K and Q came down and had to pass through my room first! They both said goodbye to me in my bed, so I couldn't curtsey! It wasn't a bit embarrassing; I feel perfectly at my ease with them now, especially the Q. She wants me to come again, as she says it's nice for both L and me. I feel I am one of the most fortunate people in the world. We went to sleep

---

* 'The Spencer boy' later became Earl Spencer. He was the father of Diana, Princess of Wales.

after the news, about nine fifteen, as we bring the wireless down.

Monday, 11 November

We got up soon after seven thirty and went upstairs like yesterday through miles of icy cold corridors and staircases. Lovely cheerful nursery breakfast. Did jigsaw puzzle and then the car came to fetch me. I said goodbye to Mrs Knight, then to Monty and Crawfie, who then kissed me with open arms. Lilibet and Margaret saw me off. I can never deny that I love all the honour and ceremony involved in a royal visit but besides that I am very happy there. I think it is because there is a nursery. I have always loved a nursery life. Right up to the war I lived in one of my own and I have always enjoyed staying with my friends most when there is a nursery. Moreover, in that Castle, with its gilded rooms and red corridors, there is an atmosphere of happy family life that I myself have never known. Ironically enough it is in the home of the King and Queen of England that I find more happiness and homeliness than I do here; it is the first Lady in the Land who has won my affection before my own mother. Let me never forget, though, that it is Cumberland Lodge that has given me all this, and, oh, dear Lord, do not let it all fade with my childhood.

Tuesday, 12 November

I got the bus into Windsor and after fitting my dress I went up to the Castle for Guides. We cooked scones and fish. Lilibet told me on arrival that Mrs Knight wanted to see me about my leg, and she put a new plaster on (from the scratch I got from the barbed wire).

Wednesday, 13 November

I woke up with a rather bad cold. I didn't go out all day and before lunch I wrote to the Queen. Grandpa had given me a copy, but as he was out for lunch, I altered it a tiny bit and put in one or two extra sentences to fill it out a bit! One was 'I am so very grateful to Your Majesty for the many happy days I have spent with the Princesses' which I thought would give her pleasure.

Saturday, 16 November

I went to dancing (in my flowered silk frock) and picked up Anne on the way. Margaret not there as she's got a cold. Nor was the Queen. Afterwards Lilibet said would I like to stay to lunch and see the film and they'd send me home. So I had to put off Anne coming back to lunch with me and sent her home in our car. Went up to the nursery and did jigsaw puzzles with M as L was doing lessons. L suddenly said I hadn't got anything to go out in so in the end I had to write a note to Billy for my thick clothes and they sent their car to Cumberland Lodge to fetch them, which was very kind. Unfortunately they didn't arrive by lunch, so besides freezing I felt rather a fool. King not there but Queen sweet as usual. After lunch I changed (in M's room) and we went out with Crawfie and messed about by the stream again. The Q joined us. Came in and tidied before going to the film, which was really very funny, though as a rule I don't like silly films. Then we had tea like last weekend, just the Queen, L and M, and the King came in late. The Q was really angelic to me and so terribly kind. She really wanted me to come today to see the film because I never get a chance to go to one now. Mummy would never have thought of that. Immediately after tea I came home in their car, because of the blackout.

Sunday, 17 November

After breakfast I sat in the smoking-room cutting out things from old magazines to stick in a scrapbook that Lilibet gave me yesterday to do for her. It is great fun, and naturally I'm trying to make it specially nice, because the Queen will probably see it. Sonia rang up after tea and we had an amusing talk. I am very happy now; I am favoured with Fortune and with God's help I shall not take advantage of it; I shall try and be happy with what I have. I only wish now for a photo of L and M for Christmas, but that I have always longed for. I would love the Q to kiss me, but I always hope for that with everyone I love. I do want more than anything in the world to be a lady-in-waiting or something when I grow up but that too has always been my ardent desire and I do feel now that it is very possible but I should like always to be Lilibet's friend whatever happens. Naturally I hope I shall go there for another weekend, apart from everything else because I enjoy it, but if I don't, I shall always retain the happy memories of this one. When I think that now if it hadn't been for the war, I should be abroad (and inevitably more grown-up) with my royal days behind me, perhaps for ever, how can I not be grateful for the path destiny marked out for me? I have gained much since I have been here, but I have lost much too. War as it is today, even from a personal point of view, is a bitter price to pay for the subtle pleasure of a royal friendship. But Fate decreed that I should pay that price and I have paid it willingly. Strange though it may seem, though, I have lost a future by the war, I may also, by the same war, have gained another future of the same nature. But, come what may, I shall always be a true friend to the Royal Family I have learned to love. No one knows how much they have influenced my life and they are far too nice for me ever to take advantage of.

Tuesday, 19 November

Guides as usual. We cooked soup and Irish stew. Lilibet is never at her best with a lot of people but then I suppose no one is, except those who have the party spirit and I know I'm much nicer by myself as I'm such a bad mixer; outside my own little circle I'm quite lost and hopeless. Deborah dropped me home. D is very nice but much too coarse. I rang up Sonia and we discussed it.

Wednesday, 20 November

Letter from Mummy saying I can stay on here another term but that she does want me to go to this finishing school in the summer to be with girls of my own age, as otherwise, she says, I will end by knowing nobody but the Hardinges and Crichtons and Princess E, who is so much younger than me. I agree about the Hardinges and Crichtons but what she would <u>never</u> see is that Lilibet is worth a hundred friends (from the point of view of the usefulness she means) and it doesn't in the <u>least</u> matter her being two years younger. If it wasn't for her I should definitely want to go to the school.

I am so afraid that if I once lose touch with Lilibet I shall never quite pick up the thread again.

Saturday, 23 November

I write for the last time while I am sixteen. It has been a year of storms and tears intermingled with unexpected joys and honours. I went to dancing in my pale blue chiffon frock, which looked lovely. It is wonderful to think that the frock I created in my imagination has now materialised in every detail. Afterwards Margaret said to me: 'You've beaten Anne this time!' I said 'Why?' and she said: 'Your dress is much prettier than hers!' (Anne had a dark green gossamer dress with diagonal gold tinsel threads, which made a diamond pattern all over. It had frills round the bottom, neck, and puff sleeves.) Personally, I like hers as much as mine.

Sunday, 24 November

My seventeenth birthday. I opened three presents in bed and looked through *Our Princesses at Home* from E.* Mass at nine. Communion. Opened all my presents after. Grandpa gave me £1. Aunt Alathea and I drove to Eton with Lady Leconfield† and Elizabeth Wyndham. Lady L said Princess E sent me her best love and said she wished she'd known it was my birthday, which pleased me very much. We had a lovely tea at the

---

* Elizabeth Wyndham was the adopted daughter of Lady Leconfield. She was an intellectual and linguist, who went on to work as a codebreaker at Bletchley Park.

† Lady Leconfield, born Beatrice Rawson, was married to 3rd Baron Leconfield and lived with him, their adopted son and daughter at Petworth House in Sussex. They were family friends and Alathea used to visit them.

Cockpit.* We would have seen a film, but I had to say that Grandpa wanted us to be back before dark, which was a bore. When we got back E sat in my armchair and scoffed at my lovely book of photographs of the princesses. Why is it that that type of girl always hates the princesses? Then she made my face up and did my hair and said I looked better like that. Brita and also Mummy would agree but I hate looking grown-up. I don't like E but we had quite a confidential talk upon that subject. She says she'd take me for about fifteen.

Tuesday, 26 November

Crawfie rang me up early to say could I stay to tea today and would I ring up Anne and ask her to come for her! Deborah met us and gave us a lift up to the Castle and we cooked scones, drop scones and jam tartlets again and had them for tea at five.

Wednesday, 27 November

We set off in the car for Arundel† for lunch. Lavinia, though rather hard and a very bad duchess, is quite sweet. Bernard‡ came and we had a lovely lunch and I got quite a lot of attention. After lunch we went up to see the children. The baby, Mary, is rather sweet but Anne is very unattractive. She is exactly like a Dutch cheese but might be rather sweet if she had her hair curled. Now it is flaxen-coloured and <u>dead</u> straight and scraped back tight. Nice nursery.

---

* The Cockpit is a restaurant on the high street in Eton.
† Arundel Castle in West Sussex, where Alathea's father's first cousin, Bernard, Duke of Norfolk, lived.
‡ The Duke of Norfolk and his daughters, Mary and Anne.

Friday, 29 November

The Tigress* has been awful the last day or two and tonight I really wondered if she had a minor brain storm because she's been madder than usual today. She went up to bed before Daddy and I had finished our game, and when I said, 'Do wait for me,' she snapped my head off. I purposely didn't say good-night to her <u>at all</u> and I came up to bed with thoughts only of bitterness and hatred in my heart and I immediately began writing this on my bed to relieve my feelings, for tonight I <u>shall</u> not cry myself to sleep. I <u>will</u> not let that woman spoil my looks for the dancing class tomorrow. She came in to say good-night and was very pleasant, though mad. I cannot like her but experience has taught me to take people as I find them. Always I have lived with hard people and so have learned what love and affection could never have taught me. Such is the lot of one who longs for the passionate warmth of love. MAY GOD GRANT IT TO ME YET.

Sunday, 1 December

How quickly the time goes! Christmas nearly upon one once again and one hasn't nearly the same enthusiasm for it as before the war. I am very sorry we shall all be separated this Christmas, except for Mummy.

Tuesday, 3 December

Didn't go out in the morning but made out my shopping list and caught the bus into Windsor as usual. Saw Zelda.

---

* 'The Tigress' was a nickname given by Alathea as a teenager to her maiden aunt Magdalen Fitzalan Howard. As she grew older she became fonder of her and dropped it.

Got *Our Princesses at Home* for Miss D for Christmas, then went up to the Castle. Only Libby there besides me. Cooked custard and spotted dick. Lilibet's hair is worse now that it is curled than before, I think, because she's got it in little flat curls close to her head all round the back, very tight in front. It ought to be longer and in loose soft curls. Margaret's is sweet.

Friday, 6 December

I said goodbye to Mummy and Aunt Alathea. I was glad to see them go. She only gave me one dry kiss on one cheek when she arrived and when she left. How unaffectionate she is! But yesterday was a wonderful day – I walked into every shop and came out with what I wanted! I would not allow the disturbance Mummy caused in my heart to spoil it. Living in an essentially disunited family has given me judgement of character, and I have now been able to form a perfectly clear view of the whole position. There is much to be said for Mummy, and also much against Grandpa – much that the world can never realise. Perhaps the future will pass a fairer judgement on this unhappy family than is at present possible. Mummy is concerned in 'bringing me to earth' and making me see life as it really is so that I shall not suffer as much when I am awakened from the dream in which I'm now trying to live. There is no doubt that she does like me better than I like her, but I cannot face facts – I must live in the little world I have created for myself and bear the consequences. She would beyond doubt think I was mad if I told her I don't think it's impossible that I shall marry the Pretender to the Austrian throne!

Saturday, 7 December

Dancing was great fun. I was lunching with the Hardinges but after the class Lilibet said could I come to a film there. She also asked Libby and there was an awful muddle about time, etc. Went to Winchester Tower and Lady Hardinge said Libby couldn't miss Guides this week, so she had to say no, which, besides being perfectly ridiculous, is very rude. I would <u>never</u> dare refuse a royal invitation. I had my Guide things there and after lunch I walked back to the Castle, shivering in my thin dress. I had a woolly and my tap shoes on. I really think they might think of these things the day before. I waited in the schoolroom till the princesses came in and I helped them paint Christmas cards. L said they were giving a *thé dansant** before Christmas and that we were to do our rhythm dance at it! Thank <u>Heaven</u> I've got my chiffon dress! Tea with the Queen. King came in after and we all went to the film. I don't like their taste in films but it's so terribly kind of them to ask me and send me home in their car.

Tuesday, 10 December

Walked up to Winchester Tower and then on to the Castle with Deborah, Anne and Libby. I made brandy snaps, Lilibet a small chocolate cake, Anne some delicious shortbread and Libby scones. Winifred also came for tea. She has just lately begun to consider herself too old for all of us and has begun to make up but she does it so badly and dresses so atrociously (so does Libby) that she's really neither one thing nor the other and also her enthusiasm over Guides does not improve

---

* Tea dance.

her. I don't like her as much as I used to and prefer Libby by far, though she's very silly and dull. Anne is charming and so of course is Lilibet.

Saturday, 14 December

I went to dancing as usual and Miss Vacani shouted across the room to me that I was holding myself better! Afterwards I went up to the nursery and changed (into my thick yellow dress) in Lilibet's room. Margaret said to me, 'You're going to get a Christmas card from me!' Lunch with the K and Q, etc. I made myself make conversation. Film was Charlie Chaplin. I sat next to L in the front row. I adored the film. When the Royal Family left the room after it was over I didn't know whether to follow or not, even though M kept on beckoning to me. In the end I had to walk across that vast room entirely by myself, which I loved when I thought of all the people I knew watching me! The Duke and Duchess of Kent had come and, though I wasn't actually introduced to them, they both shook hands with me of their own accord and once when I left the room with M I heard her ask the Q who I was, though unfortunately I couldn't hear more. We had tea at five – just the K and Q, the Kents and L and M and me. Is there anyone alive more fortunate than me? It makes up for a hundred happy homes and thousand loving mothers and I love sincerely this family, the first in all England! I came home in their car the happiest person in the world.

Wednesday, 18 December

Opened our post, which included two lovely cards in separate envelopes from the princesses with 'To Alathea from Elizabeth' and 'To Alathea from Margaret' written inside. I was half disappointed it wasn't a photograph card, as I do so long for a signed photograph, but I was thrilled all the same, and knew it was the war again! Miss D had lunch with us, and I said goodbye to her after. I do not believe it is a last farewell, I know we shall keep in constant touch with each other; over our three years we have worked together – through the happy, careless days at Hans Place, before the war, and the hard and lonely ones here, though many here have been very happy, I have known many people come and go, which only makes me feel more the transience of life. I feel too that yet another link of the old days has slipped from me.

Saturday, 21 December

Went to dancing and Miss Vacani praised my carriage. I had to spin by myself and Anne and I did a foxtrot alone, both of which she praised highly. After dancing we went to the nursery and then out for a walk with Monty; I borrowed boots from Mrs Knight and a scarf from Margaret. They'd put my cards up and M gave me a present from them both, which she wouldn't let me open. It was either a picture or a photograph and by the time I got home at seven I was convinced it was a photo, but I was disappointed to find it was a little picture. It is very sweet of them and I love it but, oh, I <u>did</u> want a photo so badly. Lunch with the K and Q and then a lot of preparation for the play. I felt great confidence in myself and my appearance (I had on my green coat and skirt and wine jersey, brown court shoes and no hat). Play very good. Afterwards, when I went along to the nursery, I ran into the King and the Duke of Kent in the dark by mistake! They were sweet to me and I had to stand there till they'd finished talking, as I couldn't get by. Then I said goodbye and thank you to them and the D of K shook hands with me too. I changed in Margaret's room and the Loyds picked me up and took me to the *thé dansant*, which was <u>quite</u> fun but I suppose I must be blasé as I don't enjoy these small rather shabby functions so much as others do, even though I try to. Zelda is very nice. It was thrilling driving home through the blackout with the searchlights and guns going.

Monday, 23 December

I went in the car with Grandpa as far as the green where I waited for a bus into Windsor. I chose a little round painted bottle of eau de Cologne at Caley's for Lilibet but they would neither deliver it for me nor wrap it up in tissue paper, so I had to go and beg a sheet from Pettle's. When I was carrying the parcel out of Caley's someone dashed past me knocking it out of my hands and never even apologised; I <u>glared</u> after him. At the Token House I got a painted bottle for sweets for Margaret but they would only wrap it up in brown paper which very much annoyed me. Then I went to the hotel to ask them to deliver them by messenger boy but they didn't possess such a thing. I said, 'Why not?' and went into a room to address them, then had to walk up to Augusta door and leave them there myself.

Tuesday, 24 December

A priest came yesterday – Father Vernon Johnson, whom we don't much like (except Grandpa) as he's so austere. I spent most of the morning doing up presents, then I went out for a walk but unfortunately I ran into the priest and so had to go for a walk with him, which was rather strained but I made it as short as possible. Embarrassing confession after Rosary. I went to bed at ten and was woken up for Midnight Mass.

Wednesday, 25 December

Had a lovely stocking when I woke up and had breakfast in bed (we all did). The rest of the morning was taken up with giving and receiving presents all round. I arranged all my presents on a table in the sitting room. Lovely lunch and I read again afterwards until three, when we listened to the King, and after that we all went out, but separated at Bishop's Gate, and Daddy and I went for a long walk by ourselves. But it wasn't a very happy Christmas afternoon, as we somehow could not keep off that <u>eternal</u> subject – after the war, which is the one thing worse than the war itself, and more than once I recognised Mummy's words coming from D's lips concerning the school and my too luxurious life here. However, I had a pleasant evening writing my diary for Tuesday and reading. Rosary at seven and the padre preached to us, which made me nearly late for dinner. I sat at my dressing table until long after eleven, thinking and dreaming of that Christmas four years ago at Wentworth,* when I danced till two in the morning! How gloriously exciting it was <u>then,</u> but how far, far more so it would have been <u>now</u>! There would have been glamour, glory, romance and even <u>love</u>! In those great parties in the spacious gilded ballrooms I now recognise a faint echo of the eighteenth century, dead now, never to be recaptured. Yet in analysing my thoughts I think

---

* Wentworth Woodhouse was a vast stately home in Yorkshire, the seat of Earl Fitzwilliam.

I know that I am <u>glad</u> for the present at least, that God has decreed otherwise. Outwardly I am far more of a child than I would have been, but inwardly the war has transformed me into what only <u>years</u> of hard experience could have achieved.

Thursday, 26 December

At breakfast this morning the priest offered to go for a walk with me and tell me about his conversion by St Theresa. Heaven forbid! Went to castle to Jackie Philipps'* tea party with Deborah in the officers' sitting room. The princesses arrived with Monty at five. L wore slightly higher heels than usual. Wonderful tea and crackers. I got a large white bone ring with flowers on it and I kept it as a souvenir of this very happy party. After tea we did the cracker fireworks in Jackie's bedroom, then we all played charades. Greatest fun in the world, I adore charades. Back at home, I put the ring in a box on my dressing-table, as I know that in future years I shall love to look back on this day, which has been, I know not quite why, one of the happiest of my life. Not of course that I would forget it without the ring but one cannot deny that sometimes substance is needed to make the shadow live, if not for you then for your children and grandchildren.

---

* Sir Grismond Philipps, known as Jackie, was equerry to George VI and commander of the Castle Company, in charge of guarding the King at Windsor. He and his wife Joan gave parties for young Grenadier officers to meet the princesses and their friends, including Alathea.

Friday, 27 December

Anne Crichton rang up early to ask me to lunch and a play today. The play was *The Midshipmaid* and I enjoyed it though, try as I will, I can never get away from the fact that I <u>don't</u> <u>really</u> like funny things like that. Not having a good sense of humour I miss many of the jokes, and it positively makes my head <u>ache</u> when I hear people <u>shrieking</u> with laughter at really stupid things which <u>completely</u> fail to amuse me. No, I seem to have a craving for tragedy and drama in <u>everything</u>. I even enjoy my <u>own</u> unhappiness, seeing in it a strange romantic beauty, which appeals to me.

Sunday, 29 December

I woke up with a cold and stayed in all day and read and wrote. I suddenly thought of the relations between Mummy and Daddy, drifting apart, each content to follow his or her own pursuits. They accept the situation as it is, and live rather as <u>good friends</u> than as husband and wife, which, if not all they once hoped for, is at least a great deal. But who, among the nobility of <u>any</u> age, has ever achieved <u>true</u> happiness? I for one do not seek it.

Tuesday, 31 December

The Royal Family have gone away to Sandringham. I think it's a very good thing as L and M haven't been away since <u>January</u> and also it'll be rather a relief to know that I shan't have to worry about missing their dance while I'm away. I got to Queen's Acre about four o'clock and sat in the nursery with Anne. I came home feeling I'd finished the year up well.

1941

Christmas 1941

PANTOMIME

CINDERELLA

written and produced by H. I. Tannar

Characters

Jemima Blimp - - -	Anne Crichton
Agatha Blimp - -	Alathea Fitzalan Howard
Dandine - - -	Elizabeth Hardinge
Buddy - - - -	Cyril Woods
Buddy's Aunt - - - -	Rose Turner
~~Baron Blimp~~ - - - -	.. ..
Cinderella - -	Princess Margaret Rose
Prince Florizel - - -	Princess Elizabeth

CHORUS

Band	No. 1 Coy. Training Battalion, Grenadier Guards
Sketch -	Guardsman Fearinside, Guardsman Goodwin
Baritone - - -	Guardsman Godwin
Accordionist - - -	Guardsman Thomas
Quartette	Sergeant Richards, Corporal Cooper, Guardsman Hathaway, Guardsman Bilson

WINDSOR CASTLE
19th December, 1941

A programme for the 1941 Christmas pantomime at Windsor Castle.

Thursday, 2 January

I knew as soon as I saw her that something was wrong with the Tigress, but it wasn't until she came up to my room just as I was getting ready to go out at eleven that I knew I was the offender. She accused me of calling her Aunt Maggie when I knew she didn't like it, of being rude and tiresome, in short of forgetting myself. Tears of bitter rage sprang from my eyes and impulsively I <u>bit</u> my hands until they almost bled. When she left me all the old bitterness swept over me; this was one of the most miserable days of my life and though I might recover my spirits tomorrow, its bitter memory will remain deep down in my heart till my dying day.

Saturday, 4 January

I set out with Taffy (walking) to meet Annabel. We were overjoyed at seeing each other again and after tea gossiped and laughed in her room.

Wednesday, 8 January

Annabel thinks I am quite mad to bite myself (I've still got the marks) but after lunch I read out to her <u>most</u> of my 'account', and she thought it very well written and that I must have much deeper feelings than her. (Of course, A is very placid and has no dramatic or romantic feelings in her.) We had a lovely gossipy afternoon and evening and I told her about some of the family rows.

Tuesday, 21 January

I caught the 10.31 and felt dazed by great melancholy London. Never have I seen it so depressing – like a city of the dead, the great empty buildings without a pane of glass, many of them in shattered ruins. Two years ago I could never have believed that such an appalling change could come over a place I have known and loved for so long.

Tuesday, 28 January

Got back to Cumberland Lodge last night. Everyone in this house depresses me, even Daddy, who has become so bitter since the war, and good God, he's had enough to make him so. Daddy showed me a letter of Mummy's and in the hurried spontaneous lines I recognised a woman who knows that her life has not been a success, that everywhere she has just missed it, through no real fault of her own. I am beginning to understand her now and whereas I can never love, I can sympathise.

Saturday, 1 February

Much nicer weather. I took Taffy for quite a long walk in the morning. Guides began today in the York Hall, with Winifred as captain. It bores me but it does make a sort of reunion of people one knows. W, of course, is at her worst at Guides, but it was nice to see Anne again. W said she was going to a film at the Castle this evening, so I expect they're back.

Tuesday, 4 February

We started for London at 10.30 (Grandpa, Aunt Magdalen and I). <u>Awful</u> day, snowing hard. I wanted to walk by myself through Hyde Park where I haven't been since July 1939, but I couldn't with Mummy there. Went to 18[*] alone and began packing the last of my belongings in a suitcase. I took *Marie Antoinette* by Zweig, which I used secretly to read before lessons, then searched Ming-Ming's room where I'd spent so many happy hours. From the nursery I collected my favourite pictures, a few ornaments and my little bedside lamp. It was all very sad. All came back here in time for tea. When I came up to bed I stood dreaming by the mantelpiece for a long time, gazing at the little picture of the bluebell wood that I can always remember, hanging first in the nursery and then in my own room, the mother-of-pearl elephant that Eileen[†] gave me, and the white Cupid that the King handed to me off Lilibet's 12th birthday cake, all reminders of a former day and I hoped they would not 'grow into' Cumberland Lodge as some of the other ornaments have. But best of all is the lamp which they're fixing up for me here to use by my bed. The shade is pale green and the

[*] 18 Hans Place in Knightsbridge was where Alathea lived with her parents and younger sister until the war, when it was mothballed, then taken over for war work.
[†] Eileen Ramsey was the cook at Houghton, Alathea's grandfather Langdale's Yorkshire house.

room blue, but who cares? In bed I once more gave way to the hot tears of POIGNANT SORROW.

Wednesday, 5 February

Fräulein* has sent me some work to do – two hours four mornings a week – German and French, which is <u>very</u> tiresome.

Saturday, 8 February

I changed into my green and white dress and went off to dancing. The princesses had the same awful blue and pink shantung dresses on. They <u>must</u> have others. Then <u>why</u> don't they wear them? After tea I made my will for fun, leaving my jewels to Elizabeth Anne, my wardrobe to Ming-Ming and my diaries to Annabel to publish them after Mummy dies.

Tuesday, 4 March

The most lovely day. Went up to the Castle at three. Joined by Libby and Anne. Met Crawfie and Lilibet in schoolroom and then went down to where we cook. Each did one thing – Lilibet did shortbread, Anne fish, Libby potato soup and I did bread pudding. We all passed. Lilibet actually likes washing up and does more of it than the rest of us put together! I am afraid I hate even putting my fingers into dirty water – I much prefer needlework, which L hates!

---

* 'Fräulein' refers to the German governess who had taught Alathea in London and now sent her work to do. We do not know her full name.

Wednesday, 5 March

Biked to meet Sonia. She read my book, while I read all her letters from Lilibet, dozens of them! I must say that she gained more in that way and in photographs, etc., by knowing her well <u>then</u>, than I do now as she never writes or gives photos now but all the same, I do prefer <u>now,</u> as I think that because we are older it is more lasting.

Thursday, 6 March

After drawing, Lilibet, Margaret and I set off for the Red Drawing Room, where we were joined by three Grenadier officers and a few others. Then all the RAF officers filed by, shaking hands with L. Lilibet finds making conversation very difficult, like me, but she did <u>very</u> well, as she had to stand by herself for over an hour talking to each one in turn. She insisted on bringing the dogs in because she said they were the greatest save to the conversation when it dropped!

Saturday, 8 March

Very few of us at dancing. Margaret didn't come. Lilibet had red dancing shoes. I got on all right till the tap and then, as I'd missed all of the new time step they're doing, I had to stand in the back row and shuffle helplessly, while Anne, Libby and Lilibet did it perfectly. I felt the tears burning in my eyes but Anne said she'd write it out for me to practise.

Sunday, 9 March

I walked across to Royal Lodge, where I found Lilibet, Crawfie and Mrs Bowlby* sitting in the saloon before driving to the Castle. L turned her hair under and asked me if I liked it and I said no. We went into the schoolroom and played cards till lunch, then went outside. We laughed a great deal and had great fun spitting over a bridge into a stream, trying to hit leaves as they floated by! Crawfie is such fun; I don't think Monty would approve of spitting! We walked back and dropped Margaret in, as this was her first time out after flu and we three went for a long walk and spent some time at the farm. Didn't get back till four thirty and we got very giggly and silly at the end because we were so exhausted! Crawfie and I were walking slowly arm-in-arm down the steep slope from the terrace and L pushed us and we hurtled down and collapsed into a bush and laughed so much we couldn't get up. Had an amusing tea in the schoolroom. Margaret was killing. After tea we played cards again – silly amusing games like Donkey, because we were in a silly mood. The more I see of them, the more fond I am of them all, and they are so much, <u>much</u> nicer when you are alone with them. I'm sure they like me too, much more than before the war.

Tuesday, 11 March

I got the bus into Windsor. Deborah was in it too. Collected Libby, then joined the princesses and Crawfie in the school-room. We went out today for quite a long walk, measuring

---

* Mrs Bowlby, née the Hon. Lettice Annesley, was a Lady of the Bedchamber to Queen Elizabeth.

time. Ran into the Queen, who looked awful. D was so bright and breezy with her that she was almost rude. Libby and I walked back to Winchester Tower and discussed Deborah. To my surprise, she does disapprove of her attitude to the Queen and also says she's <u>very</u> tactless with the princesses, talking about what she read in the paper concerning them, which one just <u>does</u> not do.

Saturday, 15 March

Dancing was <u>lovely</u> today and I managed the tap very well. Annabel enjoyed watching, the princesses spoke and shook hands with her (I <u>think</u> for the first time in her life). We drove home and discussed everything. A thinks Lilibet has an enormous chest! It is a great pity as it'll be awful one day. Aunt M came up and said that PE had rung up to say could I go to a film there today so the Ford van* came. Took our things off in L's room and then played cards in school-room with Monty and the princesses till four, when we went along to the Queen's rooms for tea. We talked and laughed a lot, then the Queen came in and just after the King. Each time we rose and curtsied and then shook hands. She and I sat on either side of the King and we all talked easily and intimately. We looked at photographs in the King's study after tea for a few minutes, then we went along to the Red Drawing Room (where we dance) for the film, which was *Disraeli,* and very good. Annabel and I sat in front row next to Lilibet. Although I've done this lots of times before, it all seemed new because A was there. I never dreamed I would ever have an opportunity of taking A there at all, let

---

* From the Castle.

alone tea with the King and Queen! I would have been intoxicated with joy if I'd been her. I am glad to know that it was entirely their wish that she should go and not my pushing, as that I shall <u>never </u>do. I hope I have by now learned the art of being in the court circle. I went to bed supremely happy feeling that I am indeed one favoured by Fortune.*

Thursday, 20 March

I started off on my bike for the Castle, down the Long Walk and in at the lodge on the right. We played cards and L asked me to stay for tea. Margaret was in very high spirits today; one can't help laughing at her, and she knows it, and so always takes advantage of it.

Saturday, 22 March

After dancing I changed in Margaret's room and read in the nursery till they'd finished lessons, then went into the Queen's sitting room before going in to lunch. The King there too. Fourteen for lunch, we had dressed crab that the King and Queen had brought back live from Plymouth. Ate chocolates with the Queen afterwards, then we went out with Crawfie before tea with the K and Q. We had Devonshire cream, which the princesses don't like but the King and Queen and I ate it, and the King told the Queen she shouldn't eat so much, when she hadn't been out all the afternoon! He asked me if I was 'hair conscious' too, as Lilibet is always fiddling about with her hair now. So I said, 'Yes!' The Queen

---

* Perhaps ironically, Annabel's daughter, Anne Beckwith-Smith, was to be lady-in-waiting to Diana, Princess of Wales.

asked me if I powdered my face. She is <u>so</u> sweet and kind and without being beautiful she has such irresistible charm one could not help loving her. She has won my unswerving adoration – oh, if only I had a mother like that. We went along to the film where I sat between L and M. It was the Marx Brothers. They all shrieked with laughter but I'm afraid I could only pretend I thought it funny.

Sunday, 23 March

Daddy and I walked across the Home Park to tea at Adelaide Cottage, which the Queen has lent Jackie and Joan Philipps for the duration of the war. I was charmed with it. It typically represents that idea of a little world within a world of its own, which is so characteristic of Windsor Castle and its surroundings. I am always told that life here at Cumberland Lodge is false; I can see now that they are right, but it is precisely that sense of unreality, that lack of connection with the outer, the real world, that appeals to me, I who have always lived in a world of my own, of dreams and fantasies far removed from the age I live in.

Tuesday, 25 March

I would have gone too to get my summer dressing-gown from Grandpa for Easter but Fear, his chauffeur, is ill so I didn't think it worth going by train. Caught the 2.30 bus into Windsor and did some shopping including a nice yellow and white check cotton blouse at Caley's. I put it down on Grandpa's account and hope it will pass unnoticed, as I can't pay for it myself. Mummy is supposed to be giving me a nice one for Easter, but I have not heard a word from her since I had measles. She really might write. I just managed to get a comb, but it was utterly impossible to get hair clips <u>anywhere</u>; we are really beginning to feel this war now.

Thursday, 27 March

Biked to the Castle. We each modelled a horse in clay, which was great fun. Margaret always tries to get me to come to her room instead of Lilibet's. On the way home, I stopped and had a long look at Frogmore as I passed it, and it suddenly occurred to me that if I was Lilibet in a few years' time, I would ask for Frogmore as my residence and when I was Queen I'd make it my Trianon. It would all fit in so perfectly, but I know it would never enter L's head to picture herself as Marie Antoinette.

Monday, 31 March

It becomes more and more difficult to hold out. I don't <u>want</u> to be a secretary. Daddy and I had a heated argument because Mrs Hill-Wood* had been to tea and said I ought to go daily to the Domestic Economy School at Ascot. It's exasperating, all these people plotting and scheming behind your back to send you to places you don't want to go to.

Thursday, 3 April

I biked to drawing and we finished modelling our clay horses. It was the last lesson for this term. Afterwards, we played a French tableau game with Monty and then cards till tea. They said something about Philip, so I said, 'Who's Philip?'

---

* Mr and Mrs Hill-Wood were family friends.

Lilibet said, 'He's called Prince Philip of Greece' and then they both burst out laughing. I asked why, knowing quite well! Margaret said, 'We can't tell you,' but L said, 'Yes, we can. Can you keep a secret?' Then she said that P was her 'boy'. Monty asked me if I had one, and in the end, I told them it was Robert Cecil, which amused L. M said she was so glad I had a 'beau'! We all laughed terribly. L says she cuts photos out of the paper! I must say she is <u>far</u> more grown-up than I was two years ago. When I left, Lilibet said, 'We part today the wiser for two secrets,' and I biked home feeling very happy and also proud at being let into such a great secret, which I shall never betray.

Friday, 4 April

Mummy is staying, so I dressed very carefully for dinner! She greatly approved of me in <u>every</u> way, face, clothes, etc, and she was very nice. I cannot say I dislike her in such moments and I'm sure it would hurt her to know I don't love her – but alas therein lies the tragedy of life; she takes an interest in me and loves me now that I am older; she would like to be loved in return but during all the years of my childhood, when she denied me a mother's affection I grew neither to expect nor want it; now that it is within my reach it is too late. I can feel pride in the brilliant figure she cuts in the beau monde. I can feel gratitude towards her for having bequeathed to me her love and knowledge of clothes, houses and beautiful things but that is all. I can never love her.

Saturday, 5 April

After lunch Mummy and I went out and picked daffodils for her before she left. Then I went to have tea with the King, Queen, Lilibet and Margaret. L and I ate some cake in the nursery beforehand, as L says they never have cake with the King and Queen, which is really rather far-fetched I think!

Sunday, 6 April

I had no room yesterday to put in an amusing incident at tea. The King, who was sitting next to me, asked me how I got to the Castle. There was an awkward pause, then I said: 'The car came for me, Sir.' The Queen and the princesses (and I) roared with laughter and the King said good-humouredly, 'Well, don't <u>laugh</u>, it was a perfectly ordinary question to ask. I've often met her bicycling in the park – a lone figure in the Long Walk!'

Wednesday, 9 April

Deborah rang up and said they were going for the picnic – to my great surprise, as the weather was awful. Biked to Forest Gate and met the princesses, Deborah, Winifred and Libby. I left my bike at the lodge and got into the royal car and we drove to a lovely part of the forest, where we stopped and went for a walk, picking primroses. Had tea on rugs, which we spread out under the trees. Lit a fire to warm ourselves by. I was very surprised that the princesses came by themselves without Mrs Knight – I think it must have been about the first time; of course, they had a detective. Packed up and set off in the cars to look for the German plane shot down in the forest last night. Took some time finding it, but when we did, it was well worth it. It was a <u>huge</u> thing, completely smashed, and we picked up bits as souvenirs. There was a guard on it. I hope to arrange a bluebell picnic in May behind Smith's Lawn with them all. There is an irresistible charm about a flower picnic.

Saturday, 12 April

Grandpa I went to church at Englefield Green. He hoped I'd always have a great devotion to Holy Week in memory of all the ones here and I thought that if he wanted me to like Holy Week the last thing he should do is to drag me round to all these ghastly what Mummy calls 'unspiritual services'.

Tuesday, 15 April

We went to Errolston,* the school, by car. It's part of St Mary's Convent in South Ascot and we talked to a <u>charming</u> nun called Mother Perpetua, who's not a bit conventy. In the morning they do domestic science, in the afternoon German, French, tennis and swimming, and after tea, current events, etc. I'd have to be there at ten, which is very reasonable but I thought staying until six very hard. I must say, it

---

* Errolston was the domestic science school, which was attached to St Mary's Convent School in South Ascot and run by the same order of nuns. It was for girls aged sixteen to eighteen who had finished their academic education. Most boarded and had been at the main school but there were others, like Alathea, who went as day girls and did not stay for a whole year.

all seemed lovely and I was quite keen. Hugh Euston* came to dinner and we had great fun.

Friday, 18 April

They had the worst blitz of the war in London on Wednesday night. Mummy said it was <u>ghastly</u> and that London was very much in ruins.

Monday, 21 April

Lilibet's fifteenth birthday, also third anniversary of Granny's death.

Houghton, Yorkshire

Wednesday, 23 April

Daddy greeted me at Houghton, then I <u>rushed</u> to see Ming-Ming and Elizabeth Anne, who was touchingly pleased to see me. Her hair is now long enough to curl up.

Monday, 28 April

Letter from Lilibet from Windsor – very nice, quite long. It was signed 'with love from Elizabeth'. I'm wondering whether one oughtn't to begin calling her Princess E now she's older.

---

* Hugh Denis Charles FitzRoy was heir to the Duke of Grafton so had the courtesy title Earl of Euston. He was a captain in the Grenadiers and later in the war was an aide-de-camp to the Viceroy of India. After the war he married Fortune Smith who has been, for many years, Mistress of the Robes to the Queen.

Monday, 5 May

Letter from Grandpa saying that Fear died of a heart attack on Friday morning. It was a shock as he wasn't a bad old man and one would <u>never</u> have believed, when I saw him last at King's Cross, that he would be dead within ten days. I <u>do</u> hope they'll quickly get another one. Letter from Sonia saying she's been to tea with the princesses and they talked about young men. L told her that I'd told them about Robert and she said she also adored Hugh Euston, so S said that I did, too, so they laughed and laughed! L told her that she had a beau but didn't say who, so I must still keep that a secret from Sonia.

Wednesday, 7 May

Bad raid on Hull and we were kept awake by the bombs for a long time. Watched the fire from the windows – the sky was all red for miles around.

Thursday, 8 May

It was too sad leaving my darling Elizabeth Anne and when she cried, I did too – it was too much for me to feel her clinging to me and crying. Back at Cumberland Lodge, the atmosphere of acute egoism is the more oppressing after having been away from it, and always there is the knowledge that I must make up to them for the sake of <u>policy</u> as well as politeness. It's no good, I can no longer <u>love</u> Grandpa and yet I must always pretend I do now, more than ever before. And poor darling Daddy is <u>so</u> depressingly pessimistic. No one <u>really</u> loves him and I'm sure he doesn't realise that I care more than all the others, though I do my best to show him that I <u>do</u> love him. Nevertheless I shall learn much from what I suffer in this house.

Saturday, 10 May

We heard that our old house poor 18 [Hans Place] had every pane of glass smashed last night and the poor door blown in. <u>Poor dear 18!</u>

Monday, 12 May

Mrs Loyd drove Zelda and me to Errolston. Grandpa told me he pays for school so I must work very hard and take it seriously. I was glad I had Z to help me for the first day or two, as I know no one else. Began by all taking notes on a lecture on housewifery. We were shown our lockers and divided into sections. She and I had to clean a lot of silver forks and spoons and then lay the table for lunch. One section cooked lunch for us all. We wore our coloured overalls for the work.

Friday, 16 May

Biked to Errolston – lovely day, so it was a pleasant ride. It was laundry for my section, but we also did sewing, which was nice. Zelda and I both loathe washing – it makes your hands so rough! I'm very glad I'm not a boarder. I should <u>hate</u> to tidy my room and make my bed, etc. I'm not made to look after myself!!

Saturday, 17 May

Both the princesses at dancing. L asked me to film this evening and to meet them at Royal Lodge first. Mrs Morshead said to me, 'Alathea, I shall curtsy to you out of sheer habit,' which was very embarrassing! I rang Winifred to tell her I was giving Guides up! She didn't take it too badly! Walked to Royal Lodge and was met by the princesses. Said, 'How do you do,' to the K and Q who were sitting on a bench in the garden and soon after the K drove us back to Castle in his own open sports car, which was great fun and also an exciting experience for me! The Q gave me her silk scarf to put over my head, which was sweet of her. If only she knew how much I adored her! We had tea out on the terrace. There were pheasant's eggs. After tea L said that Sonia had told her about her young men but I didn't say that I knew already, nor did L say about Hugh (E). We then went along to the film, *Sailors Three*. They all <u>screamed</u> with laughter, so I had to too, but I must have an entirely different mentality because I just <u>don't</u> like silly films!

Monday, 19 May

I forgot to say on Saturday that when we were in the car PE said to me, 'Have you got a comb?' and the King said, 'A <u>comb</u>! Can't you lend her a brush or isn't that <u>done</u>?' It was then that the Queen offered me her scarf to put over my head and halfway down the Long Walk, it nearly blew off and I thought with a smile what a faux-pas it would have been if it <u>had</u> blown away and I had cried, 'Oh, Madam, your scarf!'

Saturday, 24 May

Dancing went v. well. The Kents now only come alternate weeks, as they behave better when they're not together! Had biscuits and orange juice in nursery with the princesses. Then lunch alone with the K and Q and princesses, in the business room. Afterwards we went to the Waterloo Chamber to watch the play called *Up & Doing.* I saw my darling Hugh E. After tea the Q, the princesses and I played racing demon in her sitting room. I'm so blissfully happy in the Court Circle and I would gladly die for that family if there were a Revolution.

Thursday, 29 May

Changed into my pink skirt and blue striped blouse and biked to drawing, which we had under the terrace. M and I found it hard to stop talking! She said she didn't like Deborah much – too forward!!! I'm glad they see it too! Monty asked me, *'Admirez vous Lord Euston?'* and I said, *'Oui.'* She said she thought so by the way I talked to him on Saturday! We all laughed terribly and M asked if he was my beau, knowing quite well he is!!! She's very old for her age in those ways – indeed in most ways. L then went on to a Guide hike with Winifred – much against her will!

Sunday, 1 June

Grandpa's eighty-sixth birthday – I hope I never live to that age! Mass and Communion. The papers said that from today all clothing except hats are rationed! You're allowed sixty-six coupons a year, and since one dress takes eleven, God how I loathe this bloody age!

Thursday, 5 June

Changed into my yellow dress and short brown coat and the royal car came and took me to drawing. Indoors today as such awful weather. Then all went off in car to tea with Deborah. Whole family there, rather overwhelming, and they all talked at once in loud voices and made short, sharp curtsies (it's funny, everyone seems to, who aren't used to it). PE said she'd send me the first-aid book to learn for next Thursday but when Hugh Euston came up to dine he brought it with him, with a postcard inside signed 'Lilibet'. I <u>was</u> pleased! It was lovely having Hugh to dinner. Lilibet said today that he'd told her he was coming – I <u>do</u> think it's so funny us both selecting him for a 'beau'!

Saturday, 7 June

After class we went to nursery and had orange juice and biscuits. I changed in M's room as she always bags me but L says I'm to go to hers next time! At lunch, I hoped Hugh E would sit next to me but he was put between the Q and Lilibet, and Margaret caught my eye and laughed! After lunch we went out with the K and Q. The K played golf, so we strayed off and presently it <u>poured</u> with rain and we <u>rushed</u> for the tunnel and had to remain there about half an hour as we had thin shoes and no coats. The Q was sweet and very chatty to me and we all sang. Came out and the princesses ran off to collect magazines we'd left out and I was alone with the Q – first time I'd ever been alone with her but I always feel <u>perfectly</u> at my ease, though I never forget who she is. We dried ourselves in nursery and they curled their hair and M and I played backgammon till tea, with the K and Q. Went along to the film quarter to five – *Down Argentine Way*, <u>quite</u> good. Hugh E and I agree about their films and <u>try</u> to suggest others! Came back and played a few games of racing demon with the Queen — I'd do <u>anything</u> for her. M asked me again if I liked her, as she said she wasn't sure!! How could one not like her? She's inherited all her mother's charm, more than L.

Thursday, 12 June

Biked to the Castle and drew with PM on one side of the terrace wall and PE on the other as she was doing the Castle. I had my wine and yellow shoes on and L and M both said they didn't like them! Saw the Q. I said I loved coming to tea and Margaret laughed and said, 'She <u>adores</u> us,' and made one of her enchanting faces!!! M said they now take it in turns to have me in their bedrooms to get ready!

Saturday, 14 June

Went to dancing. Both Kent children there today – they're v. naughty, but very sweet. Princess Alexandra is a darling really and I longed to put my arms round her and kiss her angelic little face!

Thursday, 19 June

<u>Very</u> hot. I felt terribly lazy and my hay fever was appalling. After lunch I biked to drawing. We talked about young men and Margaret said I <u>had</u> got another 'love besides Robert, hadn't I?' But she didn't say who, though we all knew who

it was!!! Margaret was too sweet, and she always will ask me if I like her as if she's not sure!

Thursday, 26 June

Lovely drawing today. After tea I suggested going home, but L said wouldn't I come out with them to the Queen, so we went and after looking at magazines, the King came and we all went for a stroll. . . . The Queen was so sweet about my hay fever. She also asked me if I had made a plan about my coupons and laughed when I said I had already spent twenty-five!

Wednesday, 2 July

The thought crossed my mind that when I got home I might find an invitation to the Castle for the weekend – it had been a secret, though a very faint, hope all the week (since I'm going there Friday and Saturday anyway). I never really believed it <u>would</u> happen but when I heard the telephone I somehow <u>knew</u> at once that it was this, and when I was told it was PE I knew the very words she was going to say and I was right! Delirious with joy and excitement I marvelled at God granting me one of my dearest wishes and I wondered seriously whether my foreknowledge was a presentiment or whether it was telepathy, the urgency of my <u>wish</u> putting the <u>idea</u> into their minds.

Friday, 4 July

They sent the car for me and I went straight out to draw. Princess Margaret in bed with a bad throat, which is such a pity. I shall miss her. At four Lilibet and I watched their new chameleon on the syringa tree, then she and I and Crawfie walked down to Frogmore, where we punted on the lake. Rolled our stockings down to prevent tearing them. After tea we lay on the grass and talked and laughed. They're getting up a concert with Miss Vacani. They insist on bringing Mr Tannar into it but I do hope the schoolchildren'll be out of it this year, as without being horrid they really oughtn't to dance with the princesses.

Got back seven and I went to have my bath; my room is the same as last time in November, on the floor above theirs. We had supper in our dressing-gowns in nursery at eight, then L and I sat in her room and read and talked till bed. They've stopped sleeping in the shelter now but I'd hoped anyway that I could sleep in my own room, because I have such awful catarrh now at night and can't breathe properly. The King and Queen away at Sandringham. I went to bed blissfully happy.

Saturday, 5 July

Breakfast in nursery. Messed about afterwards while Lilibet did lessons, then changed into my blue chiffon for dancing. Lovely class today. At lunch, I sat next to Hugh E. I went up and wrote my diary in my room, while L practised, then she and I went out and read under the terrace wall till four, when we came in and got ready to go to tea at Adelaide Cottage with the officers. Walked over there with Crawfie. Poor Margaret still in bed. L wore a lovely green linen frock with muslin collar and cuffs and stitched with pink and yellow. She had a hat of yellow straw, with a long green velvet ribbon. We had tea with the Philipps and three of the officers and after we played the usual games and left at seven. Great fun. Sat in nursery when we got home, then did exactly the same as last night. I secretly hoped it would not be my last supper here, but nothing's been said. When I went to bed I stood for a long while gazing out of the window, remembering the other time – over three years ago now – when I did the same thing. It does indeed seem a long time since those sunny days of my childhood, when they were in the nurseries next door to me, now occupied by the Kents. And yet I haven't changed so v. much – I stood dreamily contemplating then, just as I was standing contemplating now.

Sunday, 6 July

After breakfast we sat about and also went for a little walk with Crawfie. I mentioned going away but L said nothing about me staying till Monday, so much against my wishes and secret hopes I had to resign myself to leaving this evening; L is funny in some ways – v. matter of fact and uncurious and above all untemperamental. But one can't have everything and I'm eternally grateful for this heavenly surprise. I went to church in Windsor with Monty and L went to Royal Lodge. How I wish I could have gone too! When we both got back, we fed the chameleon and then to Frogmore with Crawfie and Monty pulling Margaret, who'd just got up, in a basket on wheels. Got into punt, and then found a nice place to eat our picnic lunch. Great fun – we drank ginger beer out of bottles! Monty left after and I must say it was more fun without her – Crawfie is so much more fun. We lay out on a rug and talked and read. Discussed clothes for concert. We had great fun getting back, what with Crawfie's hat and two dogs falling into the water! Tea in schoolroom, then we just sat and looked at things. When I got up to get ready I ran into the Kents and they asked dozens of killing questions and even pushed into my room – they are <u>very</u> sweet but just like little ragamuffins! Before I left L and I took the chameleon to catch flies on the windows. Said goodbye to Mrs Knight and Bobo and then car took me home. I had that same sad lonely feeling as I had last time I returned from here, as I am REALLY HAPPY WITH THEM ALL.

Monday, 7 July

<u>How</u> I envy Lilibet's life, not only for its grandeur but for the fact that she has so many dear kind people to do everything for her, not only because it's their <u>job</u>, but because they love her and only wish to serve her but that spirit has gone from the world now with ordinary people.

Thursday, 10 July

Lilibet rang up to say Mrs Cox, our art teacher, had sunstroke but would I go over to Royal Lodge and bathe with them. The princesses met me and we dangled our feet in the pool and talked and then had tea, laid out in the garden of the little Welsh Cottage. Mrs Knight was with them – it was nice to have her as it reminded me of the old days. She so rarely goes out with them now and I don't think she and Crawfie get on. After tea we changed into our bathing things. L had a new one on but I was <u>v.</u> disappointed to see it was still a plain black Bath Club one – why on <u>earth</u> doesn't she get a nice one? We had a lovely bathe and for the first time in my life I jumped straight in and loved it. Later the K and Q came and the K bathed with us. It was fun. Came in and changed and then listened to the wireless in the saloon. The Q thanked me for my letter and said she thought it beautifully expressed, which delighted me! Heavenly day.

Saturday, 12 July

I woke up to find the sun streaming through the gaps in the curtains. I stretched lazily and contentedly and thought happily of the day in front of me. Met Annabel in Eton and had picnic lunch near the cricket ground, then A and I wandered round. Hugh Euston there with lots of hangers-on and A and I tried to make him see me (inconspicuously of course!) and succeeded! I'd love to marry him!

Tuesday, 15 July

We break up today till 8 October. Got some cleansing cream and some Cyclax Milk of Roses at Caley's, then walked up to the Castle for a rehearsal. That officious little schoolmaster was there, hopping round interfering – I could have strangled him!

Wednesday, 16 July

Went up to Castle and joined Anne C and Libby at Winchester Tower first as we had another rehearsal. Mr Tannar offered to give me lifts in his car, but as Anne said afterwards it would be better to walk than accept a lift from him!

Pouring with rain. Water hot tonight so had a bath. Dear

Billy, though she's a bad maid, is such a comfort to me here – she nearly makes up for a nannie.

Friday, 18 July

In Debenhams I found the dress of my dreams! A pale, pale orchid-coloured gauze with short, full puff sleeves, high neck at back, tight fitting from below bust to hips, then yards and yards of this heavenly stuff, and down the front panel are lengthening rows of hand-made stiff flowers in pastel shades.

Monday, 21 July

The car took me to the Castle for the dress rehearsal where we got into our minuet dresses. I adore my crinoline and somehow feel completely at ease in it, as if I belong to it, like a lady of the eighteenth century being dressed for a ball. Mr Tannar told 'funny' stories but he stayed too long today and had to be poked and told to come off! I was glad. Betty and Didi (assistants) as good as said they couldn't stand him and Didi said to me, 'Who is he anyway?!!' Tomorrow is the real day. Oh, how I adore acting and dancing – on the stage. Today was my idea of Heaven!

Tuesday, 22 July

Guests came to Cumberland Lodge so dropped me at the Castle door. I ran into the Queen in the passage who said she hoped we were going to do the minuet through twice. We dressed and were made up. I made the most of my crinoline – it was heavenly sitting down in it: it flowed so gracefully out on either side of one. Betty said I would have <u>loved</u> to live in those days and would have been in my element, which pleased me! We didn't begin till four fifteen, as the King was late, but it all passed without a hitch – we danced the minuet and the waltz through twice, as they were so short. The K, Q and the Duchess of Kent there, and five people from C. Lodge. <u>All</u> the 'artists' had tea at five round tables in the dining room. Diana Bowes-Lyon came – she's very pretty now. Lilibet had that vulgar little tadpole of a schoolmaster next to her at tea!

Wednesday, 23 July

Spent most of the morning and afternoon quietly lying on rug in garden reading. After tea, I sewed indoors, as flies so bad. At six I went up to begin the great affair of dressing! Could hardly eat any dinner and all the way to the Castle in the Barley Mow taxi I was in a state of nervous excitement. Arrived and was miserable at first because everyone had long white gloves, then I saw lots hadn't, but I should have liked to have worn them. We all filed through into the Red Drawing Room, shaking hands with the K and Q and the princesses. Then dancing began. Never, in all my life, shall I forget this evening – it was the loveliest dance I've ever been to. There were nearly 200 there and I knew almost all – it went on till three in the morning without a lull, although supposed to end at twelve! We walked out on to the terrace in between dances. Everyone admired my dress including the Queen and I got on wonderfully and danced with everyone I wanted – except the King although he did clutch my arm in the first Palais Glide. I loved the waltz best, though, by far. The Q was wonderful and danced all the 'funny dances' and Paul Jones,* etc., and looked lovely in a full frock of white tulle, covered with silver sequins and the princesses wore dresses rather the same as the Q, also from Hartnell, in white lacy stuff, embroidered with pale blue marguerites, and they had flowers in their hair and at their waist, but they were especially pretty because they <u>weren't</u> ordinary children's party frocks and were unlike anyone else's. Actually, there weren't <u>very</u> many lovely frocks and I <u>honestly</u> think that mine and the princesses' were the prettiest there. No Eton boys, for which I was glad, as we then only had the dashing young 'cavaliers'! I was <u>terrified</u> I wasn't going to dance with Hugh Euston and could have killed Libby when she had him, for ages, but then I met him at the buffet and he said, with that great charm of his, 'Oh, Alathea, I've been looking for you all the evening, we must have a dance!' It wasn't true but still!! I danced the last dance of all with him and it went on for ages – we got on beautifully and had a drink together at the end. The rooms were insufferably hot and someone fainted. PE asked me how many times I danced with him and said she was rather hurt because he only had the first one with her because he was asked to and then not again. Hugh loved my dress. We said goodbye about three fifteen – P Margaret stayed up till the very end. She was <u>so</u> sweet and everyone was mad about her. Car came to fetch me and I got home and <u>fell</u> into bed exhausted but <u>blissfully</u> happy! Never, in all my life, shall I forget this night.

---

* A 'Paul Jones' is a dance during which the participants change partners, often several times.

Thursday, 31 July

Biked to drawing. We drew in tunnel as raining. Lilibet said she had something to show me and when I went into her room to tidy, she took a letter out of a drawer for me to read – it was to Colonel Legh from Hugh E thanking for the dance – she said she'd stolen it and was going to keep it! He's got nice writing.

Saturday, 2 August

Lilibet rang up to ask me to the film. When I got to the Castle, Margaret told me that King Peter of Yugoslavia* would have tea with us. She said, with a mischievous smile, 'Lilibet thinks I like him!'

It would actually be a good marriage for me. The Q introduced me to the young king and said I was a friend of L's. He's very sweet and speaks English fluently, with an attractive accent and he's only eighteen. We were just as gay as usual at tea, though naturally I could only <u>really</u> speak when spoken to. The K and Q address him as Peter. The film was *Target for Tonight*, then the princesses and I went with the Q to her sitting room and played racing demon. The Q said how well the blue of my dress suited me. It was a heavenly evening.

We said goodbye till after the holidays – how quickly the summer's gone!

---

* Peter II succeeded to the throne of Yugoslavia in 1934 when he was only eleven, after his father King Alexander had been assassinated. He was Yugoslavia's last king. He spent much of the war in London, then went up to Cambridge and joined the RAF. George V had been his godfather. After the war he married Princess Alexandra of Greece, a cousin of Prince Philip.

Houghton, Yorkshire

Thursday, 7 August

Got to Houghton about six and I rushed up to see Elizabeth Anne and Ming-Ming and stayed with her while she unpacked for me to show her my things.

Friday, 8 August

Mummy doesn't like me so much this time. There was a note of spite and venom in many of her words – she said she was glad a button had come off my dress, as I looked less as if I was going to a garden party. She's also taken a dislike to Taffy. I'm glad I'm sleeping this end, miles away from her.

Saturday, 9 August

After tea Mummy and I played tennis and also had a talk about marriage. She is ambitious for me but not in the way that I am.

Sunday, 17 August

Mass at nine. Mummy and I went for a walk and began talking about Daddy, and she said she didn't think she <u>could</u> go on living with him after the war – he is so hopelessly vague – and could never take up <u>their</u> life again and that perhaps when both grandpas are dead they'd have a friendly divorce but she'd settle me first and E's young enough not to count. I listened with dry eyes and a heavy heart – somehow I wasn't surprised. Their temperaments differ too widely. I have my own life to make, my own ship to steer through the hopeless storms of Fate. But this has affected me deeply. I only wish that tradition demanded they should remain together and make the best they could of the wreck of their own unhappiness.

Wednesday, 20 August

Got ready after breakfast and drove into York. I've got twenty-six coupons out of Grandpa to <u>keep</u>! We had a lovely lunch at Terry's,* then we went to a very good film called *The Letter* with Bette Davis and Herbert Marshall. She commits cold-blooded murder in it and gets away with it. I thought of the Tigress. Ever since last August when Ming-Ming had that row with her, I have seriously wondered whether I couldn't poison her and get away with it! I know that I shall never dare, but I <u>swear</u> that I wouldn't hesitate if it were possible to not be found out! Mummy says, too, she'd drown her if she were alone in a boat with her! That old hag will live at <u>least</u> twenty more years.

Thursday, 21 August

Princess Margaret's eleventh birthday.

Mummy and I had a conversation about me – she said I'm old fashioned in the 'old-maidish' way, which is <u>awful</u> – I said that I didn't really belong to this century – I knew I shouldn't have said it and she answered that I have 'convinced' myself into believing that idea and that it <u>ceased</u> to be a good thing once it affected one's ordinary life. I went

---

* Terry's of York were the famous Quaker chocolate makers who also had a tea shop.

to bed in tears – life seemed to me <u>so, so</u> hopeless – the world I live in is not real – it is as far removed from the ordinary world of the twentieth-century girl as the planet Venus might be or perhaps it is my outlook on it. Anyway, I love it for that very reason.

Saturday, 23 August

Went to bed early tonight. Oh, how I longed for Hugh to come to me – but this night and the next and many more, I must spend alone, until one day when that greatest desire of every girl will be satisfied.

Friday, 29 August

Ming-Ming suggested that I should do a little mending for myself and I lost my temper and getting a needle I made long scratches on my arm till I drew blood – it relieved my feelings but still I could find no outlet for my pent-up, angry soul. I discovered I'd lost my little gold horseshoe on my bracelet, which is too sad as, besides bringing me luck, I wanted to keep it always and pass it on as an historical souvenir of Lilibet, in whose twelfth birthday cake I found it and have worn it ever since.

Sunday, 31 August

Mass at nine. Stayed in the whole morning with Mummy putting things out for her packing, etc. She's got such heavenly things – I'm longing to be grown-up and have everything of the very best. I want to marry as <u>soon</u> as possible – I don't agree with Annabel's idea that she wants to be free and enjoy herself for a few years first and Mummy agrees with me. I have always been very young for my age but I'm convinced it was chiefly the princesses, as I've always and do still, kept myself back to L's level. L of course is v. old for her age and now there is not so much difference between us, but it is a great pity she's not two or even one year older, as she could easily have been since she wasn't born till three years after the K and Q married.

Monday, 29 September

Ming-Ming and I left Houghton and got to Grosvenor Square late. M-M and I slept together in Aunt Alathea's room. I fiddled about with all her face creams! I hadn't slept in London for two years, and after the country it seemed horribly noisy but I listened eagerly for the old familiar sound of horses' feet trotting down the quiet streets and it made me happy to hear them again.

Sunday, 5 October

I suddenly decided I want to be Polyfoto'd* tomorrow with only a chiffon scarf or something round my bare shoulders, so I hunted round and Elsie [a maid at Cumberland Lodge] found me the thing – a length of blue tulle which I practised with, and found I looked lovely both with it round my shoulders and also with it over my head as a veil – also with naked shoulders. In this last pose I looked rather like Lady

---

* Polyfoto, started in the 1930s, was a chain of photographic studios with branches all over England, as well as London department stores. The client sat in a swivel chair and the photographer took forty-eight exposures. The client could later order prints and enlargements, often then given to friends and family as presents.

Hamilton! I felt once more elated with that light and airy excitement that makes life worth living!

Tuesday, 7 October

Saw in the papers that the princesses have returned south, so I do hope it's true – I'm longing to see them again and also incidentally Hugh E. If <u>only</u> Lilibet was two years older or even if she had no sister – how can I appear to H of marriageable age and to the rest of them as little more than a child at one and the same time?

Wednesday, 8 October

I bussed to Ascot and hitchhiked from there to Errolston. It was nice to be back again, as it's something definite to do and also a friendly atmosphere and I'm not there enough to bother what the girls are like. It was nice to see Zelda again.

Friday, 10 October

We cooked in the morning and I burned the sauce! The princesses came back on Tuesday, so we hope things will begin next week!

Saturday, 11 October

Had tea with Libby Hardinge. Two sweet little boys were there – how I long to have a child of my own – I should love it to be Hugh's too. L told me that he has left the Castle – my heart sank. I shall lose sight of him completely and he's sure to marry someone else and meanwhile I've got nobody! Lilibet will be sad he's gone too.

Monday, 13 October

It was a heavenly day and I sang gaily as I rode along on top of the bus to Errolston. Did a little washing in morning but knitted most of the time and looked at patterns. Saw a <u>heavenly</u> nightgown, which I decided to make. After tea we had a cookery demonstration. Bussed and taxied home. The Tigress annoyed me again – lots of little things she does drive me into a <u>frenzy</u> of <u>blind</u> hatred for this woman with the darkened mind, and then it subsides into the calmer, more odious dislike that is contempt, and always it is ready like a volcano to erupt once more, when I feel I want to scream aloud. Lord Richard Percy* dined. I'd never seen him before so I was v. excited but he was <u>terribly</u> unprepossessing in looks, though very nice. Of course I never consider a younger son seriously (God grant I never have to!) but it is good to cultivate those sort of friendships and as a last resort at the age of twenty-five it would be better than an ordinary Mr – or even Sir! His eldest brother, Hugh Northumberland, is a flame of Annabel's.

Saturday, 18 October

Went over to the Barclays and Betty and I drove into Windsor in the pony trap. It is terribly sad to think she's already a widow – she's only about twenty-two. We got quite confidential and I really want to do things with her more. She talked about Hugh, saying how much she likes him – I am a <u>little</u> jealous of her with him, as I think he likes her but at the same time it <u>might</u> be a way to see him again, if he

---

* Lord Richard Percy was a younger brother of the 10th Duke of Northumberland, Hugh Percy, who had succeeded their father in 1930.

ever comes down from London to see them. Zelda rang up at dinner time to say I am going to be the Duchess of Devonshire in the play [*Berkeley Square*]. Oh, I was thrilled. It <u>couldn't</u> be better, as apparently I only appear in one scene in a lovely ball dress, but then I completely hold the stage, so I shall have a fairly prominent part and yet only having one scene I mightn't have to stay at Errolston so much for rehearsals.

Thursday, 23 October

I biked to the Castle for drawing. It was lovely to see them again; we painted designs on our clay horses. They wore their old brown check skirts and red Aertex shirts, which they ought not to do – their clothes have gone down a lot since the war. They talked about their new lot of officers and are v. sorry Hugh's gone. Lilibet said she'd had her hair permed – it looked v. nice in front but too stiff behind. She told me that Philip, her beau, had been for the weekend and that I must come and see him if he came again! She said he's very funny, which doesn't sound my type actually – the only thing that <u>does</u> bore me about the Royal Family is that they all <u>will</u> tell one jokes that they've heard on wireless, etc. No one else I know is in the <u>least</u> interested in those sort of silly jokes, but then the K and Q and the princesses <u>are</u> v. simple people.

Saturday, 25 October

Dancing didn't go v. well today– we're doing a pantomime for Christmas and, of course, that odious Mr Tannar is helping. He came this morning, which made me <u>so</u> angry that I purposely avoided showing him <u>any</u> sign of recognition.

Saturday, 1 November

Mass at nine o'clock. Princess E rang up to ask me to stay for lunch and the film. There was a fearful hurry to get ready in time, though Billy helped me, and I was distracted to the point of tears but soon recovered my composure. The dancing class went v. well today. I changed after in Margaret's room. There were fourteen for lunch and I sat next to the King – for the first time in a large lunch. We got on v. well after a bit and talked a lot – I was <u>thrilled</u>. On my left was Sir Alan Lascelles,* who asked me if I kept a diary and remarked how interested I'd be to read in my great-grandmother's diary that she sat next to William IV or something, which I knew applied to myself at the present moment and which idea is also always in <u>my</u> mind. Afterwards we went out with the K and Q. The K asked me about the secretarial and I thought afterwards that it wasn't very clever of me to say so definitely that I hated typing, etc., in case it might help me to be a lady-in-waiting, but I don't care – I don't want to be one if I have to do that. Lilibet said she thought I was her best friend now, which <u>delighted</u> me. She said that Sonia used to be but she never saw her now – poor S, she'd almost hate me if she knew that. We had tea and the King of Greece† was there – he's <u>charming</u>. Surely I must be the most favoured girl in Europe? Surely, after such a brilliant girlhood, I could not be condemned to a life of obscurity?

---

* Sir Alan Lascelles, known as Tommy, was a courtier who became assistant private secretary to George VI.
† King George II of Greece was living in exile in London during the war.

Since God has ordained for me to sit at my ease with the crowned heads of Europe, surely he must mean me to be great? And must it not then be my duty to seek greatness and follow whosoever my ambition might lead me to, at <u>any</u> cost to myself? We walked along to the film at six. It was *Fantasia,* the new Walt Disney. It was quite the most extraordinary film I've ever seen, being a fantastical imaginary conception of the great classical music in pictures. I adored it. Afterwards, I said goodbye to the Queen, and thanked her and she said, 'Oh, but I <u>love</u> you coming.' Who would not die for a woman like that? When I got home I wrote to Lilibet, asking her to come to tea on my birthday. I probably shan't get a letter back but it's better to write than to ask.

Monday, 3 November

Zelda picked me up and we went to Errolston together. Sewed all the morning. Went up and talked to Angela in her room for a long time – she's nice and I found myself confiding in her more than I'd confide in many people I know far better. 'Aren't you miserable without your mother?' she asked. They all ask that and when I say that I'm used to not seeing a lot of her, they say, 'Don't you miss a family life?' It is hard to explain the feelings of the heart but Angela and I agreed that, for the most part, the circumstances of one's early years are given one and from them, more than anything else, we form our character, our outlook on life and even our life itself. Children quickly accustom themselves to their environment and come to accept it, as I have, as their natural existence.

Friday, 7 November

Breakfast is a nice cheerful meal at Errolston, then laundry, then sewing. German and French in afternoon. Bussed home. Grandpa got on my nerves rather, poor thing, I do try to be nice to him and not impatient – I owe so much to him and can never forget it. Without him, or I suppose Granny, I should never have known Lilibet, Lilibet who provides the very meaning of my life.

Wednesday, 12 November

Laundry lecture, then cooking all the morning. I had to do some washing-up. I have an instinctive and unconquerable loathing for touching any dirty water or dust, etc., and I'm more and more glad not to be returning next term. I do enjoy it now and it's a lovely place but I couldn't be there any longer – I'd feel I was wasting my time, restless, and as for taking the exam, I'd rather die! The officer, John Wiggin,* was killing this evening and we all laughed a lot but the Tigress was quite repulsive in her lack of control and her stupidity and all my contempt for her surged up again. That, mingled with a hotter, cleaner hatred for my mother, poisoned my soul as I went up to bed, and it was a happy relief to lie once more on my own soft pillows and pretend that Hugh [Euston] was by my side – to love me.

Thursday, 13 November

Pouring with rain. At lunchtime Diana Bowes-Lyon came. She is so sweet, and I think likes me. We started off on bikes

---

* Sir John Wiggin, another young officer stationed at Windsor, went on to marry Lady Cecilia Anson, a relation of Queen Elizabeth.

and went on to drawing. Diana is going there for weekend. I felt differently when they said that Elizabeth Vyner* was going there for a weekend sometime – I suppose it is jealousy that makes me instinctively wince whenever I hear someone else is going there because I don't <u>really</u> mind as I'm still ahead of all, except the cousins and I don't mind them. Lilibet happened to mention something that Margaret Elphinstone had written to her, calling Princess Margaret Maggie, etc., which greatly shocked me – you should always be respectful to a princess even if she is your cousin.

Saturday, 15 November

Went to dancing. Afterwards we went out with the King. Much as I enjoy these Saturdays, I often wonder how Lilibet is content always to just go out with her parents – doesn't she ever want to talk or walk alone with a friend? Much as I love Margaret, I wish L had no younger sister, as then she would be <u>bound</u> to come out more and would seek the company of people of her own age more. She doesn't know what a real friend is, as she never talks confidentially to one and she's the most ungossipy person I know. Placid and unemotional, she never desires what doesn't come her way; always happy in her own family, she never needs the companionship of outsiders; she never suffers, therefore she never strongly desires. If only she could be drawn out of her shell, she who has so much at her feet, who <u>can</u> be so gay and amusing. Margaret is far and away more the type I would like for the future queen – she has that frivolity and irresponsibility that L lacks, though one couldn't call either of

---

* Elizabeth Vyner was from a grand Yorkshire family. Her mother, Lady Doris, was a childhood friend of Queen Elizabeth.

them dull. We had tea then a film *Sergeant York* – not v. good. In the Q's sitting room after, I purposely admired a lovely photo of the princesses in summer frocks and hats under a tree and to my intense joy the Q said had she given me one and if not would I like it? Then L said they'd sign it for me, so I came home with the wonderful knowledge that one of my <u>oldest</u> and <u>dearest</u> wishes has at last been granted. I'm <u>thrilled</u> with it.

Monday, 17 November

I'm going to be here [Errolston] the whole week as we're rehearsing every day. The dresses for the play came – mine is pale green satin, trimmed with mauve. Lovely.

Friday, 21 November

Went over for rehearsal at ten. I'm <u>longing</u> for tomorrow; they all call me 'Duchess' now! I <u>love</u> being called it – it flatters my vanity and how strange it'll be if one day they hear that I really <u>am</u> one!

Saturday, 22 November

We all went to High Mass in convent at ten. When I see all this rich pomp and ceremony it makes me proud to be a RC and I feel I couldn't change, but then I realise that my worldly ambition must come first – if only the English aristocracy all belonged to it. Came back and sewed till lunch, after which we all went over to dress for the play. There was great excitement. Grandpa, Daddy and Aunt M came. I felt so happy in my dress and my part went off very well. Rushed back to Errolston to collect my luggage – some others came too and we had to get in through window as all doors locked. Letter from Hugh waiting for me which was <u>too</u> thrilling – he <u>can't</u> come to the ball as he's already <u>going</u> with Lady Leconfield but we shall meet there as he says and it was a lovely chatty letter – three pages ending: 'Yours – Hugh'.

Monday, 24 November

<u>My eighteenth birthday</u>.

I awoke early and lay staring into the complete darkness all around me, I felt myself standing on the threshold of life, eager, impatient to step out to meet that life and to fulfil my destiny. There will be sorrow, I know, because of my ambition, greater sorrow perhaps than many other people but I shall know how to bear it. The realisation of my dreams is my happiness and I ask for nought else.

The princesses arrived at four, with Monty and Libby H and Winifred and we had a lovely birthday tea, with chocolate cake, candles, crackers, etc. They gave me an amusing necklace made of painted melon pips and also a <u>lovely</u> necklace of dark red beads from the Queen! I was <u>thrilled</u> – I never expected such an honour! We played charades and other games and they all left about six thirty. It went off extremely well and I'm glad Sonia was there. After Rosary we talked in Sonia's room and sat with each other while we bathed and gave ourselves plenty of time to dress. I wore my new green dress and the Q's red necklace, which looked <u>lovely</u> with it, as it has touches of dark red in the embroidery. Played vingt-et-un after dinner. After we'd undressed I talked to S on her bed for ages and only got back to my own room at a quarter to twelve! Grandpa said I must get a good night's rest! How can <u>anyone</u> be <u>quite</u> so unimaginative as to think one wants a good night's rest on one's birthday!!

Tuesday, 25 November

Bussed to Errolston. Everyone was so nice to me about my birthday – they really do all seem to like me. I always thought I was a very bad mixer but I think now that I get on with people rather well. Crawfie rang up to say that Anne C and I are to be the ugly sisters in their Cinderella pantomime, which will be fun, as we needn't really be ugly and it means that I can be a girl in the dances.

Thursday, 27 November

I was very busy all the morning writing my birthday letters and doing some sewing. After lunch I biked to the Castle for drawing. When we were getting ready for tea I showed L Hugh's letter. She told me that she was very excited over Philip coming for weekend.

Friday, 28 November

Annabel arrived for tea, and afterwards we gossiped in the sitting room. It was <u>such</u> fun. If only Mummy wasn't coming tomorrow – but still one can't have everything.

Sunday, 30 November

Walked with A to church. Mummy said my royal friendship is not only utterly valueless but almost a menace as it 'keeps me back'. She also told me I should give up looking for impoverished young men like H. Had a lovely tea in Eton at the Cockpit with Annabel's mother and saw the Graftons there (H's pa and ma) – they're ghastly but it didn't deter me. If only H had a little money.

Monday, 1 December

A left and so did Mummy. I felt terribly depressed also over this new idea of calling people up at eighteen. It does seem unfair that girls, just as they're going to really enjoy themselves, should have to settle down to a sordid drudgery. I felt inexpressibly lonely, as one does when one has nothing in common with the rest of the house but tonight it was almost as if I sensed some further upheaval and it came with more violence than I expected. The Tigress came in and said they were just ringing up the police to find out what had happened to me – I rushed down and found Grandpa in a rare fuss and Daddy fuming as he always does on such occasions, unable to listen to any other point of view. What they wouldn't understand was that I hadn't done any different today than any other day. Oh, the fools – how can it be possible that they didn't first call me, ask if I was back, see if my bike was there, before ringing up Errolston and the police. I asked them that to their faces, every one of them, and I said things too which I would never say while I was sane, though I didn't dare tell Grandpa what I thought of him. I fled to my room and there gave vent to the wild, furious misery that tore at my heart. I scratched my arm with a penknife till I drew blood. I had to compose myself for dinner as Bernard and Lavinia [Duke and Duchess of Norfolk] came but I was glad to go to bed. I had cried too much for more tears but I went to sleep with my whole being poisoned with fierce contempt, worse than any hatred and suddenly a new bitterness filled my heart, which I felt could never be quite forgotten.

Wednesday, 3 December

I biked to Errolston. In the afternoon we had the first-aid exam. We were all in a great state of agitation. I got 34 out of 40 for bandages, but only 26 out of 60 for the oral so I didn't pass. I <u>was</u> disappointed as now I shall have to take it again as I'm going into a hospital.*

Thursday, 4 December

Daddy told me that Grandpa complained to Mummy that I read a lot of trash now, which made me laugh a lot – I suppose he thinks I ought to read the lives of the saints! We did book plates today (at drawing), which was fun. Lilibet asked me how I got the scratches on my arm and I told her that it was a cat. I wondered what she'd think if she knew the truth.

Saturday, 7 December

I spent nearly all the afternoon reading in my room. I know that my eighteenth-century daydreams will never lead me to a romantic fate only, perhaps, to social failure but it doesn't matter as long as I can keep it in control until after I've secured my position in the world, and after that it doesn't so much matter what disasters ensue – providing I can please my husband! To my great surprise Grandpa came to my room tonight and said that as I was growing up I would

---

* Alathea was going to work in a hospital for the war effort.

inevitably begin to think of marriage. I longed to say, 'Well, you are behind the times!' and then a lot of rot about Catholics being most desirable, which made me laugh a lot! Little does he know how much heed I take of his advice! I suppose though that my (to him) somewhat rebellious behaviour just lately must have made him realise that I <u>am</u> no longer a child!

Thursday, 11 December

I biked to the rehearsal. Lilibet said there's not going to be a dance on Monday now because of the two battleships sunk by the Japanese. L was v. sweet today and said she did wish she was going to the Queen Charlotte's ball.

Friday, 12 December

Went up to London by train with Daddy and went to Sloane Street to have my nails done a lovely red! I curled my hair and Mummy did my face. I'd hoped she'd lend me her lovely pearls but she said they were too old and grand for me, so I had to be content with my own, but she told me I couldn't look nicer. Anthony Kinsman* came and we taxied to Grosvenor House. We danced in between each course and later I <u>insisted</u> on going to Lady L[econfield]'s table where Hugh was (he'd already spoken to me when he first came in) – AK evidently preferred <u>our</u> dinner table but after each dance I firmly walked over to the other one – he <u>had</u> to follow! I danced with him till I could almost have screamed

---

* Alathea's mother had arranged for Anthony Kinsman be her partner for the evening. Anthony Kinsman escaped from an Italian prisoner-of-war camp during the war.

with exasperation then, with a subtle manoeuvre, I introduced him to Fenella H and we changed round, then with
another subtle move I managed to sit next to H and we
danced. He was <u>sweet</u> – I do love him so much. I must,
must marry him, but I don't see how we're ever going to
get any further! Just as they began to play a waltz – his
favourite dance – Lady L made him sit down with her to
talk! AK came up and said, 'We can't face a waltz, can we?'
so I said no firmly. So I sat out for the only dance that I
really enjoy – indeed my luck has faded lately. The rest of
the evening was deadly. The ball ended and I'd hated it all
except for the quarter of an hour with Hugh. Anthony and
I joined in a party of about six friends and taxied to a nightclub called the Nut House in Regent Street. It was the first
time for me to go to a nightclub and I was thrilled. It seemed
like entering a world that I'd never really believed the existence of for people like us! One goes through a sordid
entrance at the back of a shop and sits at an inn-like table
in a hot, heavy atmosphere and watches half-naked girls
dancing and then you dance yourself in a v. small space.
There are vulgar jokes painted all round the walls and the
whole thing fascinated me. I began to enjoy myself. I laughed
to think of what Grandpa would say!

Friday, 19 December

The pantomime began at three. The family came to watch
and of course the K and Q. I gave the princesses' Christmas
presents to Mrs Knight to give them. Afterwards they went
away without saying goodbye, which was a great disappointment, as I don't know <u>when</u> I shall see them again. PE calls
me her best friend but if friendship means seeing people on

informal but not intimate terms to her, it means more than that to me – it means confidences exchanged, joys and sorrows shared, lasting remembrance! I have offered her my friendship, I love her, and I miss her when I don't see her – but she doesn't miss me. Why should she? She has PM and the K and Q; they're all happy and have fun together – she doesn't need me. But I need her – she has made me her friend and I couldn't abandon her, even if she abandoned me, for I haven't got a home. I am a lonely stranger in my family, except for one little baby sister and she is far away and one day she, too, will be estranged from me. So I depend on my friends for the love and comfort I lack elsewhere.

Saturday, 20 December

Daddy and I went to Windsor where I had an interview with the commandant of the place where I'm going to nurse. It went quite well, only all the official-ness of it alarms me!

Sunday, 21 December

Mass at nine. Had lunch on a tray, then biked to the Castle. Had lots of photos taken both in our Bavarian dresses and crinolines. Lilibet was sweet today – her Philip came and is quite nice but not my type. The K and Q watched too and the K said in a loud voice, 'Alathea looks as if she's joined the Grenadiers!' They were all so nice to me today, and yet as soon as I get into that room now, I feel somehow <u>stifled</u> by a heavy depression – I <u>hate</u> it. I biked sadly home by myself. They're so nice to me, yet they never seem to <u>think</u> of asking me to tea – I suppose it's because they don't 'unconsciously want' people to come, like I do. It's because

I won't see them again till after the holidays that I mind so much being thus casually dismissed.

Monday, 22 December

I had a sweet Xmas card from EA drawn herself and written in French (during her lessons), which I shall always keep. Sonia gave me an enlarged Polyfoto of her, and I spent the evening writing a description of her face, which is strangely sad and expressive in this photo. I shall copy it out tomorrow & send it to her to keep, and I shall stick the photograph in my album.

Wednesday, 24 December

A present from PE arrived by hand before lunch – a sort of fancy sachet with a note inside – no, I am convinced their behaviour was in no way due to <u>me</u>, but just perfectly natural to their temperaments.

Thursday, 25 December

We sat up till midnight Mass. It was the first year that I hadn't had a stocking but there really was nothing to put in it with these coupons. Breakfast in bed and I read lazily and happily till I got up and then everyone exchanged presents. After lunch we listened to the King at three, then I went out for a bit and went up to the Barclays, where they had a tea party, which was fun.

Friday, 26 December

Anne Crichton rang up and asked me if I was going to see George Formby* at the Castle tomorrow – I said no, but that I had an idea they knew I didn't like GF. It was a poor excuse to myself, though, but I still hoped to be asked tomorrow morning and my prayer was answered as PE rang me up tonight and said the car would come for me.

Saturday, 27 December

I wore my blue angora dress and the Q's red necklace. I was put in front row next to the Royal Family, which was the only thing that made the afternoon bearable. They came in and Margaret sat next to me. She was sweet but naturally we couldn't speak much. The Royal Family went away after, without a word of goodbye to anyone – only nods and smiles. It was the first time I'd been to any show at the Castle separately from them and, though I knew this was unreasonable, I felt it deeply but I did think the princesses ought to have wanted me to stay for tea afterwards, as I know they like me. The idea that they haven't really seen me for weeks doesn't occur to them, still less that I truly do miss them. I suppose I have been spoiled, and now that I was once more treated as the rest of them, I felt offended. What was the use, I thought bitterly, of dressing up and looking nice, when the Q didn't even notice I wore her necklace? I tore up the programme of today's show because I knew it would never hold happy memories for me.

---

* George Formby was a Lancashire-born popular entertainer, best known for his comic song 'When I'm Cleaning Windows'. He was a huge star in the 1930s and 1940s.

1942

Inspection

of the

First or Grenadier Regiment of Foot Guards

held at

Windsor Castle

by Command of

His Majesty King George VI

Colonel-in-Chief

on the 16th Birthday

of

H.R.H. The Princess Elizabeth

to mark the appointment of H.R.H.
as Colonel of the Regiment

21st April, 1942

An invitation to the ceremony marking the appointment
of Princess Elizabeth as Colonel of the Grenadiers.

Thursday, 1 January

Mass, then spent the morning indoors writing – this diary arrived. It is not as nice as my last year's one but it'll do. In afternoon I went for a long walk in the forest by myself, as I couldn't face going out with Grandpa today. It suddenly occurred to me that it was selfish to deny him my company on the one opportunity I have of walking with him but I couldn't turn back and my conscience was soon eased by a prayer for forgiveness and my own excuses. If he wasn't completely lacking in imagination, he'd understand my desire for solitude. I sank into a profound melancholy – how little they all understand me, Grandpa, Aunt M, Daddy and yet they're fond of me. Rosary seemed to me more like a funeral dirge than ever!

Friday, 2 January

Breakfast in bed. Letter from the hospital – the tiresome sort of letter one <u>would</u> get when one begins war work but I refuse to put myself out over it at the moment. They can wait!

Wednesday, 7 January

Grandpa went away for a week. I must say it was a relief not to have him fussing into my room at night and, above all, no Rosary! How lovely it'll be to see the spring again – the season of love! But will it bring me love? I do envy Sonia, though I don't much care for her Micky. Annabel has no lover but then she doesn't seem to desire one. Unlike her I feel that love is necessary to my temperament. I read again on the sofa and wrote my diary and all the while the clock on the mantelpiece ticked away the minutes slowly, bearing me on towards what destiny? My aunt dozed in an ungainly attitude on the sofa, snoring occasionally and the dark, heavy velvet curtains seemed to shut out any form of love or gaiety.

Monday, 12 January

I wondered whether Lilibet was reading *Royal Flush*,* which I gave her for Christmas. I think she'll like it but it would never have the same charm for her as it has for me, as she's so very different – she's unusually <u>set</u> in her ideas for fifteen, none of her friends could ever influence her. For one thing, she never lets herself come to <u>know</u> them well enough. If she were not so placid and unimpressionable, no doubt <u>I</u> would have influenced her or at least interested her with my thoughts, so vastly different from her own. I doubt if she

---

* Margaret Irwin was a very successful historical novelist. *Royal Flush*, her most popular book, tells the romantic story of Henriette Marie, known as Minette, daughter of Charles I, who was married very young to Philippe, Duc d'Orléans, the gay younger brother of Louis XIV. She was beautiful and clever, helping diplomatic relations between her brother Charles II and her brother-in-law and cousin Louis, who was also probably her lover. She died young.

will <u>appreciate</u> the sad story of Minette, let alone compare it to herself, as I did when I read it at fifteen and <u>I</u> am not royal. It never <u>occurs</u> to Lilibet, who has every chance of doing so, to picture herself as the princesses she reads of in past centuries – her own ancestors! Dear Lilibet, what a lot you do miss! I wish you and I were more alike.

Wednesday, 14 January

Woke up to find the world white with snow! Grandpa back. I tried to show him I was pleased to see him and he irritated me almost at once by fussing into my room saying it was too cold for me to sit reading in it – that <u>maddening</u> habit of never being able to pass my room without going in and especially at night on his way to bed, so that I can never undress in peace, knowing he's going to barge in! In the morning I always lock the door but still he never fails to thump heavily on it and rattle the handle!

Saturday, 17 January

Got to Newmarket with Brita, for the dance. I wore my black. I didn't enjoy it <u>madly</u> and there was nothing in the way of love-making, as B has led me to expect! The men weren't particularly exciting.

Monday, 26 January

Elizabeth Anne's eighth birthday. How well I remember her christening, me in a green coat and velvet beret! How I loved that baby – and now we only see each other twice a year at most.

Burloes, Hertfordshire

Wednesday, 28 January

I knitted in nursery talking to Nannie and Rosalind* till they went out, then I walked to the hospital to meet Annabel. Saw a dead person carried out under a sheet!

Saturday, 31 January

I suddenly decided to ring up the matron of the Red House† and find out when I can start – she was <u>charming</u> and I'm going to go on Tuesday. I'm glad to be beginning at once, as one must have something definite to do nowadays.

Thursday, 5 February

Last night Lady Mary Crichton‡ rang up to ask me to dine there and go to a dance on Friday – so what with one thing and another my spirits began to revive.

Friday, 6 February

After tea I painted my nails and had a bath. I wore my green dinner dress with the Queen's dark red necklace. Bet fetched me in her car and dropped me at the Crichtons, where I had dinner. We drove to the dance at the White Hart. I enjoyed it awfully – they had two waltzes with the lights turned out and only little coloured lights flitting about! Regarding myself in the mirror I felt confident that I <u>am</u> pretty but somehow I have to admit that I'm <u>not</u> good in a

---

* Rosalind was the youngest Newman child.
† The Red House was a hospital and nursing home in Windsor.
‡ Mary Crichton was the mother of Anne and Barbara.

party – I feel so dull and I'm sure people have to get to know me to like me, which is a great disadvantage.

Saturday, 7 February

In the morning Princess E rang up to ask me to a film this afternoon – I put behind me all the grievances I had against them during the pantomime time and once more they became the sweetest people on earth, for I really am <u>very</u> fond of them. Drawing and dancing begin again next week. What a joy to be once more installed in the royal circle that I love so well!

Libby called with proofs of the pantomime photos – Mr Tannar swaggering with the princesses <u>infuriated</u> me and I deliberately chose ones which didn't include him! The royal car fetched me and took me to the Castle, where I was taken up to Lilibet's room. I was truly glad to see them both again and I think they were me – as much as they are to see anyone outside their own family circle! Lilibet looked v. pretty – she showed me a letter from Hugh E thanking her for Christmas card – it's miserable him going abroad – I shall never see him again now. We went along to have tea with the K and Q, who were charming, and the Duke of Kent came with Prince Edward – his sister didn't come, as they can't control both together! We went along to the film in the Waterloo Chamber and I sat in the front row and we had rugs. The film was *Dumbo* and v. sweet. As we were leaving the Queen tripped over Prince Edward and fell over my foot, which created quite a commotion and she was so kind about it to me but I must say I felt rather proud when I found a bruise on it at night!

Tuesday, 10 February

MY FIRST DAY'S NURSING.

Got up before eight and put on my nurse's uniform and biked down the Long Walk to the Red House, just this side of Windsor, where I am to work three days a week from nine to five. There are only three or four VADs on at a time,* and most of them are girls like myself including Anne C's elder sister, Barbara, who was so nice and took charge of me. The work is not <u>all</u> hard, though I found it tiring being on my feet so much. I just did odd jobs like washing the tops of the patients' lockers, sorting out things, washing up in the surgery, etc. There is <u>no</u> other washing up except the things <u>we</u> use for our tea and eleven o'clock lunch – not our proper lunch. We had tea and bread and jam in the staffroom at eleven and after helping with the men's lunch (there are about twenty men from the gun sites) we had our own which was really v. good, and the whole place is nice and warm, so I felt quite happy!

Wednesday, 11 February

Today I found I knew my way about much better. It rather embarrasses me going alone into the wards, as all the men will joke and what makes it worse is that one can't always understand what they say! But it amuses me being called Nurse Howard all the time by everyone!

---

* The VAD (Voluntary Aid Detachment) was a group of civilians who worked as nurses and assistants, organised by the Red Cross alongside military nurses.

Thursday, 12 February

I went to the Castle for drawing and we painted our china horses. Lilibet said she came down to dinner the last two nights as hostess to the Princess Royal* as the Q was away. I approve of that. I wish she could get away from the little-girl atmosphere that Margaret inevitably gives her, as then we wouldn't notice the two years between us: she's <u>so</u> much older for her age than I was. I <u>adore</u> Margaret but it <u>is</u> such a pity from my point of view that she keeps her sister back, and even apart from me, it does make her younger in many ways than a lot of girls of nearly sixteen and of course her position prevents her going out on her own so much – but what an enviable position! Why was I not born to it?

Friday, 13 February

Worked at the Red House from nine to five. It was rather slack today. One of the women said one could tell I have never done any housework by the way I held the broom when I swept their ward!

Sunday, 15 February

Listened to Churchill's speech announcing the fall of Singapore – the war is going badly for us at the moment. God help us to win in the end – I am sure we will but we seem to be so inefficient and so much <u>alone</u>!

---

* Princess Mary, daughter of King George V and Queen Mary, married to the Earl of Harewood, was given the title Princess Royal.

Saturday, 21 February

Lilibet rang up and asked me to stay for the film and to skate, so I took all my things to change into after dancing. We did elementary ballet today, which was fun, and also a Hungarian rhapsody! I sat next to the King at lunch and got on v. well, and in afternoon we all drove down to Frogmore where the K and the princesses and I skated for an hour and the Q watched. It was wonderful fun and again I felt that all this was worth the war, and also that these people were all that mattered in the world and yet I know that until I marry this cannot be so. This royal life is so much my life – the bedrooms, the armies of liveried servants, the manners and customs, all taken so much for granted, are so much after my own heart that I cannot believe I live in a world from which all this has already fled. Without the court, life would be meaningless, nothing – can it be that it will after all lead me nowhere, its sole merit a cherished memory in old age? Lilibet had the first grown-up shoes I've ever seen today – dark red suede slip-on ones and she said she's got court ones now too. I'm so glad as her shoes are really v. bad. It's strange how everyone pities her so – I envy her more than I could possibly express to anyone. I said goodbye to them all – I do wish I could kiss the Q's hand, like Diana Bowes-Lyon but perhaps one day I shall.

Wednesday, 25 February

Daddy dropped me at Priest's Hill and I bussed to the Red House where I worked till five. I walked up to the Castle to see Diana Legh in Henry VIII Gateway and we went to see Winifred Hardinge and talked about lots of others at the secretarial. I wonder if I would be the same if I was there – not that I regret it, but I <u>wish</u> I knew whether it's being alone in the middle of the park that makes a difference as I can't help feeling that people <u>do</u> think I'm excessively dull. When I got home I found a letter from John Wiggin saying he could come to the Queen Charlotte's Ball if we want him. Why couldn't it have been Hugh? He <u>ought</u> to write, but he won't. Life is hard in the way that it sends those whom one most wants to meet far away and yet I suppose those whom one is destined to meet one will do so in spite of all opposition.

Thursday, 26 February

I went up to the Castle for drawing. We had such fun, doing silly things like rolling a little wheel down the slopes into the stream below! Lilibet has been made Colonel of the Grenadier Guards* and they want her to have a uniform, which I disagree with entirely.

Grosvenor Square, London

Monday, 2 March

Got to London and went straight to the flat. Aunt Alathea went out early, so I had a good look around. I took four hankies and a pair of stockings and socks! I can't say my conscience <u>didn't</u> prick me <u>at all</u> but I do feel justified as she not only has fabulous stores of everything but she takes Mummy's things and also poor Daddy has to pay so much

---

* Princess Elizabeth had taken over as colonel from her godfather, the Duke of Connaught.

for <u>her</u> flat. I walked to Sonia's flat in Stanhope Gate – 11 – where I went to tea so often and looked through the letterbox. Yes, the hall was there, just the same, except it was once so luxurious and elegant, now bare and ruined by many bomb scars. Then I entered the park taking the same paths as I always took in the old days when it was so full of playing children and nurses. I went to the Serpentine and threw a bit of the bun I'd bought to the ducks just as EA used to do each day and I couldn't hold back my tears. In this strange new world, it almost surprised me to find the paths in the same places as they used to be – it was the absence of the railings* that altered it most. I walked slowly, stopping to gaze round me in a lost way and I felt <u>immeasurably</u> far away from reality. I walked on as if in a trance to Hans Place going through the gardens now devoid of railings and I let myself into 18 by the backdoor key that had been left hidden for me. Then I put on all the lights that would go on and made a sad, solitary tour of the house beginning from the basement and ending with Ming-Ming's room at the very top. That, and the nursery were the saddest. I looked into the cupboard that a few years ago was full of toys. I went into my own room and gazed out of the window – saddest of all to do this and reflect on what has gone and will never come again. I went into Mummy's room, but that wasn't friendly – it never had been – only beautiful. I went down the stairs and out of the front door, smiling a sad farewell to the house that was the home of all my dazzling hopes and dreams for the future. I've wanted to do what I did today for a long while and now I feel satisfied, though it is a tragic pleasure to evoke old memories and one which

---

* The railings had been taken to be melted down as part of the war effort.

shatters one's peace of mind and avails one nothing in the cruel world of reality.

Cumberland Lodge

Tuesday, 3 March

I went to nurse at Castle Mead as they are busier there than at Red House but I didn't like it much. I had a letter from Mummy saying she thought I have a vague, puffy look when in a crowd, not 'on the spot' like Brita, who though badly dressed and a ghastly figure, is 'gay and knows her stuff'. It absolutely <u>infuriated</u> me and made me momentarily hate Brita – what <u>is</u> it they see in Brita that I lack? They admit she's got <u>no</u> looks and <u>I</u> think no charm. 'On the spot' and 'knows her stuff' are typical expressions of Mummy's and they annoy me – I don't think I want to be either of them – but a terrible wave of depression came over me. I felt I couldn't be inspiring to anyone and that people must dislike me. I even wondered sickeningly whether I would grow to be a nasty person, as <u>so many</u> of my near relations are – in fact, the only one with at all a nice character is Daddy. Every <u>one</u> of the others is, to say the <u>least</u> of it, selfish and I suppose I am too. The continuous news, too, of more sacrificing to the war effort, utility clothing, less petrol, etc., was anything but cheering – it is no advantage now to be well born.

Grosvenor Square

Saturday, 14 March

I went to the rehearsal for the Cake Ceremony tonight.* Saw lots of people I knew but so hot and crowded that I was glad to return to the flat. All our party came to the flat at seven – Annabel, her partner, Brita, John Wiggin, Miles Marriott† and a friend of Mummy's, Mervyn Vernon,‡ as we were a man short. I wore my pink gauze. We drank and had great fun over a peculiar man who rang up three times asking for someone else! All drove to Grosvenor House for the Queen Charlotte's Ball and had dinner and danced. Poor Miles M was very dull though terribly <u>nice</u>. I saw <u>lots</u> of people I hadn't seen since London days when we were fifteen, including Elizabeth Lambart§ in an eighteenth-century cream satin dress which she was too small for and Ursula James¶ looking quite <u>lovely</u>. At eleven all the 1942 debs did the cake procession. At one thirty we went to the 400** but couldn't get in so went to the Nut House and there the evening really began! We had wonderful fun, singing, dancing – everyone from the ball had come on and were all in the best of spirits!

---

* Debutantes pushed a cake, made from cardboard but representing Queen Charlotte's birthday cake, and then curtsied to the chairman of the ball, who represented Queen Charlotte. Contrary to popular opinion they never curtsied to the cake.
† Miles Marriott was the only son of a rich family who lived in Belgravia. They were old family friends of Alathea's mother.
‡ Major Mervyn Vernon was a Grenadier.
§ Lady Elizabeth Lambart was the elder daughter of Field Marshal the Earl of Cavan and was a lifelong friend of Princess Elizabeth.
¶ Ursula James was the daughter of Lady Serena James, née Lumley and the Hon. Robert James. Alathea loved staying at their house in Yorkshire, St Nicholas Abbey.
** The 400 was a popular London nightclub.

1942

Cumberland Lodge

Thursday, 19 March

Biked to drawing. They were interested in the QC Ball and Lilibet said they <u>do</u> want to have one soon but that the news not being so good as in the summer the Queen thinks people will say they only think of enjoying themselves, which is quite true, but it's <u>impossible</u> to keep it out of the papers.

Saturday, 21 March

Lilibet rang up and asked me to stay and see the film after dancing. Got there early to practise a bit before as we'd both missed a lesson. My instep is always praised in the ballet, which pleases me! Afterwards we changed and had biscuits and orange juice in the nursery, then I went out with Margaret and Monty as L was doing her German. I sat next to the King – he's not v. easy to talk to but I managed to get on fairly well and like being put next to him.

Wednesday, 25 March

Walked up to the Castle. I joined the princesses outside where they were burning grass. It was the first heavenly spring day. Jackie Philipps and his four officers came to tea, so we were ten of us, with Crawfie and Monty, in the schoolroom and we had the most magnificent tea, with dishes of sweets and crackers, etc. – hardly a war spectacle! After, we went to the Red Drawing Room and played charades, acting clumps* and silly games, like musical chairs, and we ended

---

* Clumps is a team game, in which participants guess a word from its definition.

125

up by dancing a Scottish reel! It was <u>such</u> fun – everyone enjoyed themselves and the party had that air of charming, transient gaiety that the others like it last year had, which make them live in my mind for ever. I felt again the elusive sweetness of <u>life</u> as opposed to <u>existence</u> and thanked God for letting me share these moments with the princesses. They sent me home in a car at eight and I went to bed at night triumphantly happy.

Thursday, 26 March

Biked into Windsor and did one or two things before going up to the Castle for drawing. Afterwards we went out with Monty and burned grass, but there was an icy cold wind in spite of the sun. Came in for tea; Margaret was <u>very</u> amusing. Lilibet is being confirmed on Saturday and she described her dress to me. I enjoyed today.

Friday, 27 March

I went to the Queen's Head for the first-aid exam. Felt <u>fairly</u> confident and got 37/60 for practical. I <u>loathed</u> the doctor who took the oral and suddenly in the middle my mind froze and I began to cry and wanted to scream out that it was all hopeless – of course I failed with 24/60 and collapsed in uncontrollable sobs – they were v. nice and I was given some coffee and Mrs C-S* said I could, if I liked, try again if I 'pulled myself together'. I thought it was worth it while I <u>was</u> there but I had to sit on those stairs with all the other nurses waiting till they'd been up before my turn came again

---

* Mrs Chetwynd-Stapylton was the commandant of Queensmead, the Red Cross home in Windsor where Alathea later went to do her war work.

– that was <u>ten o'clock</u>! Meanwhile Mrs C-S kept telling me I'd never make a nurse and that I might be under a hospital sister, who is <u>usually</u> beastly. Why <u>is</u> it that nurses nearly always get bullied so much? You get <u>far</u> more out of people when you're nice to them. I felt sorry I'd ever joined the Red Cross – the whole, curt, official atmosphere and being called 'Howard' filled me with loathing and I've never felt more miserable in my life. The doctor was nicer this time, but patronising, and I just passed with 34 – but as long as I pass the damn thing I don't care how well. I've no interest in my work and don't mind where I go since everywhere it's just cleaning up. I was too tired even to sleep, my head ached intolerably and I cried again from sheer mental exhaustion – I shall never forget this night. Its memory was so distasteful to me that I began crying again and had to bathe my eyes thoroughly with rose water.

Saturday, 28 March

After breakfast in bed of a boiled egg and brown rolls and marmalade I felt better and got up and dressed for dancing. Lilibet wasn't there on account of her confirmation. The lunch table was laid for twenty-three, with lovely flowers in silver bowls and I longed to be there too. Dear Lilibet, my thoughts were with her during the time of the service.

Monday, 30 March

Worked at the Red House from nine to five. Got ticked off for singing, which amused me! They were all v. encouraging about my exam I went and sat on a bench in the Long Walk and did a crossword puzzle till six thirty, when I walked to

Queensmead. I wasn't so nervous this time. A woman doctor was coming, but didn't, so a sister took the oral. She was <u>sweet</u> and I got 50/60 but a v. severe old woman took the practical and I failed by two marks as I did the foot bandage wrong. It was v. nerve-racking but I forced myself not to care much, though all these official women fussing round and all their ridiculous red tape <u>almost</u> reduced me to tears again. What <u>does</u> it matter <u>how</u> one takes a cork out of a bottle? I did know how to too, only of course I forgot! I was told sharply tonight that I should <u>stand up</u> when I speak to an officer!

Friday, 3 April

GOOD FRIDAY.
Much colder. Met the Royal Family and talked for a bit while all our dogs got entangled! Lilibet is at the bad age now, rather fat, and her face puffy at the jaw and a bit stolid, though often she looks very pretty and animated. Her face is broad, though, like the Queen's, and I prefer a long face, but in a year's time when she makes up she will improve infinitely. Their clothes have deteriorated lately. I can't bear their Aertex shirts. They <u>never</u> used to wear them, and somehow now they always look frightfully ordinary – they'd never stand out among others like the Q would.

Tuesday, 14 April

Heavenly spring day but windy. Walked over to Royal Lodge at four thirty. We had tea in the nursery, which reminded me of years ago. I was sorry the Queen wasn't there – this Little Trianon of her creation needed her own great charm to make it perfect, though the house itself is deplorable! After tea we went out by ourselves, took a few frogs out of the swimming pool, then sat in their own little garden and talked. I happened to say I'd never been in a carriage and Lilibet said, 'Oh, I'll take you one day.' If only she would! Margaret was in her most spirited mood and delighted in saying things to embarrass me! They showed me the toy farm they'd laid out in the schoolroom and, once again, I was struck by the childishness of Lilibet's tastes, perhaps simple more than childish really – it shows in her drawing too, always dogs and horses yet she's far more serious and sensible than me. I doubt if her tastes and ideas will ever form differently – her whole nature is simpler and less sophisticated than mine. At the beginning of the war, when I was exactly her age, I was already well launched into the dream world of the eighteenth century, whereas she had her feet planted in less idealistic but infinitely firmer soil; consequently she can be happy as her thoughts never soar above the most ordinary, while I, forever craving the subtle, the ideal, the dramatic, all at once or separately, according to my mood, can never be truly content, as it is only rarely that my desires can be satisfied.

Saturday, 18 April

I got the train to London and went straight to the flat and unpacked. I wore my short grey silk. Miles Marriott fetched me in his car and took me to the theatre – it was *The Man who Came to Dinner*. Mummy has said I can go out alone with Miles, as he's an old friend. I think he likes me but I don't know how much and though I enjoy making myself liked I could not be in love with M – he's too boyish still, for one thing.

Sunday, 19 April

Princess E rang up to ask me to spend the day with them on Tuesday, her birthday, to watch the parade in the morning. I couldn't sleep for excitement – what a lovely few days these will have been!

Tuesday, 21 April

Princess Elizabeth sixteen today. I wore my navy blue dress and short coat with the belt and gardenias I bought yesterday and Billy pinned the veiling on to my hat and tied it in a large bow behind, with very long ends. Car took me to the Castle and PE asked to see me, then I went out into the quadrangle to watch the parade, which lasted an hour and was most impressive. PE as Colonel, Grenadier Guards had to inspect them and received a diamond cipher brooch. She looked v. pretty. They had lunch alone with the commanding officers and I went with Lady Delia Peel* to a buffet lunch with all the actors of the afternoon show and were joined by the Bowes-Lyons, the castle officers and, to my delight, Hugh Euston. After lunch we were taken to the front row of chairs in the Waterloo Chamber and I was put next to Hugh. It was a show given by Tommy Handley† and the Royal Family enjoyed it as much as the soldiers at the back.

---

* Lady Delia Peel, daughter of Earl Spencer and married to Colonel Sir Sidney Peel, was a Lady of the Bedchamber to Queen Elizabeth.

† Tommy Handley was a radio comedian whose show *ITMA, It's That Man Again,* was a wartime hit, which made him one of the best-known celebrities of the era.

I had to laugh, too, but to me it was almost nauseating and there was the added torment of sitting next to the man I loved, while he was totally unaware of it. I tried by the intensity of my thoughts to make him feel my presence and when we both sat back and our shoulders almost touched an unbearable agony filled my soul, and amid all this raucous laughter I was poignantly aware of the sadness of the world. Afterwards the Queen asked just Hugh and me to stay to tea, so we had a quiet birthday tea, with a chocolate cake and the K and Q were <u>sweet</u> to me, then we said goodbye to H. They're so pointedly nice to him that one wonders if there's anything behind it; he gets on so well with all of them – I'm sure he likes Lilibet better than me. He used to like me but now I don't think he does much – I think I've shown my feelings too plainly. I was shown L's presents; she had two lovely diamond stars for her hair from the K and Q. We went to the nursery and listened to the account of the parade on the news. The Queen admired my dress – I do so adore her and indeed all of them. I went home in their car. I lay awake and unhappy, trying to analyse my feelings concerning Hugh. I had to admit I'm <u>not</u> truly in love, I only <u>desire</u>, a passionate, agonising desire that I have long since known to be hopeless; yet it is in his power to make me love and in mine, I feel, to make him happy.

Thursday, 23 April

Spent most of the afternoon indoors – tidied up at four as the princesses were coming. Mrs Knight came with them. She is terribly grand but v. <u>nice</u> when one gets to know her. After tea we went out in the garden and had a swing for fun! We were talking of PE's birthday tea and Margaret

131

suddenly said to me, 'I believe <u>you</u> enjoyed the cake more than the show!' which of course was so true and so like her to see through all my polite praises of the show! They came up to my room, first to wash, and I showed them my necklace and I walked back with them as far as Royal Lodge gates. I returned home rather lonely, as I always do when I know I probably won't see them for a bit – I am fonder of them than my own family, but I know that <u>they</u> are happier alone with their parents than with anyone else on earth.

Monday, 27 April

I biked to Zelda's and then we went to the home-nursing lecture together – I'd changed into uniform but was ticked off for not having a belt or tie!

Friday, 1 May

Biked into Windsor and said goodbye to them at the Red House, as they're becoming mobile. I was sorry to leave there, as it was all so smooth and happy. Had an interview with Mrs Chetwynd-Stapylton at her office. I went in quite happily but she soon undermined all my courage! She was so bossy and efficient – said I must be full time when I register (in June) and when I said Thursday wasn't a good idea for me at present she said, 'Why not?' and didn't take my excuse of drawing v. well, and said I could do Saturday instead – I simply hadn't the courage to say I couldn't do Saturday either and will now have to get someone to write! I became more and more nervous as she talked and when she said, 'Poor Howard, you've got a lot to learn', and 'We'll make a nurse of you yet', I could bear it no longer and only with a great effort restrained my tears, though she must have noticed them. It's extraordinary how that woman always makes me cry – she somehow completely paralyses my spirit. I came out in a state of utter misery and cried all the way home and only just made my face presentable for the archbishop who came to lunch!

Saturday, 2 May

I arrived at West Wycombe Park at five thirty for the Dashwoods'* dance. West Wycombe is the most <u>divine</u> house – my ideal, Georgian, with colonnades, painted ceilings, terraces, lakes and follies. There were thirty people staying. Elizabeth Lambart and I shared a room and a lovely yellow satin canopy bed — it reminded me of Petworth, when Annabel and I shared a <u>vast</u> bed! E and I had great fun – she's so sweet, but v. un-self-confident. I wore Bet's pink and blue muslin dress with my new sash of pale blue muslin tying at the side and the dance began at nine in the hall and went on till three and we ate and drank in between. I <u>adored</u> it.

---

* The Dashwoods lived at West Wycombe, famous for the Hellfire Caves, which an earlier Sir Francis Dashwood had used for meetings of the notorious Hellfire Club in the eighteenth century. It was one of the first great houses taken on by the National Trust. Sarah Dashwood was the same age as Alathea and a family friend.

Monday, 4 May

Worked with Zelda at Queensmead from nine till two.* I missed the Red House – I worked in the kitchen, acting in general like the kitchen maid!

Wednesday, 6 May

At Queensmead, I peeled potatoes and cleaned some silver. They changed the duty list and I got off Saturday without me saying anything, so all is well. I'm to do nine to five now, which is really better, as half a day just messes everything up.

Thursday, 7 May

Met Bet and we drove into Windsor in the pony trap. I went up to the Castle for drawing. The princesses were in summer frocks. We sat out under the terrace and painted the blossom trees – I couldn't help feeling what a peaceful, delicious way this was of spending an afternoon: so few people do it nowadays and indeed it does seem a contrast to the hurried noisy ways of the world today. Monty has left – supposedly because her husband's returned to London but I believe it's a new husband! I don't really miss her, as Crawfie is so much easier to get on with – I loved Monty when she was with me but I never felt <u>absolutely</u> at my ease with her. We sat above the Rock Garden and talked about the Dashwoods'

* Queensmead was the former private house of Lord Edward Spencer Churchill and his family, on the edge of Windsor, and was a home run by the Red Cross, mainly for displaced civilians who had been bombed out. VADS, such as Alathea, were taken on to do the domestic work, along with some former properly trained private servants, such as the cook.

dance. PE was asked to the dance, but the Q thought her too young to go.

Friday, 8 May

Bicycled to Queensmead today. Did pantry work. Although it's not interesting it's v. peaceful and the girls are nice. They said I <u>must</u> stand up to Mrs Chetwynd-Stapylton – they all dislike her too.

Monday, 11 May

Biked to Adelaide Cottage in the Castle grounds where Jackie Philipps was having a party for the princesses. Diana Legh was there and about four officers. Afterwards we had a conjurer from the barracks who was <u>very</u> good, then we played charades in the garden. Once we dressed up as monks and used our necklaces as rosaries – it was <u>so</u> funny and we all laughed the whole evening. Crawfie was with the princesses, who were wearing their pale blue coats and skirts – they make a point now of having hardly any clothes, which I think is ridiculous. We went on playing acting and laughing till a quarter to eight but I don't know whether everyone enjoyed it as much as the princesses and I did – there is an unsophisticated charm about all these parties given by the officers for the princesses which appeals to me. It is something un-modern, something <u>unique</u> for without the princesses it would never take place. I rushed back to Queensmead for the practical part of the lecture. Mrs C-S was most amicable for once!

Friday, 15 May

Worked all morning and then in the evening. It's strange to think that before the war one would never have dreamed, looking at Queensmead, that one day girls like myself would be sweeping the stairs and cleaning the baths there and sleeping in the old servants' rooms in the attics! Strange, too, the manner in which one comes into contact with people one could never have met on such a footing but for the war. I cannot agree that it broadens one's outlook on life – in my case at any rate. It perhaps opens my eyes further to the faults of the modern world but otherwise it leaves me quite cold.

Saturday, 16 May

As I had hoped PE rang up to ask me to stay for lunch today. After dancing, I changed in PM's room and we lunched with the household and two officers but the K and Q were away at a football match! Mrs Cox [the art teacher] came and we drew out under the terrace – I made a study of a lilac bush. Margaret was in the most exuberant spirits and asked me the most embarrassing questions: 'Do you call me M or PM? It's no point calling me PM if you call Lilibet Lilibet!' I am actually rather worried as to whether I ought to begin calling them 'Princess' – it's better to be on the safe side, of course, but it's so difficult beginning. Much as I enjoy the privilege of calling them by their Christian names, I would not approve of it when they're older. Came in for tea in the schoolroom. PE lent me two books, one an adventure story about Scotland that Hugh gave her for her birthday – that sort of book bores me but I'm so afraid she'll cross-question me if I don't read it! I was delighted to see, though, that she had begun *Royal Flush* and likes it.

Monday, 18 May

Message to ring PE up and it was to tell me that they're having a dance on the twenty-ninth! I was thrilled and could hardly eat any dinner! It was so sweet of her to let me know, I thought, as the official invitations never arrive till a day or two before.

Friday, 22 May

I worked at Queensmead till four thirty, tediously but fairly peacefully, and someone told us about some oranges so I managed to slip out on a bike and get some for another girl and myself. They're like gold nowadays!

Saturday, 23 May

Breakfast in bed. Drove to dancing and wore my new navy blue and white embroidered organdie that Ming-Ming made. I think the Royal Family rather disapprove of new clothes now – the princesses have worn the same dresses for dancing for a whole year!

Sunday, 24 May

Mass and Communion at nine. Jackie and Joan Philipps came to ask for the key to the Bog Garden – <u>Hugh E</u> was with them but they remained outside and Daddy talked to them. I was in an <u>agony</u> of agitation and torment of mind and found it impossible to concentrate on the cards for the rest of the evening, so I lost! After dinner, Jackie and Joan, with Hugh, looked in. H was <u>sweet</u> to me and I was so happy, and it gave the greatest pleasure to see him in <u>our</u> house. He must dance with me on Friday!

Monday, 25 May

I biked to work. We were much busier than usual and Drusilla Maude,* who's nice, said today that she was sure the life we're leading now and lack of quality in our food, etc., will shorten our lives. It is indeed difficult when one is brushing the stairs to be philosophical and to move with the times, and hard not to reflect ironically that the people one has grown to know and like in historical books would never have done what I'm doing! I had to scrub half of the kitchen floor today, but I was beyond caring what I did and at tea time I felt better – I can never stop eating nowadays and I've put on half a stone since Christmas!

Thursday, 28 May

Drawing at Castle two thirty. We had to be indoors again but went out with Crawfie before tea and talked about the dance. Margaret Elphinstone and Elizabeth Lambart are going to stay the <u>weekend</u>. I suppose I must have a v. jealous nature, as I can't help feeling <u>terribly</u> jealous even though she has far more cause to <u>envy</u> me! The only thing they'll have which has <u>never</u> yet come my way is dinner there.

---

* Drusilla Maude was a fellow VAD at Queensmead.

Friday, 29 May

Sonia, who was invited too (I was so pleased for her because I knew that in her heart, how upset she must have been when she was left off the list last year), picked me up in her car and we drove home. Had tea, then undressed at once, prepared our faces, nails, etc. My dress was <u>perfect</u> and much admired. S had a lovely oyster chiffon over satin, simply but elegantly made. Dinner at eight and the car took us afterwards to the Castle, picking up Zelda on the way. We three wore long white gloves and were the only <u>girls</u> to do so – but they looked <u>lovely</u> and we kept them on the <u>whole</u> evening! Everyone congregated in the Green Drawing Room and then we all filed past the Royal Family, shaking hands and curtsying. The Q wore white lace richly embroidered with pale blue and silver, and the princesses pink taffeta picture frocks, embroidered with seed pearl bows – <u>quite</u> pretty but they <u>ought</u> not to have been alike. PE didn't look pretty tonight somehow – she's v. Hanoverian and has reached the age now when she <u>needs</u> make-up. The dance was a great success but somehow it <u>wasn't </u>the same as the one last July – perhaps it was the military band, which played so <u>pitifully</u> few of my adored Viennese waltzes that rendered it more like other<u> dances </u>and deprived it of that magic charm. I found myself regretting having so impulsively torn up the sketch I wrote of it, as there was certainly nothing to inspire me tonight. We had a series of Paul Jones tonight but both S and I failed to get the King, though we strove as hard as we unobtrusively could! However I enjoyed myself and Hugh was there. He sought me out to dance with him and we sat in the White Drawing Room after and talked easily and happily for quite a long time. He's been so nice to me the last twice and I am so v. happy but <u>everyone's</u> talking of the way in which the Royal Family single him out – he's staying the night there and he sat by the princess at supper and <u>she</u> began liking him at the same time as I did, though quite unbeknown to each other! She was so sweet tonight and told me that it was she who pointed me out to him when he was <u>vaguely</u> looking for me to make sure he danced with me! But is it possible that Fate intends to entwine us in a far deeper bond than any of us could ever have imagined? If it is their intention that PE should marry an English commoner, then I think this match quite probable – he is <u>not</u> in <u>love</u> with her, but I believe fondness of them all would greatly tempt him. If this be the case I would make a willing sacrifice of him to my future sovereign but to have loved the prince consort in itself would be enough to lend colour to my youth! And meanwhile it gives a zest to life to combat my charms with hers!

Saturday, 30 May

Sonia and I had breakfast in bed together and got up at ten. PE had asked me to staff concert this afternoon but had said no more about it, so acting on Hugh's advice last night, I bravely rang her up. It was most awkward as she'd forgotten and there were no more seats left, so I felt disappointed and humbled but she was v. nice and it was her fault. To make us laugh S and I thought we'd climb up on the roof like we used to before the war and we had such fun and found we weren't <u>half</u> as supple <u>or</u> brave as we used to be! She had to leave soon after lunch and I felt depressed as one always does after something one has longed for has happened and is over. I felt almost sick with love for Hugh, too, and I wondered so much what'll happen in the end. I was also worried as to whether the Royal Family think I'm overstepping the line – from now on I'm going to take a firm line with myself and call them 'Princess' and try to make myself a discreet and valuable friend to them. It is my most ardent desire that after the war when we're no longer near each other she may not forget me and still keep me as her friend – I would make a good one to her always but she doesn't seem to need friends and is <u>so</u> careless with the ones she has, though quite unconsciously I know.

Monday, 1 June

Grandpa's eighty-seventh birthday. He was so sweet today and I felt how much happier we'd all be if he were always like that. It was the first <u>summer</u> day and it seemed such a waste to be indoors working all day! I biked home afterwards and had my sandwiches and Horlicks before going to bed.

Tuesday, 2 June

Princess E rang up and asked me to stay next weekend as they're going to be alone. I could hardly believe my good fortune as I have been praying the last few days that I might stay there again soon.

Friday, 5 June

After work, I walked slowly down to Frogmore, where I was told the princesses were picnicking, and I met them and Crawfie, just as they were leaving and we walked back and sat under the terrace wall, talking about the dance for a bit.

Then we came in and played a game of Monopoly in the schoolroom till we all went to our baths. I had the same room as last time, on the floor above theirs; came down to supper in the nursery in my dressing-gown and nightdress and PE had a lovely sort of housecoat of blue-flowered shantung with a long sash of orange. When the Q is alone she now dines with her but they are away this weekend. Supper was so good and Mrs Knight and Bobo so nice. Afterwards we went to PE's room and PM and I both lay on the spare bed under the eiderdown and read and talked. After she'd gone, PE and I went through the dance list and I went to bed about ten fifteen. She also gave me one of her birthday parade photographs and I went to sleep almost unbelievably happy! The engravings of the old royal weddings round the walls, the whole atmosphere here, all seem so much part of my life, that I can't believe that a little way away lies the <u>ordinary</u> world where, in spite of all this, I live <u>most</u> of my life.

Saturday, 6 June

The only thing I <u>don't</u> like about here is that they always have the wireless on during breakfast and supper. After breakfast in the nursery, we went to the schoolroom and I wrote my diary while they did lessons and then we went for dancing. It was rather fun today. We had orange juice in the nursery after, then put on cotton frocks and straw hats for the picnic. We, the princesses, Crawfie and I, walked down to Frogmore, pushing our lunch in a cart, then went in the punt to a good spot where we ate our lunch under a tree on the lawn and afterwards read, lying in a row on the rug. We came slowly back and after tea we did the hypnotising card trick* and it worked! Then the princesses and I played Monopoly till seven when PE and I went for a walk with the dogs in the comparative cool of the evening. Came in and had baths and then PE and I sat on the floor in her room by the open window (they are v. low in these rooms) watching people and gossiping. We saw Winifred below the terrace with her dog but we didn't let her see us. We talked about Hugh and other men, and in the warm summer evening in the intimacy of her bedroom, we talked more freely than ever before, as she's naturally v. reserved, but tonight she seemed as if she liked a friend to talk to. We heard that poor Elizabeth Vyner had died of meningitis – she was only eighteen and pretty and charming and it gave us both a shock. PE looked pretty tonight too – she has lovely eyes.

Sunday, 7 June

Breakfast eight fifteen again – much cooler. The princesses wore new dresses of silk with pattern of autumn-coloured maple leaves on a blue ground – v. pretty and PE's was a different shape. We did the card trick after and played Consequences till ten thirty when we got ready for church! They went to Royal Lodge and I longed to go with them but that, I suppose, is something I will never do! In after-noon we sat out and read and had to hide in the tunnel from the Australians who were shown round the Castle and I had an attack of sneezing and we all got the giggles! Came in and got ready to go to tea at Adelaide Cottage. There were six officers there, including Jackie Philipps, and we had great fun playing all the usual games. Walked home and

---

* Alathea learned the card trick from Sonia.

had v. quick baths – I use the one the princesses had whenever they stayed at Windsor before the war and I remembered it from the first time I stayed here. Had a last lovely supper in nursery, then PE and I went to her room and lay on the beds talking. We began about her family, which she's never breathed about before, and I said things to her I would never had thought I would say! She said she wondered if she'd ever marry, and I assured her she would, and she said if she really wanted to marry someone she'd run away, but I know she wouldn't really – her sense of duty's too strong, though she's suited to a simpler life. I would love to know how far she or her family have gone into the marriage question for her but I would never go a step further than she leads me herself. She may be right in her position, in not making too intimate friends. But tonight I learned to know a new Lilibet: I saw behind the outward calm and matter of factness into something lovable and sincere – I knew this aspect of her would fade with daylight but it is one I shall never forget and my affection for her has become the deeper for it. We said goodnight at quarter to eleven and I lay awake in bed for ages, thinking. I've made a great effort since I've been here to call them PE and PM and as they haven't told me not to I concluded it must be right. It's sad the old Lilibet days are over but I know the time must come when it would be impossible.

Monday, 8 June

Came down to my last breakfast in the nursery. I said goodbye to them all about nine, which was sad but I shall see them again so soon. They sent me down to Queensmead in the Ford and when I got there I changed into my uniform and began the day's work. They were all v. interested in my weekend, but I didn't volunteer much.

Thursday, 11 June

Biked to drawing after lunch and spent a lovely afternoon – it was warm under the terrace wall. The Queen came out dressed in pale mauve and looking lovely. Princess M told me today to call her 'Margaret' but PE hasn't said anything. So, I'm in rather a mix-up about it!

Friday, 12 June

Worked all day. Had the dreadful home nursing exam! We all sat in a row waiting and I was dreading the practical more than the oral but to my intense annoyance, though I knew all the questions but one, the odious little woman failed me by three marks, and Mrs C-S said there was no point me doing the practical as it would not count if I did pass, as one must pass both together. I can't pass exams – this is the fourth I've failed since November. Although I know most of the things, my answers never seem to please them. But I've got quite hardened to failing now!

Sunday, 21 June

Diana Bowes-Lyon came to Mass and we both wrote after breakfast and rang up people and talked about the princesses. She adores them and we share the same opinions of their characters; she and Margaret Elphinstone know them better than anyone of that age does.

Friday, 26 June

Biked to drawing after lunch. V. hot so after we ate wild strawberries on the slopes. Margaret was v. sweet: she suddenly asked me to give her a kiss!

Grosvenor Square, London

Saturday, 27 June

Got to London and unpacked and did my nails and then lay on bed reading till Barbara Crichton came. We bathed and dressed (I wore the pink and blue muslin Bet gave me and two little silver bows in my hair). We went to Grosvenor House and joined the Loyds, who had a party of about sixteen, including Angela Stokes and Flavia Drake[*] from Errolston. Alastair Graham[†] came as my partner. It was, of course, the summer Queen Charlotte Ball. The dinner was good and so was the cabaret. At one moment, some of us started writing verses about each other and I wrote such a good one but a little unsuitable owing to the Champagne I'd drunk! The one about me said, 'Her face had grace and seemed sincere'. I loved doing this. I saw <u>hundreds</u> of friends from all directions.

---

[*] Angela Stokes and Flavia Drake were pupils at Errolston whom Alathea liked and later kept in touch with.
[†] Alastair Graham was another Grenadier officer.

Friday, 3 July

I biked to the Castle for drawing, which was indoors today
as raining. We did imaginary pictures – mine was to illustrate,
'Oh Mary go and call the cattle home across the sands o'
Dee'. PE v. characteristically chose 'The Market Place'! She
scribbled on a piece of paper to me that Philip was coming
for the weekend.

Sunday, 5 July

At seven Miles Marriott fetched me in the car and we drove
to Maidenhead to the Boat Club, where I watched him swim,
then we took a boat and he rowed me down the river to
Bray. We had dinner at the Hind's Head, which was fun,
then rowed back again. It was lovely now in the setting sun
and M told me I 'looked handsome with its glow on me'! I
like him v. much and Mummy would like me to marry him
because he's rich, but I could never love him and would
never be content. I wonder v. much if he loves me at all; I
would have considered him too immature to love – but he
does seem to like me.

Thursday, 9 July

Mass at nine. Billy washed my hair after breakfast and after
curling it I lay out on a rug in the garden writing to Annabel
while it dried. Biked to drawing after lunch. Went out with
Crawfie at four and ate hundreds of wild strawberries – it
was quite hot now and we sat on a seat and Princess Margaret
sent us into fits of laughter by imitating the actions of all
the members of the Household, especially Lady Katie

Seymour* coming in rather late for lunch! Came in for tea and we had melon which was quite delicious. I biked home and called to see Bet on the way. She was just taking the pony back, so we went for half an hour's drive in the Park, which was so pleasant.

Saturday, 11 July

Drove to the Castle. It was difficult to believe it was the last time I would ever come here, into the Red Drawing Room to dance with the princesses. I am really sorry to be giving it up but all things must end.

Monday, 13 July

Of all the officers who come up to dinner to Cumberland Lodge, not <u>one</u> of them asks me out in return, so how <u>can</u> I get to know anyone? Him on whom my thoughts dwell is nowhere near me, and even when I do see him, it avails me nothing save bitter anguish of soul and yet it is my <u>belief</u> that my time is not come yet, that I am destined to know great love.

Thursday, 16 July

I biked to the Castle for drawing – indoors again as windy and dull. PE said she thought it v. bad for me to scrub floors and I ought to join the WRNS at once – she's crazy on them and thinks I'm v. odd and they aren't in the least interested

---

* Lady Katherine Seymour, née Hamilton, was born in 1900, the daughter of the Duke of Abercorn. She was married to Sir Reginald Seymour, and became a Lady of the Bedchamber in 1930.

in what I'm doing! I had to fly back to Queensmead at five thirty and change back into uniform and was on duty till eight.

Saturday, 18 July

It seemed v. strange to be working on a Saturday; it was v. painful, too, to reflect while I was sweeping a carpet that not far away, in a room which has so many memories for me, was a row of red and gold chairs, each with a pointed foot in a pink satin slipper beside it – it was hard to believe I had been part of that for so long and now have left it for ever. I wondered if they missed me. It is just a year ago since our minuet show – but there is no time in the world of today for such charming diversions and I wonder if ever again I will dress up in a crinoline to act. All the same I quite enjoyed today – it was different from other days. All the guests depart and we have to <u>thoroughly</u> clean all their rooms, which I found exhausting but we had a nice lunch with Mrs Hovell* and there wasn't much to do in the afternoon, as there were two voluntaries on. So we went up to the sitting room where Rosamund Foster† was 'receiving' the new guests as they came in; I practised bandaging for Monday, and then we had our tea in there. I wondered if they'd had a film at the Castle – I shall have to let them know somehow that I <u>can</u> still get off at teatime. It's so like them not to find out for themselves!

---

* Mrs Hovell was the Red Cross official in charge of running Queensmead on a day-to-day basis.
† Rosamund Foster was another VAD.

Monday, 20 July

Put on clean cap and apron for the home nursing exam! I just passed the oral with 31, in spite of saying one should boil junket! I hadn't told Grandpa anything about exam in case I failed but he was pleased now.

Thursday, 23 July

Bussed to the Castle for drawing – indoors. PE said there was horrible space on one side of her at dancing last Saturday, which she did not like at all! We went out at four with Crawfie and spent some time making the dogs jump the tennis net, which I thought boring, but it's so typical of the Royal Family's simple tastes and perhaps they are the happier for it. PM was in her usual exuberant spirits and we had a v. gay tea.

Sunday, 26 July

I went up to see the Barclays and Bet said Hugh is returning to Windsor – my heart leaped and I tried not to look interested but I could not help thinking God must mean something, either for PE or myself, by preventing him from going abroad and now sending him back here. Perhaps PE will tell me something on Thursday – if only I could get her to work for me to bring us together. She has got Philip and if I let her know seriously that she alone can help me and that it means a lot to me, the idea might appeal to her – but I hardly ever see her without Margaret or Crawfie and one can only treat it as a joke then.

Monday, 27 July

Aunt M offered to lend me her diamond bow brooch, which I <u>adore</u>; she has got some lovely jewels but I'm afraid she'll never give me any, though I think she'll <u>leave</u> them to me – most of them, anyway, are <u>bequeathed</u> to me. I'm v. fond of the old thing now – strange after <u>hating</u> her so for so many years.

Thursday, 30 July

Zelda and I did housework in the morning. She said she received her summons to an interview at the Labour Exchange today and I found mine when I returned home. I changed for drawing and biked up to the Castle – at least it is hot again and we were outside, finishing our pictures. It is the last lesson, but as my day off is Saturday this week I asked if I might come to <u>watch</u> the dancing class and PE persuaded me to dance, so I agreed. PE showed me two new pairs of shoes, which delighted me – they were grey and wine suede and navy blue suede lace-up ones with crêpe soles – v. smart and v. unlike her. I was so glad. She's also having three of the Q's evening dresses altered for her.

Saturday, 1 August

They rang up from the Castle to ask me to spend the day there, and I felt that indeed Fortune was kind to me. Car took me to dancing and I wore silver slippers and pink ballet shoes to dance in a gilded drawing room – how strange after all my sad farewells! I went out with the princesses and then I sat next to the King at lunch; I must say he is <u>not</u> easy to talk to and yet I never feel shy with him. We read papers in the Q's room afterwards and she admired my dress (it was the pale blue with the muslin frilling), and said I ought to wear that colour a lot, as it suited my colouring so well. Later we went out and lay in long chairs under the terrace where we draw. Lilibet and the King went for a walk and the Queen and I talked a lot and so naturally. She asked me all about Queensmead; she is so sympathetic and I love her so very much. I read bits of *Royal Flush* which PE is now <u>really</u> reading and I felt blissfully happy sitting out here under the shady trees with this so very happy family – here was peace such as I have never known in my own home – four people who mean <u>everything</u> to each other, whose lives form <u>one</u> spiritual whole, independent of the aid of all outsiders, or even relations. I could not help feeling as though I were <u>intruding</u> on this perfect family unity and yet how privileged I am to be allowed to partake of it! Deborah Green-Wilkinson came round the terrace with her platoon of ATS (people are taken round sight-seeing every Saturday) and the Q, P. Margaret and I got up and hid behind a yew bush as otherwise they hang over the wall and stare but we were too late to choose a good place and afterwards realised they must have seen us quite well through the gaps, dancing about behind the bush in our light-coloured frocks and wide straw hats! Came in for tea with the K and Q and then went along to the film which was *Mrs Miniver*. It was <u>very</u> good, I thought, but v. sad and we all cried. It was strange to look back at all the <u>tremendous</u> events, suffering and tragedy that went on in the world all through that summer of 1940, while I was still sitting here doing my lessons and gathering wild flowers in the afternoons with Miss Dunham, being so desperately unhappy at times over my first taste of sorrow, which then seemed so unbearably great! I said goodbye to the Royal Family after the film, which was not over till eight and I shall not see them for some time, as they hope to go away to Scotland, and I <u>do</u> hope they do for their sakes.

Saturday, 8 August

I bussed with my luggage to Queensmead. I am to stay for a fortnight and take Drusilla's place while she's on holiday. I'm sleeping with Elizabeth Christie-Miller,* which is <u>far</u> nicer than right at the top, with writing table, washbasin and everything!

Wednesday, 12 August

I've never worked so hard in my <u>life</u> as I did this morning! I was so exhausted by lunchtime that I could not eat anything and felt I should just drop! I'm sure it can't be good for one and it's annoying to think one would never have done any work but for the war.

Friday, 14 August

Elizabeth C-M has gone away – I miss her and feel lonely, but she is now in the train on her way to Scotland. How I envy her, and I think they must be such a nice family. I wish I was going up to Kinharvie this year, but how <u>wonderful</u> it would be to go and stay at Balmoral! I wonder if this dream will <u>ever</u> come true one day?

---

* Elizabeth Christie-Miller, sometimes called Christie to differentiate her from the many other Elizabeths, was slightly older. Alathea sometimes visited her family at their idyllic home near Henley.

Wednesday, 26 August

There was the most <u>dreadful</u> news – Duke of Kent was <u>killed flying</u> in the north of Scotland – it seems incredible, one cannot believe it. I wrote to Lilibet, which was rather difficult, but I thought it was the right thing. How <u>awful</u> for the duchess.

Houghton, Yorkshire

Friday 4 September

Letter from PE, which was passed round the table – it was sweet but so like that of a child of eleven. I think it is the <u>greatest</u> pity she cannot compose a good letter – it is such an asset and in royalty it is <u>invaluable</u>, and it gives such a bad impression of her to outsiders, and it is even frightening when one considers she is sixteen and might be Queen tomorrow. Until she has trouble and sorrow she cannot hope to be great . . . Mummy came up to nursery in morning and talked to me about my character – she says I lack force and reality.

Monday, 7 September

Mummy, Daddy and I went mushrooming in the morning – I've got to the stage now when I can hardly bear to be with them together: poor D <u>cannot</u> stop irritating her with every word and action almost, and she can't or won't exercise patience with him any more. It's dreadful to see him unhappy, as I know he is. I can only play a silent part by being nice to Daddy. I wondered, too, with a sickening grip at my heart, whether one day far ahead <u>I</u> might be the central

Alathea aged three, with her grandmother Viscountess Fitzalan of Derwent.

Viscount and Viscountess Fitzalan of Derwent at the wedding of Princess Mary, later the Princess Royal, sister of George VI, to Viscount Lascelles, later the Earl of Harewood.

Alathea's mother Joyce, with her baby daughter Elizabeth Anne, Alathea aged ten and Joyce's mother Mrs Philip Langdale.

The Hon Magdalen Fitzalan Howard, Alathea's aunt, described by Alathea as 'The Tigress' in the diaries, with Alathea's father the Hon Edmund Fitzalan Howard, always known as Boydey.

Left: Alathea's mother Joyce in 1942.

Right: Alathea's sister Elizabeth Anne with Taffy the corgi.

Ming-Ming and me on beach at GRIMSTON in Yorkshire. August 1933. Me aged 9.

Left: Alathea with her beloved nanny Ming-Ming.

JAN. 1939. LEICESTER-SHIRE.

The two Alatheas: Alathea with her aunt Alathea, Lady Manton in hunting clothes.

Sonia Graham-Hodgson (above), Zelda Loyd (below), two of Alathea's closest friends in Windsor during the war.

Cumberland Lodge, Alathea's wartime home.

The Royal Family at Royal Lodge in Windsor, April 1940.

The Royal Family inspecting Boy Scouts at Windsor in 1938, with Alathea in a white collar behind them.

A Polyfoto of Alathea taken in Windsor in 1941.

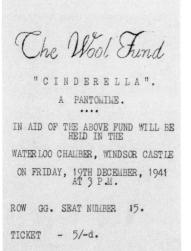

The Wool Fund

"CINDERELLA".

A PANTOMIME.

. . . .

IN AID OF THE ABOVE FUND WILL BE
HELD IN THE

WATERLOO CHAMBER, WINDSOR CASTLE

ON FRIDAY, 19TH DECEMBER, 1941
AT 3 P.M.

ROW GG. SEAT NUMBER 15.

TICKET - 5/-d.

A ticket for the production of the pantomime 'Cinderella' (above), starring the princesses and Alathea, in December 1941. (right) Princesses Margaret and Elizabeth (standing) in costume in 'Cinderella'.

WINDSOR CASTLE

24th Nov 1942.

Many happy returns of the day. From

Elizabeth, & Margaret

A birthday note from the princesses to Alathea for her nineteenth birthday in November 1942.

Alathea in her VAD uniform in 1942.

(left to right) Princess Margaret, Princess Elizabeth and Queen Elizabeth photographed at Windsor Castle on Princess Elizabeth's sixteenth birthday, 1942.

The Maidenhead boat trip. Back row, left to right: Lt Colonel Sir Grismond 'Jackie' Philipps, Michael Farebrother, Billy Whittaker, Sandy Ramsay. Front row, left to right: Crawfie, Lady Joan Philipps, Princess Margaret, Virginia Hall, Alathea.

A Christmas card from the princesses.

A portrait of Alathea, aged thirty-four, in 1957 by Dorothy Wilding.

figure in a similar tragedy – oh, God preserve me from such a thing whatever else I suffer.

Tuesday, 8 September

We spent the morning in the usual way and in the afternoon I made Mummy come on the lake with me, and we spent a more interesting afternoon than I've known for a long while – she told me of her own childhood and a lot about herself, too, while I listened as we rowed contentedly up and down. She put into words what I have so often silently felt, that I am not intended ever to be peacefully happy and contented – there is something in our blood, inherited from Grandmama Langdale* and perhaps, too, from our distant Langdale ancestors, that denies us <u>all</u> – and surely this is the way to live? She said, too, that we come from unquiet blood and therefore all of us are, in different ways, interesting, unordinary people. Give us position or power and we would be among those who are remarkable in history.

Cumberland Lodge

Thursday, 10 September

Early breakfast, then once more the poignant sadness of farewells – another year may pass before I return to this home that I now love, and who knows what may happen in that time? Cumberland Lodge seemed unspeakably lonely and dreary. Grandpa with his fussiness and deafness and continually saying how thankful he was to get me back

---

* Alathea's maternal grandmother, née Gertrude Derriman, daughter of an admiral, had died in 1939.

irritated me beyond endurance after being away from it. There was nowhere to go, no one to talk to, and I felt depressed and unhappy to an unbearable degree. To make matters even more cheerless, there isn't enough coal to make the bath water hot at night.

Tuesday, 22 September

At Queensmead all day. Drusilla told me Geoffrey Pallow* had written to her to say he's getting married, and the poor child was so upset that she was actually sick. I sympathised with all my heart and I tried to believe the sudden and complete dampening of my own spirits was due to the effect of hers, but somehow I knew it was because I was selfish – in a queer, odd way, jealous of another's unhappiness, of her having known, having had something, in her life that has so far been denied to me, even though she has lost it now. That I have nothing in my life to upset or disturb me, annoyed me, and then I felt that my profound boredom and restlessness are due to the lack of love and deeper emotions, that my temperament, perhaps more than most others, requires these things to appease and feed it. All my defiance of yesterday disappeared and I wandered dejectedly round my work all day. Since I've been away they've put red marks in the baths at five inches for water lines, following the King's example, and moved the dining-room table to one end of the room, so as not to have so many lights on – by degrees we are losing every comfort of civilisation. The gloom of this house increases and Grandpa becomes more and more nerve-racking.

---

* Drusilla had been in love with Pallow.

Thursday, 24 September

Queensmead was torture today. The heavy nameless cloud that has settled on my life will lift – depression never lasts for ever and quite soon mine must pass away, and in the sanctuary of my own room I did find some comfort alone with my diary and my own possessions – a comfort that if I lived at Queensmead I would lack and therefore it is worth the loneliness and the pain I sometimes endure here.

Sunday, 11 October

I got off at four and met Daddy in the Long Walk and we walked across to Adelaide Cottage to tea with the Philipps. To my intense joy Hugh [Euston] came in and spent the rest of the evening till we left. I felt and talked easily and naturally with him and he was sweet to me. He looked ill, though, and I could see he was depressed and unsettled – I felt I could make him happy and that he needed marriage to give him interest and security in life again. I did not think he was in love with anyone and that if he wanted to marry he would as soon choose me as anyone. Why doesn't an idea occur to him that is the object of my most fervent prayers, night and day?

Thursday, 22 October

Daddy gave me a lift as far as Beaumont.* I bussed on to Windsor and walked up to the Castle. Princess E was just the same but PM had grown a lot taller and her face seems a bit longer. We didn't settle down v. well to drawing for

---

* Beaumont was a public school for boys run by the Jesuits.

157

the first day. I washed in PE's room and we had tea in the schoolroom. 'Toni'* now lives there as Libby Hardinge has gone to boarding school and Winifred is in the WRNS. My life felt full and happy and the future no longer seemed so black and barren.

Friday, 30 October

In the afternoon I went for a walk with Bet. We discussed getting married, and I hinted to her about Hugh, which I'd meant to do for some time as I think she'd be capable of helping me – she agreed he is the only person I've met here who I could possibly marry but she said she knows he doesn't <u>want</u> to get married yet. I returned feeling depressed. If he feels like that, how can I hope to make him change?

I dressed for the dance in my green crêpe. We drove to the White Hart, picking Zelda up on the way. Joined the rest of our party there – Sonia, all the Queensmead people and one or two others. The men were quite nice, and I enjoyed it more than I'd expected to.

Thursday, 5 November

When I got up to the Castle I found no one there and then PM appeared and said there was no drawing because Mrs Cox had earache but they hadn't let me know on purpose. We went out with Crawfie and took the two new ponies for a walk, plus the four dogs, and we got <u>soaked</u>! I had to

---

* (Marie) Antoinette, neé Willemin, known as 'Toni', was a Belgian married to Vicomte Pierre de Bellaigue. She taught the Hardinge girls, then Princesses Elizabeth and Margaret until 1948 and remained close to the Royal Family and Alathea.

borrow Mrs Knight's slippers and PE's skirt for tea! It fitted <u>perfectly</u> round the waist, and I had thought I was much bigger made than her. That dreadful Mr Tannar came to tea, which I considered totally unnecessary, and afterwards we discussed the Xmas pantomime, which is going to be *Sleeping Beauty*. I am truly relieved that I am going to be out of it this year, as I really couldn't bear all that I went through last year again. I was v. disapproving of the whole thing, though as I can do nothing about it the best thing is to appear enthusiastic. <u>No one</u> is more in favour of, or would more enjoy taking part in, <u>some</u> sort of private theatricals at Christmas than me, since they are the only people able to do it now. *Sleeping Beauty* could be made so charming with a completely fairytale atmosphere but how can PE with her sense of her non-exalted position bear to act in a rowdy variety show? Now, especially as she's older, she ought to assume a more regal bearing. As for getting guardsmen in with low comedian jokes, it is beyond my comprehension. One thing, however, that did please and excite me was that they've been photographed by Cecil Beaton[*] in their taffeta frocks and I <u>do</u> so hope they'll give me one!

Friday, 6 November

Had an early lunch at the Cordon Bleu.[†] As I had plenty of time I suddenly thought I'd walk to Lenare, Hanover Square, where I intend being photographed. I loved their portraits and discussed what to wear with the girl. I also thought how

---

[*] Cecil Beaton was the best-known society photographer of the era and often photographed the Royal Family. He was much favoured by Queen Elizabeth, who first summoned him in 1939.
[†] Petit Cordon Bleu was a restaurant near Sloane Square.

I'd love to have Elizabeth Anne done in her white muslin bridesmaid frock – perhaps in colour – if only they'd pay me at Queensmead I <u>could</u> do this quite well.

Sunday, 8 November

I wired to Miles Marriott and got a reply to say he'd love to come next Saturday, so that is a great relief, even though he does rather bore me.

Monday, 9 November

Biked to work again after three weeks' holiday. It seemed v. strange and I <u>hated</u> house-maiding again, but I was quite glad to be back as one soon gets bored nowadays. Had a lovely tea today with two sorts of cake, as it was Drusilla's twentieth birthday yesterday.

Tuesday, 10 November

My day off, which I only obtained by saying that I had to go to the dentist! All went to the House of Lords, where Grandpa was one of the four peers selected for the Royal Commission for proroguing Parliament. It was an interesting ceremony and I revel in the many old customs upheld there. I rang Mummy up this evening – she got on to the subject of my job and said I'd 'missed the bus' by not going to the secretarial college and that if I fail in the world it will be because I persistently oppose her. I feel v. bitter towards her tonight, verging once more on hatred, and when PE rang up to ask me to tea tomorrow I reverted even more to the circle Mummy disapproves of – I felt as long as I have them nothing matters and could I turn back two years I know I would do exactly the same again.

Thursday, 12 November

I went up to the Castle but Princess M and I alone as PE had gone to Caterham. We had an amusing tea. PM made me laugh by saying she dreamed that Margaret Elphinstone was sitting on Hugh's knee and that PE and I were sitting at his feet v. jealous! If only I could rely on them not forsaking me, were I to leave here, but I cannot blind myself to the fact that I might lose in a day all I have gained in years.

Saturday, 14 November

Biked to Queensmead at nine with my case. Soon after I'd arrived, Barbara suddenly said to me, 'Perhaps you'd rather work by yourself if you don't consider us good enough for you.' Flabbergasted, I demanded what she meant and she went on saying the most dreadful things to me. I rushed downstairs to Drusilla and amid sobs and tears made her explain it all – she was v. sweet and sympathetic but she admitted they'd all thought me rather snooty since the dance and that I said things that offended people, though <u>she</u> knew I didn't really mean them. Mrs Hovell saw me crying and I had to go and tell <u>her</u> the whole story – she took my part, though, to my horror, she said someone outside once told her <u>I</u> thought I ought to be working with people of higher rank. No doubt it was some malicious old gossip who, because I go to the Castle, assumes I must be like that for that very reason – but nevertheless it is disconcerting for never in my wildest dreams have I uttered or even <u>thought</u>

such a thing. It is awful to have that reputation and once got it is hard to live down. I think it is cruel that people should say things about me that aren't true at all but the world is unkind in the things it says of one.

I changed into my navy blue and white muslin dress, and got the quarter to five train to London. I wished I wasn't going at all – my eyes ached intolerably from crying and it was all <u>such</u> a rush. I changed my shoes and stockings in the taxi. When I got to Grosvenor House and met Annabel, Miles Marriott and another boy there, we all rushed off to see *Lilac Time*, which I <u>loved</u> but I'm afraid they were rather bored. We went on to dine at the Savoy where we danced and laughed all evening at a v. drunk but quite harmless man. We left at about one and were dropped at Grosvenor House where A and I had a room. We were 'mobbed' in the hall by about ten Americans who asked us to go out with them. Of course we didn't go, but we had a good laugh out of them first!

Sunday, 15 November

I had to rush off and all my misery flooded back on me. Everyone was v. nice, including Barbara, yet I was unhappier today and felt suddenly overcome for no particular reason and my tears gushed forth uncontrollably and silently. I longed for the moment when I could be alone. Too tired to cope with the world and all its intricacies, I fell into bed without even doing my hair. Barbara might have been sorry if she had seen the tears I shed at her expense and as I wept I thought how unhappy I was, how alone in the world, incapable of facing its hard injustice. Then suddenly I got up and fetched my knife and tore the flesh on my forearm till I was exhausted and couldn't cry any more. By some sinister coincidence Aunt Magdalen, who never comes to my room after we've said goodnight, opened the door and spoke to me but I pulled up the sheets and spoke in a faraway voice and she went away again. No one will know what I did tonight and even at the moment I asked myself why I did it – it gratifies some strange impulse and succeeds more than anything else in abating my grief and anger.

Monday, 16 November

Today passed better than I expected. Z was there and of course I told her everything. She said she hoped I'd try and get on with B and forgive her, as it's only her temper and she's really quite good-natured, though life hasn't treated her kindly, which has had this effect on her. This is true, and though I can never quite forget the things she has said to me I shall no doubt learn a valuable lesson by hiding my feelings day after day towards a person whom I can never like.

Tuesday, 17 November

V. interesting post for once – one was an 'Afternoon Party' at B. Palace on <u>26</u>. I was <u>thrilled</u>, though <u>very</u> curious to know the details. I hadn't heard a word about it, but it must be a large affair for it to be in London. Also had a letter from Miles saying, 'My Dear' and 'With love' – if only that could be someone else how thrilled I would be! But much as I like Miles, I <u>can't</u> take any <u>interest</u> in him – it's strange he likes me.

Thursday, 19 November

Changed after lunch and went to the Castle for drawing. I told PE and PM about the white lace I'm thinking of buying and when I mentioned a Victory ball they both said I'd look <u>so</u> conspicuous and that everyone would be in rags by that time! Their tastes are <u>so plain</u> since the war and I'm sure they slightly disapprove of me in some ways. We went out with Toni to see the ponies, and I suddenly fell to wondering what fate awaited this girl, who was in character and tastes so much simpler than I. Will she stand out in history as another great Elizabeth, or will she merely be a commonplace puppet in a rapidly degenerating monarchy? She seems to have no desire to win fame for herself but what a waste of one who has unbounded scope in both the social and political world.

Monday, 23 November

Zelda and I had the housework to do alone, which was nice. We began discussing when we would like to have lived and came to making a story of it – who we were, where we lived, and what we did until, to me at least, it became more real than my own life. My dreams were rudely shattered, however, when Drusilla told me I am so jealous and that she really <u>dislikes</u> me in those moments – since I've been at Queensmead I've heard a great many 'home truths' and hardly one of them has been pleasant, though they've told me nothing I did not already know. The fact is that working <u>day after day</u> with a lot of other girls is a severe test of one's character and one to which in ordinary circumstances one would not be subjected. I don't think anyone else's character has stood up to it, least of all mine. Rang up Sonia and told her all about it, and we laughed over it, as she has gone through exactly the same thing on the rare occasions she has mixed with girls en masse – she thought she was so popular and she asked for criticism and when she got it, it found its mark more surely than she bargained for. It serves only to harden and embitter our hearts and, if anything, increases the vices we are accused of.

Tuesday, 24 November

<u>My nineteenth birthday</u>. Mass, and breakfast after. I opened a few presents and felt v. happy – after yesterday it was an almost unbelievable change! We all went to London by car and I bought chocolates at Fortnum's for the party; then I taxied to Lenare, where Sonia met me and helped me change for my photograph. In the end I was done in my new frilly white muslin blouse and I do hope they will be a success. We then went and had lunch at Gunter's and collected my birthday cake, which we were unable to make at home this year, and car came and took us all home, with Sonia. I changed into my pink skirt and muslin blouse and Zelda, Drusilla and Eliz [Christie-Miller] all arrived at four fifteen. We waited downstairs for the princesses to arrive and Patricia Beauchamp suddenly turned up, which was most embarrassing! The princesses came with Crawfie and Joan and Jackie P. Francis Legh* and Francis Wigram† all came with

---

* Major the Hon. Francis Legh was another Grenadier. He was later an equerry to the Queen and Princess Margaret's private secretary.
† Francis Wigram was a captain in the Grenadiers, who was killed in action in 1943 during the Allied invasion of Sicily. He was the son of Lord Wigram, a senior courtier at Windsor, who had been private secretary to George V.

them. They gave me a lovely green suede bag, the Philipps a book token, Sonia a scarlet leather belt, Eliz and D a book token and several other things from other people. We had tea straight away, which went off v. well, though we were all rather stilted, but afterwards when we played charades everyone relaxed and it was great fun and we all enjoyed ourselves and laughed a great deal! Played another acting game and then they all left about seven. Spent the rest of the evening quietly and I was quite exhausted! PE had rung up the night before about Thursday and said they'd take me with them to London, which thrilled me and tonight I was blissfully happy. Everything had gone right once more and there were no shadows to darken my joy. My other presents were a pigskin bag from Grandpa, the green wool dress from Daddy but it isn't ready yet, pink satin lace-trimmed underclothes from Mummy, which I think are too bright and am going to change them, chintz work bag from Aunt M and several other smaller ones.

Thursday, 26 November

A memorable day. Car took me to Castle at quarter to ten where I joined the princesses and drove up to London with them and Mrs Knight. I left my case in PE's room at Buckingham Palace – it was strange being there again after so long but I had never actually been in either this room or the nursery and I liked them better than any of their rooms elsewhere that I've seen. Went down with the princesses but then there was the usual muddle as to where I was to have lunch, which was both embarrassing and humiliating though I have grown so used to it now! Anyway, it appeared I was to lunch with the Household, so I was escorted to a vast empty room, where I waited alone for some ten minutes. Then they all came in and, to my surprise and delight, the Duchess of Northumberland* was there too. We had a v. amusing lunch. I was taken up to the nursery again, where I changed into my dark blue wool frock and tidied and waited with the princesses till three, when we went down again and I alone went into the Bow Room, where there were already several people awaiting the party. I was told to go over by the ladies-in-waiting, etc., and the duchess was <u>angelic</u> to me putting her arm round me and being so kind, whereas she might have taken no notice of me at all and made me feel miserable and out of it. The Royal Family came in later and received all the Americans and the rest of the guests. How different the scene in this room was from those summer evenings when we had Guides here! We then went into the long corridor outside where a buffet stretched the whole length of it and talked to the Americans. There were about 300 people altogether; the K and Q moved about among them and the princesses stood together talking to everyone who was brought up to them. PE wore that awful blue silk frock, with the little pleated cape, which is the <u>worst</u> thing she could possibly wear with her figure. PM had a nondescript little silk frock on – they <u>are</u> so badly dressed now but I was glad they weren't alike today. We all found conversation rather difficult, but I enjoyed it, and there was lovely chamber music playing in a corner. I reflected how disappointed I would have been but a short time ago not being with the Royal Family personally much today but now suddenly I was glad to be classed, as it were, with the

---

* The Duchess of Northumberland was Mistress of the Robes to Queen Elizabeth.

ladies-in-waiting rather than following <u>them</u> about like a child. Joined the princesses upstairs at six and we drove back to Windsor in the dark and discussed everything and everybody, which I enjoyed. They sent me on home afterwards and so ended a day that will remain happily in my memory all my life.

Tuesday, 8 December

Met Daddy at the New Gallery (in London) to see Noël Coward's film *In Which We Serve*, which was brilliant. Drove home, when I had to begin ringing up people for this damn ball on Saturday – without success and I was so tired and fed up I just ceased to care.

Friday, 11 December

Went up to the Castle for the pantomime – we sat in the front row and the Queen came and sat next to Elizabeth [Christie-Miller], much to her joy and she shook hands with me. It was *Sleeping Beauty* and I must say I loved it – it was all beautifully done and Princess Margaret especially looked divine as the Good Fairy, though PE looked <u>slightly</u> old among so many children and it is a pity she is always the boy.

Saturday, 12 December

Went to Queensmead with my luggage and got the quarter to five train to London. Took Mummy's fur coat as I hadn't brought mine, and when my partner arrived, we went straight off to someone's house in Oxford Square where we had a delicious buffet supper. We went on to the Grosvenor House for the Queen Charlotte's Ball in a party of twenty-four. We danced Scottish reels, which were the <u>greatest</u> fun. Sonia was there in white net. Hundreds of others I knew, so I really enjoyed it <u>far</u> more than I ever expected and almost more than any other Queen Charlotte's I've been to. The ball ended and a party of us tried to get into the 400, but it was full, so we were all dropped home in turn.

Thursday, 17 December

I rang Sonia up in their new house near Bray – she confided to me that she'd heard a young man say I 'run through the list' too much when I ring up barracks to get someone for a dance and also that I ring up too much anyway, 'which is a pity, as I'm so nice really, and it makes me rather laughed at'. Actually it's Aunt M who 'keeps on' ringing up and not in a v. clever way but, since she does it for my sake, how can I say anything, but I wish they wouldn't think it is me. Sonia hesitated to tell me this, but I persuaded her as, after all, what is a friend for if not to tell one things for one's own good? I am grateful to her, and though slightly perturbed, I'm not hurt – perhaps because I've got used to hearing ungratifying things about myself, and S, I know, would help me a lot if she has the chance. Nevertheless I went to bed once more at odds with the world I live in – how can I ever hope to get on in it, when I am so rarely at peace within its boundaries?

Tuesday, 22 December

Work in the morning. In afternoon I went out to get presents. Came home and found lots of cards, including one from Miles with a special photograph of PE by Cecil Beaton, and a lovely one from the princesses, of a little eighteenth-century girl, picking bluebells in a white frock, with a wide pink sash and a picture hat.

Wednesday, 23 December

The morning seemed to drag by – I am so terribly bored with work and long for a few days rest. It doesn't seem credible that I have <u>got</u> to go on working every day over Christmas. When I think of it, my soul rises in rebellion; the only thing is <u>not</u> to think of it and let my mind dwell on other things. That is why Daddy is unhappy, because he can never get away from realities – we both hate them equally and in the same manner, but I am able to push them from me and be comparatively happy in a world of my own creation, and it is only when they flood back on me, or take possession, that I lose all hope and interest in life. Now I always try and think that however bored I am, the day must come to an end, and even though the next day may be just the same as the last, it must inevitably bring one nearer to those that, one hopes, will bear in their train the realisation of at least <u>some</u> of our wishes. Elizabeth [Christie-Miller] and I had tea alone, and we had one of those discussions which somehow never fail to upset me – she praised the idea of the modern woman taking a more active part in the world and deplored my view of marriage as the only vocation of any well-born girl but I have been brought up in that tradition and never can I understand that anyone should entertain <u>other</u> ideals.

Thursday, 24 December

Very busy all day but quite a nice day. Heard that Myra Wernher's* brother, Alec, had been killed abroad – how broken-hearted they will all be and how much sadder this war must be to some than to me who have really suffered so little from it. I should like to have heard from the princesses, as it seems so long since I last saw them. It struck me as sad that she counts so little on her friends – she must miss such a lot and it would seem that she will never change: she will marry and be a model wife and mother, devoted to her family and dogs and never desire anything more – but then again, who can know what lies ahead of this princess?

Friday, 25 December

I had breakfast in bed and opened several of my parcels, including a lovely flowered china basket with pot-pourri from Aunt Gwen.† I got up at nine thirty and, after giving all the servants their presents, I biked to Priest's Hill only

---

* Myra Wernher was the younger daughter of Sir Harold Wernher and Lady Zia, who was the daughter of Grand Duke Mikhail Romanov but also related to Pushkin. The family were very rich and lived at Luton Hoo. Myra and her sister Gina were brought up with the royal families of Europe and were particularly close to Prince Philip. She went on to marry Major Sir David Butter.

† Gwendoline, dowager Duchess of Norfolk, née Constable Maxwell, was the second wife of the 14th Duke of Norfolk and was Lady Herries in her own right. A member of a huge intermarried network of Catholic families, she liked gathering all the cousins at Glenharvie, her house in south-west Scotland. She was Alathea's great-aunt.

to discover there were no buses today, so I had to bike all the way to Queensmead from there. Exchanged presents with everyone there – Eliz gave me a lovely large black velvet bow for my hair – then they all went to church and I just had to skim around the top floor with a duster and then we prepared for the Christmas lunch! It seemed strange working on Christmas Day but had a <u>lovely</u> lunch – turkey and plum pudding, etc. I spent the afternoon in the staffroom with Rosamund and Eliz, listening to the wireless and the King's speech at three, which was <u>v.</u> good. Tea at four thirty, with an iced cake, and then I biked home. It was almost dark and I <u>loathed</u> it – it was so lonely and dreary and cold and I'm terrified of the dark alone. We had benediction when I got in at six but Grandpa annoyed me so much just before by fussing and bellowing that all spirituality was banished from my soul, which is the effect he always has on all of us. I wore a long dress for dinner, which was v. Christmassy in the way of food but everything seemed so dreary and inadequate – probably because there were all old people.

Tuesday, 29 December

Nothing in the least happened all day.

Thursday, 31 December

Slight fall of snow in the night and <u>icy</u> cold. A letter from Myra Wernher came and she said what a miserable war it is and prayed God it ends soon, and in such moments I feel selfish, for no one can really claim to have suffered in war unless they have lost someone they have loved. I close this diary, then, with three great wishes in my heart, and may God grant them.

1943

A group photograph at Queensmead, the Red Cross
home in Windsor, where Alathea did her war work.
Alathea is fourth from left, wearing her uniform.

Friday, 1 January

Mass, then worked till five. Drusilla on with me, so we had a good gossip about everything and everyone! Stayed the night in a nasty little attic room and I thought crossly how I hated being subject to these sordid conditions. I prayed that this year might be a good one and indeed I have more confidence in it.

Monday, 11 January

I felt v. nervous beginning my fifty hours* but I was put on Mary Ward (women's medical) and the sister and other nurses were v. nice to me. The only thing I was ticked off about was standing with my arms folded! At first I was shocked by the sight of so many white, ill faces but I soon got used to it and I even managed the bed pans well, though I retched out of the sluice-room window once or twice!

Tuesday, 12 January

Biked round to the hospital. I was allowed to stand by and watch the sewing up of a great gash in the back of a woman,

---

* This was Alathea's first real hospital work.

caused by a huge carbuncle. This was under an anaesthetic and I had to help hold her head. It was so new and fascinating that I didn't feel queer at all!

Sunday, 17 January

I went off to the hospital for the last time. I was sorry in a way, especially to leave the patients, many of whom I have become really fond of. One of them gave me half a crown, which of course I wouldn't take, and another two toffees, which I <u>did</u> keep! But I had such a sense of <u>freedom</u> as I rode back to Zelda's – wrong though I know it is to think thus – such a <u>relief</u> to be returning to easy-going Queensmead tomorrow! There was an air raid after dinner and we heard the guns for the first time for ages. I only <u>hope and pray</u> they won't begin bombing London seriously once more.

Wednesday, 20 January

All went to London by car and I was dropped at Grosvenor Square where I saw EA and Mummy. She was v. excited about going to her new school, and we took her to the station to see her off to St Giles. There was a warning and heavy guns just before the train started, which terrified the mothers but thrilled the children!

Tuesday, 26 January

Elizabeth Anne's ninth birthday.
How I hope she is happy at St Giles and that she will learn to love that ideal child's life, which will fall behind her so quickly.

Thursday, 28 January

Spent the morning hectically preparing for the party. We had intended wearing short frocks because of those who would have to walk but Mrs Bathurst* suddenly created an almighty row saying it was an <u>insult</u> to her. So altogether everyone was in a furious temper and Drusilla angry with Z and me, for some reason – just before lunch it came to a head and I flung some forks down on to a table, which fell on to the floor and one of them hit D's ankle and made it bleed. She hit me on the shoulder, I spun round and hit her on the face; I burst into tears and fled from the room, not having the <u>least</u> idea of what had really happened! I cried all through lunch and in the afternoon, and Mrs Hovell asked to see me but she was v. kind. I had never felt more miserable before a party and we all wished we needn't go. Went back with Z but while she titivated herself and became more enthusiastic I still felt utterly desolate. I was glad after all to wear a long frock and as soon as I was dressed I had forgotten my ill humour. Major Loyd drove us to Queensmead. There were over sixty and we had the Grenadiers' Dance Band – Sonia came and lots of officers I knew. I got on v. well with Julian Lyttelton† and they played lots of waltzes and we had a wonderful fork supper, so altogether it was a <u>great</u> success and for once I felt that I was too!

---

* Mrs Bathurst was the owner of Queensmead and she lived in the house next door.
† The Hon. Julian Lyttelton was the son of Viscount Chandos and a lieutenant in the Grenadiers. He died in 1944.

Tuesday, 2 February

Sonia came at five. She told me she'd often heard Hugh talked of as the 'Prince Consort'. I know how much he'd hate that, and if only, if only, he'd marry me before he gets further compromised, by way of escape – it would be so sure, and so simple a way for him – but, alas, things never work out as one plans them.

Wednesday, 3 February

Princess E rang up tonight and asked me to drawing tomorrow. They returned on Monday and it will be lovely to see them again.

Thursday, 4 February

Biked with my case to Queensmead. Afterwards, I biked to the Castle for drawing. I was glad to be back with them all again and it made me sad to think I only share their life for one afternoon a week – so little, and yet I feel I am part of their world or, rather, that their world is part of me, so truly in my element do I feel there.

Wednesday, 10 February

I went to Queensmead by bike and then bus. Had to polish the pantry floor by myself in afternoon which nearly killed me! There was an air raid at tea time with guns and I went home directly after it. Grandpa in London for the night – what bliss it was! With no Rosary, no telephoning, and no one fussing into my room at night!

Thursday, 11 February

Rode up to the Castle for drawing. PE had a pleated skirt and PM one of plain bottle green. I was glad they weren't quite alike, though I do think they ought to break away altogether now. We took it in turns to ride the little cream Norwegian pony, Hans, bareback, which was fun. Came in for tea and I got ready in PE's room – for the first time I was struck by the odd mixture of nursery chintz and elegant striped brocade, of monstrous Victorian wardrobes and graceful Rococo chairs!

Saturday, 13 February

I had tea with the King and Queen and the princesses in the Queen's sitting room. It seemed like the old days to be doing this again. We went along to the Waterloo Chamber after for the film *Casablanca*, which I enjoyed <u>far</u> more than I expected to. We sat in the front row with rugs over our knees, as it was cold in there. When we came out PM said in her own sweet, innocent voice, 'What I couldn't work out was who was married to who?' Lady Katherine Seymour and I laughed over this – she is so sweet. Letter from Mummy when I got home – it wrecked my evening and left me, as usual, in an odd, unsettled state of mind. For safety's sake I burned the letter but the sum of it was that young married women would be more help to me now as friends, as they have more to offer men, in the way of material amusement, than girls. She feared young men consider Cumberland Lodge as one huge joke and v. boring. She couldn't <u>bear</u> me to be associated with it, and that I ought to encourage people to think I am here by force and <u>not part</u> of the atmosphere.

Monday, 15 February

When I got home I heard that poor Lord Fitzwilliam is dead.* How sad so many people must feel over this – it must seem to them, even more than it does to me, the passing not only of a man but of an epoch, of a representative of an existence which, even in <u>his</u> day, was almost unique. I, in my generation, am privileged to have partaken of that existence, in those days before the old order in England, though fast crumbling, had not completely fallen!

Wednesday, 17 February

Sonia and I rode out to her new house at Oakley Green, and we had tea with her mother. I felt v. happy and the ride home, up the Long Walk, was curiously pleasant instead of frightening – the great park, lying tranquil in the silence of dusk seemed more my own than it ever does in the garish light of day. Unspoilt by tourists, it seemed once again to be the happy playground of kings and princes of bygone days – I was not afraid because I knew all its secrets. I was at one with those royal personages whose fair hunting ground this used to be.

Thursday, 18 February

Biked to the Castle for drawing. It was the most lovely spring day. We discussed what fun it would be to have a fancy dress ball and Crawfie said she would come as a man and flirt with us all! We would all wear masks and I said I would come in a crinoline and powdered wig. PE vaguely hinted

---

* The 7th Earl Fitzwilliam, known as Billy, was the father of Lady Joan Philipps.

that they might be having a dance and she said something about 'lengthening' it, in the hope that Philip might get leave.

Sunday, 21 February

I stayed in bed all day, idle and happy since there was nothing to miss by being up. I wrote a long letter to Sonia, sending her a book to read and also to Miles Marriott, who <u>can't</u> come to Queen Charlotte's but said he was just going to write to me anyway to ask me to a theatre in London with him – I suppose it is wrong to feed and encourage a man's affection when one has no intention of returning it but I have need of some excitement in my life and I see in this my only possibility for the moment.

Thursday, 25 February

Biked to Queensmead. Worked until lunch and then biked up to drawing. I continued my little eighteenth-century figures. Took the ponies for a walk at four and the princesses rode them. It rained and we sheltered under the portico of Frogmore for a bit. Left after tea and was on with Drusilla in evening, which was <u>so</u> much nicer than alone. She told me I dance much too far away from my partner always – it's probably old-fashioned influence and instinctive desire to avoid the 'cheek to cheek' look that I hate so much but it doesn't look graceful. I don't mind trying to alter myself.

Saturday, 27 February

Bussed to the Castle. I had tea with the K and Q and the princesses. I long to tell PE something of my dreams, as she, too, vaguely shares my feelings and I feel she would <u>enjoy</u> being confided in and trusted but I never seem to be with her alone without PM. It's odd she doesn't mind being accompanied <u>everywhere</u> by her little sister and that she never seems to desire to talk alone with a friend. We went to the film after tea – a farce called *George Washington Slept Here*, which they all thought the funniest thing they'd ever seen, and I secretly couldn't bear! I just <u>don't</u> like funny films.

Monday, 1 March

We now have to give up hot cans in our rooms – yet another symbol of the old world that has slipped out of one's existence for <u>ever</u> – the next generation will regard such an arrangement as unheard of, as we do hip baths! Drusilla told me she'd heard Tony Bethell* had fallen completely for Sonia – it is unfair, embittering, that the young men I ask up to dinner should admire my friends and ignore me. <u>Why</u> is that I attract no one?

Tuesday, 9 March

Colin Davidson† has been killed – <u>poor</u> Rachel. Somehow one never expected this. In the face of another's sorrow, I forgot all my petty hurts, and at the thought of so many

---

* Richard Anthony Bethell was a Yorkshire neighbour.
† Colin Davidson had married Lady Rachel Fitzalan Howard, sister of Bernard, Duke of Norfolk.

happy unions severed by death in the very prime of their existence, I became truly sad. How cruel indeed is the world and how selfish I must be to think that I have ever really suffered.

In the afternoon Grandpa, Aunt M and I drove to the House of Lords and had lunch, then went to our places for the ceremony of the introduction of the new Speaker. Afterwards, Aunt M and I wandered round Westminster Abbey; we prayed in the little chapel of St Faith and I felt v. near in this old historic church to the tragedy of life – it had seen so much that was joyful too, I suppose. I wondered suddenly if Lilibet would be married here and if I would come to it.

Friday, 19 March

Tonight was Queen Charlotte's Ball. Caught the train with Drusilla. I wore my blue and gold brocade. I saw hundreds of others I knew and enjoyed myself v. much. It is a pity I get no pleasure from dancing itself and I think why I am a little disappointed in dances is because I <u>expect</u> too much of them. I think I always vaguely hope someone will fall in love with me and instead I often sit alone, with no one taking any notice of me. What is it my personality lacks, for I flatter myself I <u>look</u> as nice as anyone else?

Monday, 22 March

It was v. hard work as two families arrived today who were in the Bethnal Green Tube disaster,[*] so we are now nearly full up.

---

[*] 173 people were killed in a rush for shelter on 3 March.

Wednesday, 24 March

Worked solidly from seven thirty till five and felt a complete wreck! Then went to see Barbadee Meyer and her baby.* My envy knew no bounds when she held her baby in her arms in bed! I thought this must be the most supreme moment of one's life and I could not understand how <u>my</u> mother could have refused to see me for three days and told the nurse to throw me out of the window because I wasn't a boy!

Thursday, 25 March

Biked and bussed for drawing at the Castle after lunch. PE showed me the list and we talked about all the men who were coming and then I left as they were not expecting me to tea today, so I had some at home and then read on the sofa till six thirty, when I began to get ready. Wore my orchid gauze and my diamond and aquamarine necklace, with silver bows in my hair. Put on my long white gloves after dinner and left, picking up Bet, Zelda, Anne and Pat Crichton on way. Got to the Castle and waited as usual in the Green Drawing Room before being presented to the K and Q and the princesses. The Q wore black net and black gloves and looked divine, though I prefer her in white. PE had her white lace and PM white muslin, with white appliqué flowers, an old dress of PE's that I'd seen at the last BP children's party. PE looked v. pretty and wore a little lipstick and PM was as entertaining and high-spirited as ever! There were about a hundred and fifty people and I knew most of the girls though v. few of the

---

* Barbadee had married Sir Anthony Meyer in 1941.

men. Hugh was there, having just returned, and I had almost despaired of dancing with him, when he asked me, <u>without any</u> manoeuvring on my part! But I could not get away from the bitter fact that my case is hopeless – he loves <u>no one</u>, let alone me, but prefers the friendship of older married people, except that I think Diana Bowes-Lyon appeals to him with her vivacity more than I do. Yet he does <u>like</u> me and if only I could kindle that into something more! He is still in great favour with the princesses – I <u>do</u> hope he'll stay in Windsor some time. We had supper and Champagne and the dance went on till four – later than ever before! Everyone was happy and gay and I enjoyed it more than last year, though nothing has yet equalled the idyllic happiness I felt at the <u>first</u> dance – in July '41 – perhaps because that was still in the days before disillusion had spread a chill over my life, the days when I never doubted my success and that the world was at my feet. We said goodbye and the K and Q were charming to me. Dropped the others home and I myself got into bed at five!

Saturday, 3 April

Caught the quarter to five train to London and went straight to Claridges, where I joined Lady Newman and Annabel for tea. It was lovely to see them again and A and I were sharing a room there. We began dressing at six thirty – I wore my long black. We dined then went to the Red Cross dance (in the hotel). When it was over, we all decided to go on somewhere. We started walking, Miles Marriott and I in front. M and I got separated from the others in the dark and landed up at a place called the Cabaret – I was rather annoyed, mostly with myself for not being firm and insisting on waiting for the others. Since I didn't want to be alone with M, it would have been so much more fun all together. He showed me tonight that he is in love with me, though he said nothing, but I kept wishing he were someone else and I do not feel true harmony in his company.

Sunday, 4 April

Elizabeth Anne staying and it was a perfect spring day and I felt happy – life suddenly seemed more exciting. In afternoon I took EA to the spot beyond the wood, behind the larches, where one day last year I lay and dreamed of Hugh, and I came here again to think of him – I read aloud to EA but in odd moments I sat silent and thought Miles is not the sort of man to go out with lots of women. He has always liked me, I know, but he is not passionate enough to love as I want to be loved – he lacks something whereby to hold me and I could never, oh, never, spend my whole life with him!

Thursday, 8 April

Everyone rather depressed because so many of the Grenadiers we knew here two years ago have just been killed in Tunisia, including Hugh Trenchard,* who was so nice. My Hugh should have gone out with that lot – thank God he didn't! I biked to drawing after lunch – it was the last lesson and I finished painting my little figures. One that I especially

---

* The Hon. Hugh Trenchard was the son of Air Marshal Viscount Trenchard, who had effectively started the RAF. He was killed in action in Tunisia aged twenty-one.

love is of a girl in a green and white striped poplin dress. They're going away next week, I think to Sandringham, so won't be here for PE's birthday.

Tuesday, 13 April

Caught the train to Paddington, where Miles met me in the car he's hired for his leave. We dropped my luggage at Grosvenor Square, then went to the play *A Month in the Country,* then went to dinner at the Bagatelle. At first M was inclined to be amorous but it seemed to me that he cooled perceptibly after I started flirting with him! I don't think he likes flirtatious girls. We left with the intention of going to the Embassy, but it was such a lovely night that I suggested going for a drive – anywhere, everywhere, my sense of adventure was aroused! We drove round Regent's Park and the trees cast clear-cut shadows on the ground from the moon, the soft April air blew in my face, romance stirred in the atmosphere, and I thought if he wanted to make love to me, if he wanted to kiss me, I would let him, but irony had to follow me even here – just as the mood grew on me, it seemed to pass off him. Surely if this scene was enough to stir my senses, I who bore him no love, surely it should have stirred his, for even if he does not truly love me he has shown a v. marked preference for me. We went on driving down the river through the City, to the Tower of London, over bridges and back again and then down to Chelsea – but still there lacked harmony between us. He was so quiet and passionless, so careful – perhaps of my reputation – while I longed to do something mad and reckless and thought of all the people I might have been with now. Perhaps he guessed something of this, knew that I only wanted to play with his affections, and therefore turned away from me. He took me back to Grosvenor Square at one and I went to bed feeling half pleased with myself and half disappointed in the evening, wondering too why I do not want to marry M. He is so nice, so good-looking, so rich – he would give me everything I wanted – I should be the spoilt, pampered wife of an only son, but how dull life would be! So soon would I be discontented, seeking elsewhere what he failed to give me.

Wednesday, 21 April

Princess Elizabeth's seventeenth birthday – I thought of her a lot during the day and missed her. I have spent so many of her birthdays with her, since she was ten years old and next year she comes of age.

Friday, 23 April

Went to church [it was Good Friday] but I do not care for the Windsor church and everyone around me was so un-attractive and smelt, so that I lost all my spirituality.

Sunday, 25 April

Mass and Communion. Quick breakfast after, then I biked to Queensmead. What a different Easter to all others I've known! No eggs, no presents, no frivolities anywhere, so devoid of joy and pleasure. The day passed uneventfully. No one doing much work because of all going to church at different times and I returned home at five, struggling against the wind with my bike.

St Nicholas Abbey, Yorkshire

Tuesday, 4 May

Yesterday was the beginning of my week's leave and it was lovely to be at St Nicholas again. Ursula [James]and I sat in the nursery after breakfast while she did her hair, then we went out in the garden. The lilac-scented air everywhere and I thought how <u>wonderful</u> it would be to be in love here. A little world of its own, St Nicholas seemed to me today, a wholly charming world of flowers and frills and gaiety, one <u>believes</u> in happiness here – it flooded over me today, a blissful contentment that lately I had thought had ceased to exist.

Thursday, 6 May

Ursula's nineteenth birthday. We stayed in all morning curling our hair in the nursery, discussing what we would wear, writing letters and playing all the music of Strauss waltzes on the wireless. Everything seemed to have magic charm today, and we discussed the usual topic of getting married! What a perfect wife U will be! Gentler than me, untroubled by any motives or ambitions, seeking neither drama nor tragedy, she will, I think, be happier than me. I hope I shall love her all my life. After tea we looked for flowers in the garden to put in our hair, then dressed for the dance. She wore a simple white lace frock, with a small dark red flower in her hair and I my painted net, with the black velvet bands and a sprig of azalea in my hair. We were twelve for dinner. About thirty to forty people came to the dance, which was <u>great</u> fun and I got on v. well, asking for the tunes we liked, and we had lots of Viennese waltzes, which at least here there was room to do with comparative ease!

Monday, 10 May

After such a peaceful, happy week it was dreadful to be back again in the impatient, bickering core of the family, trying to be with Grandpa again, and yet to live here that I would sacrifice all! Daddy told me that Mummy said to him up at Houghton that I ought to be put in a museum, because I'm so old-fashioned – he said it as a joke, but it hurt me, and I think Mummy is unkind.

Tuesday, 11 May

I <u>hated</u> being back at work again and I had to scrub the kitchen floor too! Drusilla told me that Miles M. has apparently told Michael Stoop* to probe <u>my</u> feelings through <u>her</u>, just as I told her to probe <u>his</u> through Michael! D showed me the letter and it said that Miles declares I show him nought but a polite indifference! I was v. amused but I also wondered whether I haven't perhaps played my cards badly – had I been clever, I might have kept him on the tapis till I find someone else, thereby gaining experience to deal with others but I am so unversed in matters of love and am quite incapable of conducting an affair properly. But I do consider it was <u>his</u> fault that night we drove round London, especially as <u>I</u> suggested it. I <u>even</u> mentioned getting out of the car in the park – <u>there</u> was a chance for a man seeking love. It was

---

* Michael Stoop was another young Grenadier officer. He was later an accomplished backgammon player and successful gambler. Lord Lucan borrowed his car when he disappeared in 1974.

up to him to take it and he didn't and I can only believe he was angry with me.

Wednesday, 12 May

D and I did the house and pantry between us. She told me that Michael said Miles asked his advice as to how to proceed with me – hence taking me out to dinner and the play and when he returned he flew at M for giving him false hopes and said I was 'as <u>cold</u> as last fortnight's potatoes'! It is a most unattractive description, though of course it <u>mightn't</u> be his own words but it amused more than disconcerted me. After all, I never really meant to be anything else towards him and it was <u>he</u> who was cold when we were driving – short of behaving like a tart I could have done nothing else then. The only thing that worries me is whether I know how to be warm when the occasion demands it – no one has ever yet truly stirred my <u>feelings</u> and where I have <u>tried</u> my arts I have received no encouragement.

Thursday, 20 May

Biked to QM with my case. Worked in kitchen, which was hectic but managed to get away at quarter to two. Bussed up to the Castle for drawing. We were outside and I drew Princess E. We saw little Prince Michael of Kent aged ten months – he's an adorable baby and has a great look of <u>all</u> his family by turns! We then tidied ourselves and drove up to Royal Lodge in the Ford with Crawfie, the Philipps, <u>Hugh E</u> and another officer. I had hoped we were going in pony traps but the officers couldn't get off early enough. We had a wonderful tea laid out on tables on the lawn, with a canopy to shade us from the sun and little rose-patterned lawn napkins. Afterwards we walked round the garden, which was divine, and I did my best with Hugh, which was mostly, actually, to leave him alone this evening. He happened to say that he would never allow his children to go sailing alone – he was walking beside me and I wondered if he guessed at all how passionately I was thinking and wishing that <u>his</u> children might be <u>my</u> children! Looking at his delicate, gentle face, I knew I could marry him more easily than anyone I've yet met, with the exception perhaps of Robert Cecil. PE took a photograph of us all, or rather Crawfie took it with PE's camera, so I <u>do</u> hope they'll let me have one! After this we played Consequences in the garden using names we all knew and laughed a great deal! It only needed the pony traps to make it perfect today. They drove back to Windsor and I walked across here. But no dreams of love softened my heart as I went to bed, like they used to after I'd seen H, yet nevertheless, I slept restlessly – life took on a bewildered, distorted form and I could not see where to turn. Fear of disillusion haunted me – where shall I be if none of my wishes come true?

Thursday, 27 May

Changed after lunch into my blue spotted muslin blouse and pink skirt for drawing. Painted some delphiniums. PE told me that <u>Winifred Hardinge</u> is engaged – to someone called Murray,* a Grenadier.

---

* Major Sir (John) Antony Murray was later adjutant of the Grenadiers, and after the war a businessman and adviser on trade to the government of Barbados.

Sunday, 30 May

Biked to work at ten after Mass. We all put on clean caps and aprons after lunch and went to Combermere Barracks, where we all had to assemble for the parade (for Wings for Victory Week). It was rather exciting and we certainly found plenty to laugh at! Daddy was marching, too, with his Beaumont Officer Training Corps. I'd never marched before and kept on sneezing because of my hay fever! We went up to the Castle and round the quadrangle where the King took the salute – the Queen and the princesses were with him, the latter both dressed in bright pink frocks and hats but I found it so difficult to 'eyes right' and keep in step at the same time that I couldn't take in nearly all I wanted to! But they did recognise me and we smiled faintly at each other! After that it was most dreary, hot and exhausting and we got back to the barracks half dead!

Tuesday, 1 June

Grandpa's eighty-eighth birthday. Went to Rosary tonight to please him. Daddy and I had a joint letter from EA – she's no longer bottom of the school and also is head of her bedroom, which pleases her!

Wednesday, 2 June

On the wireless tonight we heard that an air liner with Leslie Howard in it has been shot down – presumably in the hope that it was Churchill's. It made me v. sad as he was my favourite actor – he was so perfect in all those old-fashioned parts I love so well and I think he believed he'd lived before as I do.

Monday, 7 June

Mummy is coming here next Monday till Friday. Thank heaven she at last sees she ought to, but Lord! What a strain for me. Here is the <u>worst</u> place for her to see me – I haven't seen her since February and I dread the trial I know her visit will be, the biting criticisms, the acid reproaches and warnings, the strain of hiding my true thoughts from her, but I shall bear it and will make a success of it – I must for my own sake.

Thursday, 10 June

We drew at Frogmore today – the drawing things were brought down in a little pony carriage driven by two grooms; Crawfie and Mrs Cox walked and the princesses and I bicycled. We settled ourselves on the corner of the lake by the little mock ruin and then had a picnic tea. PE said she'd heard from Winifred H. and her wedding is to be 10 July and she is going! If only they'll take me with them! I shall go anyway, as it'll be quite a big affair. If she goes to W's wedding surely she will come to mine?

Wednesday, 16 June

My day off. Mummy didn't want to go to London so we stayed at home. She said she's become socialistic lately, a fact I'd noticed last year. I felt wretchedly unhappy – something within me dies when my mother brings me to earth, an element that is choked by her realism and yet <u>her idealism</u> is far greater and deeper than mine. We heard that the <u>King</u> is in <u>N. Africa</u>, which is thrilling. Mummy leaves tomorrow.

Thursday, 24 June

I changed into my pale green and white frock and biked to Frogmore for drawing. PE was sweet today and said it was a pity that they didn't see more of me now (whose fault is that?), but I wish she wasn't so dispassionate – royalty are not always like that. No such things as vows of eternal friendship could ever pass between us – I happen to be part of her surroundings, taken for granted while I am there, but she shows no desire to talk or exchange thoughts and ideas with one of her own age. Her temperament is quite unsuited to forming strong or violent attachments – no doubt this is a blessing in one of her position and she is wholly fitted for being a queen nowadays but I believe her sister will be quite different and I think, were it not for the difference in our ages, I could make a greater friend of her, though I shall always be deeply devoted to PE.

Wednesday, 30 June

On all day. Taxied to the Ritz where I met Brita. It was lovely seeing her again – I had never realised I was so fond of her. She is going into the WRNS and will get on well, as she can adapt herself to new and different situations and people. Her only object is happiness, which, after all, is the main thing. Why are some human beings made otherwise?

Thursday, 1 July

Joined the princesses at Frogmore for drawing. PE wanted to 'braille'* the Guide tents, which I thought quite unnecessary and a perfectly <u>hateful</u> task on such a hot afternoon. But we went to eat raspberries in the gardens afterwards, which was far more pleasant! I heard nothing about the wedding, so I must wait another whole week in suspense. It is strange that when I am <u>with</u> them hope always diminishes and yet they are so charming. I think it is because they are so matter of fact that they don't lend themselves to dreams!

Friday, 2 July

My day off. Letter from Joe Dormer† asking me to go out with him. Aunt M also had one from his mother, Lady Dormer, suggesting we should all go to the theatre! Obviously she is looking out for eligible Catholic girls for her sons, as they have made such a line for me since I met him at St Nicholas. We refused, as they are <u>such</u> boring people, and he <u>so</u> ugly! Why must it be <u>them</u> to chase me? But it does make me laugh!

---

* 'Braille' is a nautical term, referring to rolling up the lower sides of the tent.

† The Hon. Joseph Dormer was the younger brother of Lord Dormer, of an old Catholic family. At a time when marrying non-Catholics was frowned on, he was in search of a suitable wife. He never found one and died unmarried, aged eighty-one, in 1995, having inherited the title from his brother who had only daughters.

Saturday, 3 July

Saw in *The Times* that Rachel [Davidson, Alathea's cousin] has been appointed Extra Lady-in-Waiting to the Duchess of Kent. I am so glad for her and it also interests me because it shows they have overlooked the question of religion.

Thursday, 8 July

Changed and went up to drawing, which was in the Castle today, as the weather unsettled. PE said that Winifred is driving to the church in a royal carriage – why are some people so lucky?

Saturday, 10 July

I started for London in car. I wore my new green flowered voile frock, beige coat and wide cream straw hat. Went straight to the Guards' Chapel for Winifred's wedding at two thirty. She arrived in a royal brougham, which unfortunately had to be closed, as it was wet. She looked v. nice in white net and satin, but the bridesmaids, Libby and Mary Anna,* looked ghastly. The reception was at St James's, in the very room we used to have the dancing class! Saw a great many friends and Robert Cecil was there. To my delight he remembered me and was charming. He is more attractive than Hugh Euston, even though the latter's nature might be more suited to mine, and today I can imagine nothing in the world easier or more pleasant than being in love with him. But what use is it? He

---

* The Hon. Mary Anna Sturt was the daughter of Lady Shaftesbury's daughter Mary Ashley-Cooper and Lord Alington of Crichel. An orphan, she was the Hardinges' ward. She later married Lieutenant Commander George Marten.

will never give me another thought and at the moment I have given up hope of all good fortune. The wedding service depressed me. W is the first of the old circle in London to marry – how little one thought she would be! One wonders who will be the next but I am now resigned – wishing and hoping have served me an ill turn. It is hopeless to struggle in this alien, unsympathetic age.

Cumberland Lodge

Tuesday, 13 July

Mass at nine. There <u>would</u> be on my day off when I might have lain in bed! Biked and bussed to the Castle. Anne Crichton and Domini Lawrence* there, and we all went along to the Red Drawing Room with the princesses, to greet the thirteen Eton boys and four officers, then we had tea. Hugh was there but no longer now am I tormented by passion for him – I did not seek him out and if he should choose to seek me then I shall respond with ardour and devote my whole soul to loving him but it is useless to waste my heart since artifice is out of the question. I shall not marry him, nor will PE, and I feel now that I shall wait till another, perhaps unknown, comes along. It is a relief to be free of anguished thoughts concerning Hugh.

---

* Domini Lawrence was the daughter of the Hon. Alfred Lawrence. She became an Olympic dressage rider.

Thursday, 15 July

Drawing in the schoolroom again as raining but went out with Crawfie at four and ate wild strawberries on the slopes. PE told me about her weekend – it will be the first time in her life for her to go away for a weekend alone. I suppose either Allah or Bobo will accompany her. I thoroughly approve of the whole thing and PE has promised to tell me all about it. Crawfie told her she must take her prettiest dress and choose her nicest jewels – she can look so nice if she tries. How fond I am of them and how happy are these days when we laugh and talk together – with all my heart I thank God for them. They make any amount of drudgery at Queensmead worthwhile.

Friday, 16 July

We are making wonderful progress in Sicily – God grant it may be a complete victory! How I wish this war would end and I wonder what my fate will be after it. Now it seems full of foreboding.

Thursday, 22 July

Drawing was indoors again and PE had to go to London, which was sad, as I wanted to hear about her weekend, but Princess Margaret was sweet. We played croquet then walked round. They all liked my hair better – Crawfie said it reminded her of an old picture.* I wish PE had seen it but I shall keep it for a bit.

---

* Alathea was trying a centre parting, which her mother disliked.

Sunday, 25 July

Biked to Frogmore to where the Guide Camp was. I was made to play rounders, which I hated, and was quite futile at! But I enjoyed coming and we had tea on the grass at which the K and Q joined us! The Q looked charming in a mauve and white silk frock and white straw hat. PM was sleeping in the camp for the weekend with Anne Crichton and two of the Park Guides, which I <u>thoroughly</u> disapprove of – it's outrageous and undignified and I think the Queen is wrong to allow it. Thank Heaven PE didn't – she only came down for a bit each day, in her Sea Ranger uniform. I suppose democracy is responsible for this, but if it is carried to this pitch, royalty will lose the last remaining prestige that still remains to it. But the modern world is not suited to kings, and if I were one, no doubt I should cause a revolution!

Monday, 26 July

Mussolini has resigned, and the King of Italy and Marshal Badoglio have taken command and martial law prevails in Italy.

Friday, 30 July

EA is spending the week. It was v. hot and I bathed her and put her to bed as soon as we got in. How I do long to have a child of my own!

Tuesday, 3 August

Everyone departed from Cumberland Lodge today. Grandpa, Aunt M, Daddy stay in London for a fortnight, I go to Queensmead. I was off at four and went straight to London. EA was wild with excitement at her first dinner <u>and</u> her first visit to the Ritz, which took away some of the sadness of parting.

Queensmead

Wednesday, 4 August

My day off. I biked over to Sonia's. We gossiped to our heart's content. She told me that Tim Barclay kissed her in the car coming back from that party, and as they were all sleeping on each other's shoulders she too pretended to be asleep! I wonder if I am unique in not having been kissed.

Thursday, 5 August

I worked, then biked up to the town. Looked in an antique shop, Sheldon's, to find a birthday present for Princess Margaret and saw the most exquisite Dresden china figures, which I couldn't resist – I bought two, one to keep myself. One is of Venus and the other a lady in a Grecian robe carrying a pot of flowers, both white tinted with delicate colours – I would rather keep Venus and give PM the lady, but unfortunately I afterwards discovered this was <u>slightly</u> damaged so I must send her the Venus.

Saturday, 14 August

Rosamund flew at me at breakfast, saying I tried her patience to the end of its tether and everyone else did their best, except me. It was for a quite trivial reason but I knew this has been brewing ever since she's had to be doing a little work herself and she was only waiting for an occasion to vent herself on me – even old Mrs Hambrook and Blucky* say it's always me she's unkind to and I'm no worse than the others. Enraged, I wept and couldn't stop and in the kitchen I scraped all the skin off my forearm with a knife – it poured with blood and I was ashamed but it was done on an impulse of misery and fury. I have had cause to hate R too often now ever to wish her well again, for she is <u>unjust and spiteful</u>. I've never harmed her and I don't deserve her rebukes – anyway, it's for Mrs Hovell to deliver them, not her. Sonia came again, which was a mercy for me, as she took my mind off it a little and, above all, she fully sympathised with me. I wished Z had been there too, for she has often been a fellow victim. I was off at five and spent the rest of the evening alone upstairs – I couldn't go down and have any supper, I couldn't even read, I was so wretched. But I wrote my diary, which always affords me consolation and I thanked God I am going home on Tuesday. <u>Everything</u> seemed so futile. I could not see how life could ever possibly hold any success or happiness for me.

---

* Mrs Hambrook and Blucky were both trained professional cooks, as opposed to the 'young ladies' who served as VADs.

Sunday, 15 August

Today has been little better, though R has been pleasant – she could hardly be anything else and I consider she ought to apologise to me for hurting me so. I was on all day till five and I broke into an awful uncontrollable fit of crying when I got to my room – I know it is only the result of overwork but it <u>vaguely</u> frightens me to get into this state.

Monday, 16 August

The whole world seemed happier today. The thought of no longer sleeping at Queensmead was bliss, even though I do have to go back there every day. Sonia had been to London with Myra Wernher who told her she thinks PE will marry Prince Philip of Greece, though as yet he is not in love with her. I do hope so, as it would be <u>so</u> suitable a marriage for her.

Wednesday, 18 August

It has occurred to me lately that I no longer crave marriage as fervently as I used to. When I think of marriage, I think of an ancestral home waiting for me, with servants already there, only wanting me to step in and impose my personality on the place and to redecorate my own rooms. I realise now that I am mistaken: the fate of brides at the moment is to shift from one tiny house to another, near military stations, cooking for themselves, or at <u>best</u> to be paying guests in neighbouring houses. Would love compensate for all this? How much better to remain here, clinging to the last remnant of <u>security</u> left to me, and wait till all men may perhaps have something a little more stable to offer one. I am willing to make sacrifices but the sacrifice must be worthwhile!

Saturday, 21 August

Princess Margaret's thirteenth birthday.

Wednesday, 25 August

Letter from Princess Margaret, thanking me for the statue – very short but quite sweet.

Wednesday, 1 September

Had a letter from Brita, who has just arrived at her WRNS depot. Her descriptions filled me with horror but she says she is getting used to it and quite likes it. She has to drive a heavy lorry round Piccadilly Circus and is <u>sworn</u> at by 'a swine of an instructor' – <u>not</u> my cup of tea I feel!

Friday, 3 September

The fourth anniversary of the war and a day of National Prayer. We had mass at nine and I biked to QM after. They are cutting down more and more of the old elms in the Long Walk that were planted in the reign of Charles II, which is very sad.

Wednesday, 8 September

When we got home we heard the most wonderful news – Italy has unconditionally surrendered. On the nine o'clock news we heard more details and everyone all over the world listening to it must have felt aware of the great momentousness of the event. It is icy cold here tonight and I am shivering as I write this, and there is still such sadness in the world, yet everything suddenly seems a hundred times more hopeful, and one knows, more than ever before, that God is on our side, however hard the struggle be.

Kinharvie, Scotland

Monday, 20 September

Arrived at Kinharvie to stay with Aunt Gwen. To my surprise it was almost empty but I believe more come later. We changed for dinner and I sewed after – they all used to be so gay here and now sorrow has come to almost all of them. I hope they have a gay party here soon, as I feel I need it, having come all this way to seek it.

Wednesday, 22 September

The men went shooting. I went for a walk with Winnie,* It is still a mystery to me how she married, and such a charming man too, as she is the plainest person I've ever seen and does not make the best of herself – it must have been through her great unselfishness.

Friday, 24 September

We talked about ghosts till teatime, then Rachel talked about her duties as lady-in-waiting (R goes into waiting on the Duchess of Kent soon), and it was amusing to hear her side of it.

---

* Lady Winefride Fitzalan Howard was the sister of Bernard, Duke of Norfolk and Lady Rachel Davidson.

Burloes, Hertfordshire

Wednesday, 29 September

Arrived in Carlisle yesterday and this morning Mummy said E.A loathes coming to C. Lodge and I know she is secretly pleased at this. Mummy doesn't know that she has the power to sometimes make me almost hate E.A, whose likeness to Aunt A terrifies me. Mummy now likes my hair parted in the middle and she was nice to me; why then does her presence always <u>wither</u> my spirit in such a manner? After lunch I went to Royston by train, arriving at Burloes [Annabel Newman's family home] in time for tea. Annabel got back from her hospital. Two Americans came over after supper and we played cards with them. They amused us but I can't say I like Americans – nor does A really but they serve as a diversion and all the Newmans love anything and anybody to laugh about!

Friday, 1 October

Francis Wigram has been killed in Italy. How sad it is – he was so nice. One wonders who will be left at the end of this ghastly struggle, and the Guards have suffered specially heavily. Annabel and I stayed indoors in the afternoon gossiping and knitting. What I find so refreshing here is the way one laughs all the time, how all the simple, ordinary things of everyday are made a joke of in a good-natured way. I laugh from the beginning of each meal to the end of it and over such silly things!

Monday, 4 October

Annabel came with me to the station and saw me off – how many times have I done this sad journey away from Burloes, and I mind it only a little less now than when as a child I could never say goodbye without tears. The family were all well but how dreary it was getting back even though they were all so pleased to see me. Aunt M told me that Hugh Euston is going out to India on Lord Wavell's staff, as he is unfit for fighting. I am glad for him and for myself I no longer care – I bade farewell long ago to this romance that never bore fruit. God grant I may be married to someone else before he returns.

St Giles, Dorset

Monday, 18 October

Arrived at St Giles and saw Elizabeth Anne. She was wildly excited and seems to be happy here. It is such a lovely house, full of pictures of people one has read about and I felt again that urgent, impelling desire to marry someone with a beautiful, historic home, for there is something indefinable in the atmosphere of a great English country house that I feel is <u>part</u> of myself that I have always known in another life, and again in this one, and have loved more than anything else. There is even a liveried footman here! It made me laugh the way we dressed for dinner tonight, too – there was Lady Shaftesbury in a long satin gown, carrying as always long kid gloves with pearl buttons, and then her daughter Dottie in the most awful corduroy trousers and tweed coat!

Friday, 22 October

EA came to say goodbye to me – she is so brave, and just managed to restrain her tears, though I could see it was a struggle.

I think she is happy on the whole, though she is a bad mixer.

Tuesday, 26 October

Staying at Queensmead. Eliz [Christie-Miller] and I got up and cooked our breakfast, and Z came and we cleaned all morning. Had time to tidy before Martin Fitzalan Howard* and his sister Miriam arrived. The play was *Hi di Hi* and quite good. At Bagatelle for dinner, I had oysters for the first time in my life and loved them! It was Martin's twenty-first birthday and we had Champagne and a birthday cake and were all v. gay. We went on to the 400 and I have never enjoyed it so much, as it wasn't at all full and there was nothing sordid about our party, as there so often is now. No one thought of dancing cheek to cheek, which so many people consider essential to a night out and which I loathe. Miles Marriott was there with a girl and it pleased me to see him embarrassed when he saw me but he knew Martin and came over and joined us later. Sarah Dashwood was also there, looking rather fat. We bought a <u>banana</u> for £1 and cut it into six – the first we'd had for nearly four years. We left about four and it was such a thick fog that we had to walk halfway down Piccadilly before we <u>luckily</u> got a taxi.

---

* The Hon. Martin Fitzalan Howard was the third son of Lord Howard of Glossop and his wife Mona, Lady Beaumont in her own right. His elder brother, Miles, became Duke of Norfolk after Bernard died, a title that would have gone to Alathea had she been a boy.

I found a note in the flat saying would I sleep on the drawing-room sofa and imagine my horror when I saw someone asleep on it, and I dared not put the light on to see who! Breathing was coming from both the other rooms, so I undressed in the hall, put on my VAD clothes, washed and packed as quietly as possible and lay in the armchair close to the unknown body and dozed off – only for an hour and a half as then I had to leave to get the train. What a night but for once it was really worth it! Owing to the fog the trains were late and I didn't get to QM till nearly ten but it didn't matter and Eliz made me have some breakfast. It was fun telling Zelda and her all about it. I was on edge, though, about drawing as I'd heard nothing, and yet as they rang up while I was away, I concluded they must be having it, so every time the telephone rang I fled to it, and was <u>so</u> disappointed when it wasn't what I wanted that I was rude to whoever it was! The last time it was Daddy just after I'd got into bed at nine thirty and I regretted not having sounded more pleased to hear him, as I think he is just as lonely as I am alone with Grandpa.

Sunday, 31 October

It was Daddy's birthday and we drank Champagne at dinner. My own birthday is worrying me, as I <u>must</u> ask <u>now</u> about my dinner party.

Thursday, 4 November

Biked up to the Castle for drawing – we began posters for the pantomime, which is to be *Aladdin*. PM has her hair parted in the middle now too but I'm not sure that I like it. When they were getting ready to go out I asked Crawfie about my dinner party and she said she'd ask the Queen and thought it a v. good idea. We went out to see the two new Norwegian foals they bought in Scotland and took them for a walk through Frogmore. How they do love their ponies! And how happy I was to be with them again. Margaret Elphinstone is <u>living</u> with them now and going to Clarence Lodge* every day – I saw her at tea. What <u>wonderful</u> luck for her.

Tuesday, 9 November

At dinner Daddy told us an amusing story about the King in Africa – he asked General Alexander how he got on with General Montgomery.† Gen A said he thought he coveted his job, and the King replied, 'Oh, really? Last time I saw him he talked as though he'd <u>got</u> mine!'

Thursday, 11 November

Biked to the Castle for drawing. Poor Crawfie was taken ill last week and sent to London to have her appendix out. That ghastly Mr Tannar was there for tea to talk about the pantomime but of course I have to be charming to him. PE was rather distant today – she takes v. much after the royal

---

* Clarence Lodge was a secretarial college.
† General Harold Alexander, later Field Marshal Earl Alexander of Tunis, usually called Alex, was noted for his victories in North Africa against Rommel and later campaigns in Italy and western Europe. General Bernard Montgomery, later Field Marshal Viscount Montgomery of Alamein, was the commander of the Eighth Army and later of all Allied troops in France. Usually called Monty, he was the most senior British general in the Second World War and the most famous.

side in this way: she does not often give much of herself to her friends. PM is more friendly and I nearly always go to her room to tidy, which to me is v. strange, but I know her too well now to be hurt by it.

Saturday, 13 November

After dinner PE rang up herself and was charming. She said she'd love to come to dinner but could it possibly be Thursday instead of Wednesday, and she's going away for a few days this week, so won't be at drawing. I was full of interest but could not ask where!

Sunday, 14 November

I'm sleeping with Drusilla tonight – she won't be _so_ bad. When we were in bed we got on to the subject of kissing somehow; she would not at first believe that not only have I never been kissed but that no one has ever even attempted to do so to me! I feel that Z and I must be unique and I would like now to be able to tell my husband that he is the first – I wonder whether this will be so. Yet the reason never ceases to intrigue me – D could sincerely think of no other that I am aloof and give a false impression of primness. I thought of PE – she, like me, talks with men without ever encouraging them nearer but then she has people to look after her career and I haven't. I used to say I couldn't live without love, but I have forgotten it for so long now that perhaps it isn't true.

Thursday, 18 November

I went to drawing and heard that Mrs Cox could not come as she was ill, so PM and I were left alone to get on with our posters. I loved being with her and she told me that PE had gone to Badminton,* to have her <u>first day's hunting</u>. I was thrilled.

Tuesday, 23 November

This is the last time for me to write in my teens. Tomorrow I shall be twenty but I do not feel as if I were having a birthday, nor do I now regret leaving my young days behind. It has not been a happy year for me and perhaps the coming one will be better, as I have missed the gaiety of youth anyway. I feel I might as well go forward and get older.

Wednesday, 24 November

<u>My twentieth birthday.</u>

I didn't work v. hard but it didn't seem at all like a birthday and I was alone for tea. Christie returned, however, just as I was leaving and gave me her and D's joint presents, which were two pairs of white woolly knickers from Scotland! But when D came down she was furious with me because I quite forgot to do the laundry this afternoon. Eliz gave her the present to give me and D thrust it at me saying: 'Here you are as it's your birthday, but <u>I</u> call it the <u>limit</u>!' and stalked away. It was a miserable moment. I couldn't help crying but the others were angelic to me. To be in a position to be ticked off by one of one's own age for forgetting something

---

* Badminton was, and is, the seat of the Duke of Beaufort in Gloucestershire.

on one's <u>twentieth</u> birthday is what <u>I</u> call the limit, but apart from that I can't <u>bear</u> anyone's ill will and I wouldn't mind so much if I thought she was sorry but I don't feel she is, not taking the slightest interest in my party, which also hurt me. When I got home I forced myself to forget her and Queensmead and rejoiced in all my presents – the loveliest of which are some diamond and pearl earrings from Aunt M, which belonged to Granny.

List of my Birthday Presents, 24 November 1943

Handkerchief sachet of white lace and pink lace	<u>P. Elizabeth</u>
Earrings consisting of a round diamond flower with a pearl in the centre, hanging on several small diamonds	<u>Aunt M</u>
Small round tortoiseshell box with coloured picture on enamel on lid	<u>Grandpapa F</u>
Very old edition of Jane Austen's novels bound in blue leather ornamented with red and gold	<u>Daddy</u>
Pale green satin hot-water bottle cover	<u>Sonia</u>
Several <u>tiny</u> glass animals	<u>Annabel</u>
Small pot and jar of old-fashioned white china with flower pattern	<u>Ursula</u>
Photograph of herself in white lace frock	<u>Zelda</u>
Charles I, Patron of Artists (book)	<u>Miss Drummond</u>
Powder puff	<u>Margaret Elphinstone</u>

Yellow thimble	<u>Billy</u>
Two pairs white woolly knickers	<u>Christie and Drusilla</u>
Book tokens	<u>Joan and Jackie Phillips</u>
Glass plaque of Madonna	<u>Mme de Bellaigue</u>
Cheque for £1	<u>Grandpapa Langdale</u>
Book token	<u>Mrs Pearson (at QM)</u>
The Corner Stones (book)	<u>Kenchington (at QM)</u>

Thursday, 25 November

Mass at nine and Communion. Drusilla rang up to wish me success, so I forgave her and appreciated her thought. Wrote out the cards for the table and arranged my presents in evening. The servants were wonderful and got out all the silver and best china, etc., and the table looked lovely. I began dressing at seven – wore my blue and gold brocade and my own pearls, with two rows of Aunt M's and also a <u>most lovely</u> brooch of hers of a large pink topaz surrounded to form a diamond, by white and green filigree enamel work and pearls with one pearl drop. Princess Elizabeth arrived just after eight. There were twelve of us altogether including Margaret Elphinstone and Joan and Jackie Philipps. We had a delicious dinner of celery soup, pheasant, chocolate soufflé, apples, confectionary and my cake, with twenty red and white candles on it. PE sat next to Grandpa. It was the <u>first time</u> PE had ever been out to dinner and she said it was lovely to come here first – it is certainly a great honour for <u>us</u>. She looked absolutely charming in a dress of pale yellow chiffon, simply made, and her pearls and two diamond stars either side of the neck. Her face was made up and she looked v. pretty, with a dignified grace peculiar to herself. After dinner I showed her my presents, while the men were still in the dining room and she gave me the most lovely handkerchief sachet, made of pink net and white lace with pot-pourri inserted. I am delighted with it. We began by playing a paper game and then went on to acting clumps and charades, which were a great success and we all laughed a lot. They didn't leave till quarter to twelve, so they <u>must</u> have enjoyed it and there certainly never was a dull moment. I went to bed radiantly happy and shall remember this day all my life – it was <u>my</u> idea and it all happened just as I could have dreamed it, and it could <u>not</u> have been a greater success. <u>Everyone</u> was pleased; Grandpa and Aunt M were so kind and Daddy loved it too, I think, and it was indeed a wonderful birthday.

Thursday, 2 December

Biked to the Castle for drawing and found that there was none and Mme de B <u>thought</u> she had told me so last week! However, PE asked me to stay, which was lovely and I went to watch the pantomime rehearsal. I think at least the princesses ought not to <u>touch</u> the schoolchildren – to have them as a chorus is bad enough, instead of which PE and the awful little boy who plays the mother of Aladdin actually pat each other on the back and link arms – as Z says, nobody but Mr Tannar would dare to be the cause of such familiarity. We went out afterwards for a bit with Monty, who has arrived there for a month, while Crawfie is ill. Came in and I tidied in PE's room and then we went along to the Queen's sitting room to have tea with her. I hadn't seen her for such a long time and she was so nice to me, saying how much Lilibet enjoyed my birthday party. Margaret E was there, and I was astonished to hear her call the Queen 'Peter', which is a family nickname for her. I do think she ought to say Aunt E, or even Ma'am in public. She is so lucky to be there – to be kissed by the Q, always one of my own wishes! – treated as one of the family and included in many of the public events is to my mind unutterably enviable.

Friday, 10 December

Began dressing at six thirty. I wore my brocade again and Aunt M's topaz brooch this time as a pendant on a gold chain, and after dinner, I put on my long gloves. Picked up Zelda, the Crichtons and Sarah Dashwood on way to the Castle. Waited as usual in the Green Drawing Room. The King had flu and wasn't able to appear. The Queen wore black like in March, PE the yellow chiffon she wore to my birthday, only tonight in the bright lights it hardly showed up at all, and PM the beautiful white lace. I saw a great many friends but only knew a few of the men, most of whom are raw youths, with whom it is no pleasure to dance. Nearly everyone is abroad now. But I loved it and there were enough waltzes to please even me (and far too many to please most of the other people). I had one lovely dance and supper with one of the gentlemen of the Household, which I enjoyed most of all. He told me it was such a relief to hear a young person say they don't like jazz, which pleased me. I danced with David Milford Haven* in a Paul Jones but I don't really

---

* The 3rd Marquess of Milford Haven, David Mountbatten, was a cousin of Prince Philip and (on his mother's side) of Myra Wernher. The princes of Battenberg had taken the more English-sounding name Mountbatten and been given the Milford Haven title because of anti-German feeling during the First World War.

like him. I wonder sometimes whether I shall ever marry, I seem to have so little success at dances, yet I feel I shall. All the same I did enjoy it as much as last year and I felt happy in my dress. It ended at three fifteen – we had another supper and again shook hands with the Royal Family before departing.

Saturday, 18 December

Zelda and I rushed up after lunch to change and her mother took us in the car to the Castle, for the pantomime. We had seats in the second row in good places. The K and Q came with the Duchess of Kent, who looked a <u>dream</u>, all in black and Prince Philip of Greece, who is very fair and older-looking than when I saw him last year. He seems so suited to PE and I kept wondering today whether he <u>is</u> her future husband. I think it is the most desirable event that could possibly happen. <u>She</u> would like it and, though he could not be in love with her, I believe he is not averse to the idea. The pantomime was good, even though one does disapprove and the princesses act and sing beautifully. I think the K and Q saw me but didn't have an opportunity to speak.

Wednesday, 22 December

The Dashwoods have given West Wycombe Park to the National Trust – how sad that people should be forced to give up their homes to strangers through no fault of their own. It is indeed an unhappy era for us.

Saturday, 25 December

Biked to Queensmead. Everyone went to church and little work was done. The Christmas lunch was <u>wonderful</u> and we all grossly overate! Went home at five. I looked up Christmas Day in my last diary and remembered that I felt v. sad and depressed then, for no real reason. But tonight I felt quite happy.

Thursday, 30 December

To my surprise, Miles Marriott rang up to say he'd love to come to the Devonshires' dance with me on 8 January, and would I like to stay with them, as it's so close. I was greatly relieved, as I was v. worried as to how I was to get myself, without a partner, from Grosvenor Square to Eaton Square at ten. I <u>do</u> so hope I shan't be stranded with M all the evening and not able to dance with anyone else. I couldn't bear that and that's why I <u>infinitely</u> prefer going to these dances alone, like one used to, and meeting people and trying one's success there. Then one's under no obligation and it's far more exciting.

Friday, 31 December

I read most of the evening in gaps between work. This is the last time for me to write in this and I have ended the year, as I began it, at Queensmead. I wonder where we shall all be next year. There are moments when I dread to think!

1944

WINDSOR CASTLE

The Master of the Household

has received

Their Majesties' commands

to invite

Miss Alathea Fitzalan Howard

to a small Dance at

Windsor Castle

on Friday, 5th May, 1944

at 9 p.m.

Dress:-Short jacket, black tie

Officers--Uniform

This invitation must be presented

on entry to the Castle

A reply is requested

An invitation to a dance at Windsor Castle.

Saturday, 1 January

Worked and was able to get off for church and biked there at eleven, to find that Mass was at ten today, so I missed it. I was upset as I'd somehow wanted v. much to go today but I remained there some time and lit a candle and prayed that <u>some</u> of the things I desire may come my way this year. Bicycled home to wish the family a Happy New Year, after which I had to hurry back to be on duty at five. There is little to do in the evenings. I am now writing this before going to bed. It is strange to think of all the pages in front of me and what may be written on them.

Tuesday, 4 January

Had a letter from Mummy, who told me PE is 'keen' on David Milford Haven, who is in love with Bridget Elliott[*] and trying his best to escape from PE, whom he thinks <u>deadly</u>. This hurt me, as Mummy speaks from her own and her friends' opinions, without any real knowledge of the sentiments and feelings of the people concerned. Personally, I doubt that PE does like David MH in that

---

[*] Lady Bridget Elliott was the daughter of the Earl of Minto. She went on to marry three times but not to David Milford Haven.

way and I certainly think Prince Philip would suit her far better.

Saturday, 8 January

My weekend Christmas leave began. Went to the Marriotts' in Eaton Place, where I was spending the night. Played backgammon with Miles and after dinner changed into my blue and gold brocade and Mrs Marriott said I looked charming. Miles and I set off for 99 Eaton Square, where the dance was. The Duchess of Devonshire was charming, and so were Elizabeth and Anne Cavendish. They wore hideous frocks. I knew practically all the girls there, but v. few of the men with the result that I did dance with M. the <u>whole</u> evening! I was miserable and it wrecked the dance for me, as in no way could I call it a success. I think it is <u>outrageous</u> to only dance with one man all the evening. <u>Never</u> again shall I drag one man along to dance with me, though in this case it was convenient. Unfortunately there were <u>no</u> Paul Joneses, which would have been my one saving but there <u>were</u> a great many Viennese waltzes, so I could forget M and imagine I was the Empress of Austria at a State Ball in London, wearing the most beautiful of dresses and jewels. I even go so far as to design these dresses in my mind – alas, my happiness seems always to exist only in dreams. At twenty I have not excited the love, the admiration, nor even the <u>friendship</u> of one single man, except Miles, who is <u>so</u> boring and lukewarm that I really would be quite pleased if I never saw him again.

Sunday, 9 January

Had breakfast with Miles, then to my surprise he announced his intention of coming to Mass with me. I would far rather have gone alone. We walked to the Oratory where I prayed desperately for many things and once again, feeling M beside me, I wished I could be loved and love in return. Mr and Mrs M are so charming and very amusing. I knew <u>she</u> would like me for a d-in-law but I am sure that one day M will marry someone v. nice and far more worthy of him than me. When I got home, Aunt M asked if I danced with Marriott all the time, I said, 'Lord, no, I danced with hundreds of people.' I <u>couldn't</u> tell anyone, except a few great friends, the truth – it is like an admission of defeat.

Friday, 21 January

We had a hectic evening at work and after supper I had to rush and change for the concert we were having for the guests. I recited a short poem about England and also danced the Highland Fling! In the middle of it all, there was an air raid with v. heavy gun fire – we had to go flying round turning lights out and it was a terrifying, yet chilling feeling to be running down pitch-dark passages, with the whole house shaking from the thunder of the guns – which are quite near, at Queen Anne's Gate. We looked out too and the whole sky was livid with light. The raid was over London and we shot ten planes down.

Sunday, 23 January

Mass at nine. After breakfast I went up to the Barclays' to give Bet her present (a blotter). Brian Rootes,* her fiancé, there and I thought him v. nice and quite good looking. There are moments when I wonder if I shall marry but I realize that <u>background</u> is the chief factor in <u>most</u> marriages and of that, at present, I have none, or rather, such as I have seems to be more detrimental than otherwise to me, since they appear to associate me, too, with everything that is both dull and old. It is sad, as I would make such a good wife for someone who could captivate my interest. Jim Lees-Milne† and a friend of his came to lunch.

Wednesday, 26 January

Today is Elizabeth Anne's tenth birthday, the same age as I was when she was born. I sent her a gold fox pin. Lord knows whether she'll like it or not! Lord Dormer, brother of Joe who tried to chase me, is engaged to Maureen Noel‡ whom I knew years ago. He's forty and she's twenty-six, so perhaps that's what I shall do! A very nice boy, John Grigg§ dined – <u>rather</u> conceited, but intelligent. We played backgammon and I won six shillings.

---

* The Hon Brian Rootes, son of Lord Rootes, became Bet Barclay's second husband.
† James Lees-Milne, who worked for the National Trust, was a family friend and co-religionist. He is best remembered today for his diaries in which visits to old Lord Fitzalan at Cumberland Lodge are mentioned several times.
‡ Lady Maureen Noel was the daughter of the Earl of Gainsborough.
§ John Grigg, later Baron Altrincham, was then in the Grenadiers. Later he became a journalist and historian and criticised the court for being too upper class. He was godfather to Alathea's nephew Sir Philip Naylor-Leyland.

Sunday, 30 January

My day off. How I enjoyed it today – being able to live an ordinary life, even for a short time. That is the one advantage of having Sunday off. Changed for dinner and played bezique with Dick Molyneux* after. He said the Royal Family return on Tuesday. He also said that when he asked Lord Linlithgow† what struck him most here after five years' absence in India. He answered, 'How much more <u>experienced </u>the King has become since the war' – which is a very good thing to hear.

Thursday, 3 February

Biked to Queensmead. I've had something the matter with my throat all the week, which makes me cough all the time, without it being a cold, and today I felt quite ill and bored beyond endurance with the endless round of housework. There are times when I could <u>gladly</u> strangle everybody there.

Thursday, 10 February

PE is not taking drawing this term, as she feels she is not doing very well and would prefer an extra music lesson. I think the truth is that she is discouraged by her sister's greater quickness at it, and now that she has <u>less</u> time to spare it would be better to devote it to music, which she is really good at. Crawfie said PM would be disappointed if I didn't come and that we shall meet for tea afterwards. It is v. kind of them to want me and I only hope that PM won't take it into her head to stop too because her sister has! They

---

*   Dick Molyneux was an equerry to Queen Mary.
†   Lord Linlithgow was a former Viceroy of India.

also asked me to another officers' tea party on Wednesday, which will be lovely. I returned to Queensmead in the best of spirits and began planning how I could fit everything in – always a difficult problem now!

Saturday, 12 February

Drusilla asked me today why I couldn't be natural with men as I am with women – that I talk to them in quite a different manner. This rather shook me, though perhaps in my heart I have known it all along. So that is the secret of my failure to attract people, why no man enjoys talking to me, why they never want to see me or bother about me at all! And yet what can I do about it? I am not consciously affected – it's just that I never know what to say to them because I have no brothers or cousins and we are leading such an abnormal life now, no house parties or continual social life to bring one together. How can one wonder one grows up unnaturally? It is very sad and I seem destined to find everything an effort that comes to others as a matter of course. Life will always be hard for me because of my own conceptions of it, which differ so widely from the reality. Yet still I believe that all will be well with one in the end.

Monday, 14 February

Worked all day, then hurriedly bussed to the Castle, where I saw the princesses, and Margaret Elphinstone, who was staying the night, was there and several others including the Philipps and a most amusing Russian friend of the Duchess of Kent's, whom they all call Zoia.* We were fifteen in all – had a wonderful tea, then went to the Red Drawing-Room and played clumps, a wild game of stone and charades where Michael Farebrother† dressed up as a parson in a tablecloth that we found in the dining room and a napkin tied round his neck!

Tuesday, 22 February

Read in *The Times* of the engagement of Rupert Nevill and Camilla (known as Micky) Wallop.‡ Rupert happened to be dining with us tonight and to my delight he asked me to the wedding – on 22 April. He is certainly one of the most charming young men I've ever met. She is not at all pretty, though has the small person's attraction and quick bird-like gestures, which would appeal to him. I felt filled with envy of <u>her</u> – how excited she must be and how wonderful to become so soon a married woman, while all her friends are still knocking round the world with, in many cases, not the remotest hope of marriage. I do wonder how she managed it.

Thursday, 2 March

Biked to drawing after which we went out with Toni and had spitting competitions in the lake at Frogmore! PM was quite unmanageable while we were out – in some ways she

---

* Zoia Poklewska-Koziell, daughter of Baron de Stoeckl, lived in Coppins Cottage in the garden of the Kents' home, Coppins.
† Captain Michael H. Farebrother was another Grenadier officer.
‡ Lord Rupert Nevill was the younger son of the Marquess of Abergavenny. Lady Camilla Wallop, always called Micky, was the daughter of the Earl of Portsmouth.

is so v. young and childish – <u>quite</u> unlike PE – yet one cannot help laughing at her. PE was in London today – it is sad, I never see her now that her life is becoming so less and less her own.

Friday, 3 March

I forgot to say that Toni told me yesterday that in a conversation at dinner in which they were discussing who ought to be painted by whom – of the old masters – Mr Kelly* said I should be done by Velázquez. I suppose this is a greater compliment than Gainsborough, though of course the latter is more after my own heart. By him and by Angelica Kauffmann† I should like to have been painted, even more than by Reynolds.

Thursday, 9 March

Changed after lunch and biked to the Castle for drawing. Afterwards, I went out with PE alone for half an hour. It was only the second time I've done this and Crawfie apparently thought it a good idea. She was so nice and she told me the Duchess of Kent took her to lunch at Claridges last week, which <u>fascinated</u> her, as she'd never been in a hotel before. She asked me to a tea party on Monday with a treasure hunt – the <u>very</u> day of the ghastly <u>affair at Queensmead</u>, which I cannot <u>escape</u> from under any circumstances. It seems dreadful to have to put the Red Cross

---

*   Gerald Kelly, later Sir Gerald Kelly, was president of the Royal Academy, a well-known portrait painter who spent the war years in Windsor Castle.
†   Angelica Kauffmann was a Swiss-born artist who became well known in London in the late eighteenth century, when she became one of only two female founder members of the Royal Academy.

before royalty and to me it is the symbol of the new world that one is not only <u>able</u> to but, as in this case, <u>must.</u> I could have wept with fury and disappointment – it does seem hard. However, as a consolation PE asked me to the film on Saturday.

Saturday, 11 March

V. busy day but I got away before five and bussed up to the Castle, with the result that I was too early and had to dawdle about! Waited in St George's Hall before going in to the film. The King and the princesses came but the Queen was not there – the K shook hands with me. The film was Tommy Handley in *Time Flies*, which I thought I was going to hate, but to my surprise it was quite amusing, the people in it travelling in a 'time ball', an invention of the future, back into Elizabethan England, quite absurd, of course, but it made me wonder whether one day we may do something like this in all seriousness and I might really see my beloved eighteenth century.

Wednesday, 29 March

Mummy and Elizabeth Anne arrived at seven. EA has grown enormously. Talked to Mummy after and it was nice to have <u>someone</u> say how hard I work and how tired I look!

Thursday, 30 March

Bussed to the Castle for drawing. It was the last lesson. From remarks dropped, I gathered that Mrs Cox will not be returning next term but another artist will be teaching PM.

I could make out nothing of it but perhaps I shan't be included in these lessons? If I am, I shall regret Mrs C, who has been so kind and patient with me. And my pathetic little eighteenth-century sketches. I shall never have the face to do them with some great landscape painter! Crawfie and I went down to Frogmore and sat in the boats that are tied to the bank. I felt terribly sad, as though the old carefree days I have had with them here were gone now for ever. PE wasn't there and the only consolation of today is that Mrs Cox recommended me a woman who does watercolour portraits and I hope to be done by her in my new velvet frock.

Friday, 31 March

Found Mummy at home when I got back. She has been so nice to me this time yet her presence <u>here</u> is such a strain that I cannot but long for her to go. She picks on things the whole time and asks me <u>why</u> – well, <u>I</u> can't help what doesn't concern me. She thinks I am becoming too old-fashioned by being here.

Saturday, 1 April

EA and I biked to the Castle to watch the dancing class. PE was in bed with a bad cold, so only PM was there, in a delicious dress of pale grey silk and white muslin that used to be her sister's. Both she and Crawfie asked me to a film in the evening but I made the excuse of Mummy being home – had I been alone I might have gone, but with PE not there and it being so cold, I didn't feel inclined. I don't know when I shall see them again and in my present run of ill luck I dare not hope for anything for her birthday. Life at the moment is indeed cheerless.

Sunday, 2 April

EA wants v. much to take painting at St Giles and between us we succeeded in getting Mummy's consent. I am delighted as she really shows promise and if she wants to she <u>should</u>.

Tuesday, 4 April

Had a heartrending farewell with EA and I find it so hard not to cry myself when she clings to me and sobs.

Sunday, 9 April

EASTER SUNDAY

Worked seven till eight, then biked home for Mass. It was v. tiring having been up so long without food* but I liked being home for it and derived a measure of joy and of hope that I have not known for a long while. Had breakfast with the family before returning to Queensmead. My only present was a tiny satin lily of the valley sachet to put in my night-gowns from Aunt M, which I love. Mummy's and Daddy's are to come. Miss Cobban's† watercolour paintings had arrived (examples of her work to show me).

---

* Fasting overnight was then compulsory for Roman Catholics before Communion.

† Rose Cobban was a portrait painter who had studied at the Royal Academy School at the turn of the twentieth century.

Monday, 10 April

Opened drawings and was enchanted with them. I wrote to her at once – this will amuse me, distract me. One has so little to add zest to life now.

Monday, 17 April

There was a good article in *The Times* on PE. My thoughts are in such confusion but I do not speak of it to anyone. Why does Lilibet cause such havoc in my mind? She has promoted by far the greatest pleasure in my life, represented by far the greatest happiness that I have ever known, and in proportion I suppose I must suffer when she appears to fail me for I could never mean to her what she means to me. At the moment I want more than anything else to take part in her eighteenth birthday and it is agony to wait and wait in silence and then perhaps be bitterly disappointed. Since there seems to be no official celebration, or at any rate not a ball, which is understandable now, she may well spend the day with her family – they may all gather together for it – why should they ask me or any outsider to share this great day with her? Yet still one goes on hoping – that unquenchable trait of human nature that carries one through existence at sometimes cruel expense!

Tuesday, 18 April

I had the most charming letter from Jim Lees-Milne saying I must use his house in Cheyne Walk for sittings whenever I like. The pleasure I hope to derive from this picture will make up for a lot – it's the one and only thing I have to look forward to.

Wednesday, 19 April

I went up to the Castle to leave PE's present – they weren't there and I gather they only arrive Thursday.

Thursday, 20 April

Spent the evening quietly. I cannot say I did not hope for a message about tomorrow, but I succeeded in persuading myself into a more reasonable frame of mind. It is obvious that they are now having a family party at Windsor – she would not on such an occasion have friends to tea and it is obvious, too, that if they <u>did</u> have a theatre show or something I would be invited but as they all went to the theatre in London yesterday I conclude that any celebration they may have tomorrow will be entirely <u>formal</u>. I must content myself with the honour of having given her a present and one I hope that she will like. All the same the anxiousness of the family and the enquiries of my friends on the subject all make it the more painful to me. And I cannot help thinking of the wonderful ball there <u>would</u> have been at Buckingham Palace had there not been a war. I might even have been married and gone in lovely jewels.

Friday, 21 April

Well, here is the day on which I counted so much, the blank page that I so often looked at and wondered what would be written on it and it's ended in my having nothing to do and plenty of leisure to think of my dear princess and wish her well. I read everything I could find about her in all the papers – she certainly has received much attention and her character described really well. Today I envied her nature

– normal, rational and simple but then the contrast between her home life and mine! I thought of her on the threshold of a life, not, it is true, at the moment of gaiety but of busy activity and pleasant interludes – whereas the days drag so heavily for me with little pleasure for months on end. I wrote letters, then took my book out to the Spring Garden and sat in the sun till lunchtime. In the afternoon it grew cold so I stayed in. Grandpa went out and three royal cars passed him – they stopped and he was told the King would like to see him. Queen Mary was there and they talked for some minutes. He was so pleased, most honoured that they should have stopped. I was right – they had a complete family luncheon party and it was really most unlikely that they would have had anything else.

Saturday, 22 April

Wore my enormous brown hat and the pale green bag that the princesses gave me. Went to St George's, Hanover Square, and sat on the bridegroom's side. It was a lovely wedding – Rupert Nevill and Camilla Wallop's. She looked v. sweet, though nervous going up, in a v. plain white satin, and tulle veil held in place by a pearly coronet. The reception was at Claridges, which was beautifully done. They looked so touchingly young to be married and so <u>wildly</u> happy.

Thursday, 27 April

It was the most lovely day – like summer. Had a letter from PE. It was a most charming one ending with best love and saying had I heard – 5 May! I think she was really pleased with the clothes cover. She said Rupert Nevill gave her a corgi puppy.* I felt so pleased and happy tonight. The coming two weeks promise to be all they might be and I long for the dance more than I've longed for such a one for ages – the last one or two I <u>didn't</u> enjoy <u>quite</u> so much, I don't know why, perhaps because I have <u>now</u> entirely given up expecting someone will fall in love with me at a dance.

Tuesday, 2 May

Elizabeth Anne arrived today. I spent rather an exhausting evening with her. She was in v. high spirits but I got all the gossip out of her from Houghton and she told me <u>all</u> that Mummy had said on the subject of my taste, which she says I have caught from PE – it isn't true, actually, as I think I would anyway have always loved frills and pretty things though I <u>did</u> imitate the princesses a great deal when we were children. EA makes a most faithful reporter!

Friday, 5 May

Worked till five, then biked home. Mary Lumley† and Sarah Dashwood came, and we all bathed and dressed. I wore my orchid gauze, pale blue satin shoes and a flower in my hair to match those on my dress and my aquamarine necklace. Called for Zelda and the Crichtons and got to the Castle at nine. We filed through into the Red Drawing-Room and

---

* This puppy was Susan, who was to be the progenitor of the many corgis who stayed with the Queen until the death of the last of the line, Willow, in 2018, seventy-five years and fourteen dog generations later.
† Lady Mary Lumley was the elder daughter of the Earl of Scarbrough. She and her sisters, Elizabeth – known as Skip – and Anne, were all family friends.

made <u>five</u> curtsies this time, as the Duchess of Kent was there. She looked lovely, though v. sad and more drawn than she used to. The Queen wore black again, PE a new dress of red and green check organdie, which I thought ugly, though a pretty shape, and she herself looked charming. PM's dress was perfect – cream organdie with a v. full skirt and puff sleeves ornamented with green velvet bows and one in her hair. I danced all the evening and danced with the <u>King</u> in the Paul Jones, when I was least expecting it – I was thrilled and it made my evening. He was in naval uniform and we talked quite a lot. The supper was delicious though I was next to Richard Stanley,[*] who is so snooty. When I had at last got rid of him, the King, who was dancing with Anne Anson,[†] came up to the sofa on which I was sitting and said, 'Who <u>was</u> that man you were with?' Heard all about Billy Hartington's marriage to the Kennedy girl[‡] – what a pity it is. I was <u>most</u> surprised to find Elizabeth[§] v. talkative and amusing – she used to be quiet and rather stodgy. This time the Royal Family all went to different tables for supper. I was at the Duchess of Kent's. We ate salmon mayonnaise, chicken mousse and white soufflé with jam sauce and drank Champagne. There were a hundred and fifty there – just a perfect number for the size of the room.

---

[*] The Hon. Richard Stanley was the younger son of the Earl of Derby.

[†] Anne Anson, later Princess Anne of Denmark, was the daughter of the Hon. John Bowes-Lyon, brother of Queen Elizabeth. She was married to Viscount Anson, a colonel in the Grenadiers, but they divorced in 1948. She was the mother of Patrick Lichfield, the photographer, and Lady Elizabeth Anson of Party Planners fame.

[‡] Kathleen 'Kick' Kennedy was the sister of John F. Kennedy.

[§] Lady Elizabeth Cavendish was the daughter of the 10th Duke of Devonshire. An almost exact contemporary of the Queen, she went on to be a lady-in-waiting to Princess Margaret and the long-standing companion of the poet John Betjeman.

There were lots of waltzes, which was heaven – I was introduced to Margaret's brother Andrew Elphinstone whom I
danced with and thought <u>madly</u> attractive. Rupert and Micky
Nevill were there. She wore her wedding dress. I could go
on for ever writing about this evening, which I <u>adored</u>.

Sunday, 7 May

The clock was striking <u>six</u> as I got into bed, and I had to
get out of it again at seven thirty and bike to work, so you
can imagine what I felt like all day!

Friday, 12 May

We all worked frantically all the morning and after lunch
changed into clean caps and aprons, etc., and were given
long instructions as to what we were to do. We were lined
up in Mrs Bathurst's drawing-room and the Queen arrived
at three. We were each presented to her after all the Red
Cross officers, who'd been asked to meet her. She was
charming to me, calling me Alathea, which I hope was
noticed by people like Mrs Woolcombe,* who are so fond
of treating me like dirt. The Q had tea in the hall and there
was a buffet for everyone else, which when they'd gone, we
devoured in the pantry!

Saturday, 13 May

Annabel at Cumberland Lodge last night. It was lovely to
see her again. She came along to my room at nine and we

---

* Mrs Woolcombe was the regional head of Alathea's branch of the Red
Cross.

both had breakfast in my bed and lay there gossiping. I saw in the paper that Princess Margaret has begun drawing lessons with Charles Knight.* I felt certain then that I would not be included and, to my own surprise, I <u>accepted</u> this fact almost at once, without further hope – perhaps at last I have learned my lesson where hoping is concerned.

Monday, 15 May

Annabel left this morning, but I had to go to Queensmead early. Drusilla asked me today when drawing would start again. I told her about it <u>naturally</u>, and yet not <u>too</u> carelessly, for that points to one's real feelings as much as <u>telling</u> them. There is a certain satisfaction in hiding a grief from all the world, in letting people believe you think lightly or not at all of something that gives you intense pain and humiliation. Indeed, I can't truly realise that one great pleasure, the circumstance that made life most worthwhile to me, has now dissolved into thin air – I try to understand that PE is now grown-up and has given up her lessons, and that PM is now to study seriously with a famous artist. It is, then, only natural that I should withdraw – I am happy in the knowledge of not having offended them, so why should I worry? But I feel I shall never see them again, that they will forget my existence – they are so busy and so happy; they can't realise my loneliness, or how I love and depend on them. But I did not feel like tears – it seemed suddenly as though life were not worth any of this, that the grey flatness into which it has subsided will not allow of any emotional disturbance, for good or for evil.

---

* Charles Knight was a highly respected landscape painter.

Tuesday, 16 May

Day off. We all drove to London. Taxied to Jim Lees-Milne's house, where I am going to have my sittings. It is a dear little house, overlooking the river. Miss Cobban arrived and I changed into my blue velvet frock and she began my portrait, sitting half sideways in a chair with my hands clasped loosely, one arm resting over the back of the chair. She is a charming little woman, rather like Mrs Cox, and I enjoyed my afternoon immensely – there was something peaceful and appealing about sitting there quite still for two hours, far away from everything and everybody. But for the traffic outside, it might have been a hundred years ago, and here it was so easy to imagine horses and carriages in the street. The setting of the drawing room, too, with its four long windows and pale green walls was completely of the past, so that all else faded into oblivion.

Wednesday, 17 May

Crawfie rang me up after breakfast and said would I come to drawing again! There <u>are</u> going to be some others there – children – but what could I care when my prayer had been answered.

Thursday, 18 May

Worked till two, changed and biked up to the Castle. Found PM, Mary Morshead, Louise Cockcroft and Dawn Simpson* sitting in a row with Mr Knight showing them little pictures. We had to practise mixing a few simple colours. I think it

---

* They were all children of people who worked in various capacities in the Household or lived in Windsor.

will be v. interesting but the other girls are rather silly and the poor artist himself is so shy. He is a quiet, nice little man, v. arty with a terracotta shirt and little curls over each ear and not at <u>all</u> frightening. At four PM showed us the corgi puppy, Susan. Poor Carol was put to sleep recently and she was my favourite. The others left then, and I was asked to stay, which I deeply appreciated, as I had wondered what would happen. I wonder also what made them think of asking the others, as they obviously do not intend to make more than war-time <u>acquaintances</u> of them for PM who, herself, pays little attention to them. We went out with Toni to see the ponies and returned for tea – PE was there, having a music lesson. I was so pleased to see her again and we had a gay tea. I began calling her Ma'am for the first time!

Friday, 19 May

Had a letter from Brita, who is terribly lonely at times at Dartmouth, and says they're treated worse than servants.

Monday, 22 May

Worked all day and changed – wore my brown skirt and pale yellow blouse. Biked up to the Castle and met the princesses. Joined the rest of the party outside, the Philipps, Michael Farebrother, Wing Commander Townsend,* the King's new equerry, who was charming and v. gay. We all piled into the brake, driven by two large grey horses, with the hampers of food, and started off for Royal Lodge, the

---

* Peter Townsend had been a decorated hero in the RAF, and became an equerry to King George VI in 1944. He was later involved as a possible husband for Princess Margaret.

Queen watching us from a window. We walked round the garden till tea, which was laid out on a long table on the lawn just below the terrace. There was a huge birthday cake for Jackie, with chocolate icing. After tea we played clumps, charades, twos and threes, and the time passed v. quickly. We were all gay and informal, yet there was simply dignity about it, which is lacking in most of the parties of today, making them a touch on the sordid. We went into the house to tidy and had dinner outside at eight – it was all cold, and <u>delicious</u> – sausage rolls, lobster and venison patties, asparagus, sandwiches, jam puffs, cold drinks and strawberries and cream and coffee. Again, it was to me a *fête champêtre* of long ago, something unique and remote from this hurried, noisy world – one of the officers said as much and I laughed. Then someone said the <u>carriage</u> was ordered, and the picture was complete – except for our dark, dull clothes and I wished it had been summer weather. PE had a blue and green check coat and skirt and a hideous yellow silk Aertex shirt and PM a deep pink coat and skirt, which was prettier. But they were both so happy and charming. After dinner we went into the Little House to show the two officers, who had never seen it, and then set off back to the Castle. It was so much fun going back with them, because one is at one's merriest at the end of a party and it was lovely driving through the park as it grew dusk. We sang all the way, mostly old songs including French ones. We passed a few people but no one recognised the princesses at that hour, though they did earlier in the afternoon and all seemed astonished at our party! We all said goodbye at the Castle, and I biked back to Queensmead, having had a blissfully happy evening.

Thursday, 25 May

Biked to the Castle for drawing. We did studies of pansies, for the colour only. Afterwards I went out with both of the princesses and Toni to see the ponies. It was a v. dull, windy day. PE took me to her room to tidy and showed me some of her birthday presents – a beautiful diamond and sapphire bracelet from the King, a pin-on watch in diamonds and rubies, which I adored, from the Beauforts and Cambridges – she also told me Queen Mary gave her a bracelet and necklace, the King of Norway* a dressing case and she had a small diamond tiara too.

Friday, 26 May

Went to Cheyne Walk, where I had my sitting in Jim's house and was delighted with the portrait. Miss C told me that all the people she'd shown it to said that I do not look like a girl of today, though they couldn't quite decide where I belonged. No one could pay me a greater compliment than this, yet it has the unfortunate result that my own generation pass me by.

Saturday, 27 May

Worked till two, changed quickly into my blue flowered silk frock and my navy blue straw bonnet. Grandpa and I drove down to the horse show in the Home Park. PM was driving in a class of utility pony carts. All the Royal Family were there, in an enclosure some way from where we were sitting. Drusilla was there and came and tacked herself on to me,

---

* King Haakon was in exile in Britain during the war.

which was maddening. PM won the cup and then PE drove Hans, the cream Norwegian pony, in a little phaeton that Queen Victoria used to use, and behind squatted a tiny groom in a top hat – it was the most perfect turnout. I was thrilled she won the first prize for it.

Thursday, 1 June

Grandpa's eighty-ninth birthday. I biked to QM at eight thirty and changed after lunch and went to drawing. PE told me about three VADs who had hitchhiked to the horse show and were picked up by the Duke of Beaufort, who knew them, and took them all the way. Then the King and Queen heard about this and invited them to dinner with them at Royal Lodge and to spend the night at the Castle, so that they could go back with the duke the next morning, instead of hitchhiking in the heat. They were so thrilled apparently and I can well understand it! Victor Canning* has been killed in Italy – he was one of the nicest who came up here, I thought, and I remember so well at a dance at the Castle, when we both agreed how much nicer it was when ballrooms were lit by candlelight. How sad it is.

Monday, 5 June

ROME HAS FALLEN!
I heard this when I arrived at QM at eight this morning. The city itself has escaped unharmed which is indeed a mercy.

---

* The Hon. Victor Canning, younger son of Lord Garvagh, was another Grenadier.

Tuesday, 6 June

During the early hours of this morning our forces landed on the coast of Normandy – the long expected <u>invasion</u> has <u>begun.</u> It was my day off. I made my way to Cheyne Walk, where I had lunch in Whistler's House before going to 104 for my sitting. I was an hour early so after changing I looked at Jim's lovely books on art and houses. I went home and in the evening listened to the King who spoke at nine – he hesitated slightly more than usual but the main theme of his speech was the need and call for unceasing prayer. The news was thrilling – the first town we have occupied is Caen. How glad I am to be at home on this great day.

Thursday, 8 June

Went to drawing after lunch. I enjoyed it v. much today – Mr Knight and all of us are becoming better acquainted and the five of us doing entirely different things makes it rather amusing. I went out with PE and Toni to see the foals. PE told me how terrible a strain it was for the King over the weekend waiting for the invasion and then living through it all for a further twenty-four hours, when it had to be put off from Sunday till Monday night and also that the Queen spent almost the whole of Monday night at the window looking at the planes, unable to sleep. She, PE, said she did <u>not</u> know beforehand and was thankful. We came in for tea and laughed a great deal over Crawfie imitating people.

Saturday, 10 June

It was a frantically busy day. Had an invitation to a cocktail party from Jean Wills,* Margaret Elphinstone's sister, who now lives at Adelaide Cottage – on Saturday, which I'm greatly looking forward to.

Thursday, 15 June

Worked till two, then biked to the Castle for drawing. We were outside today, for the first time, and sketched views from under the terrace. Afterwards, PE joined us with Miss Lander, the music mistress and we all had a picnic tea under the wall. PE said they were going to Jean Wills's party on Saturday.

Friday, 16 June

There was an air-raid warning last night from midnight till <u>ten</u> this morning! A bomb hit an inn in Old Windsor and apparently they sent over their new pilotless planes. Our guns went off at five but we stayed in bed.

Saturday, 17 June

I changed into my green voile frock and brown coat and biked to Adelaide Cottage at six for Jean Wills's party. There were a great many people there, all fairly young. The King and Queen came with the princesses and the Duchess of Kent and also Prince Bernhard of the Netherlands† with an

---

* Jean Wills was a niece of Queen Elizabeth.
† Prince Bernhard was the husband of Princess (later Queen) Juliana. He was working for British intelligence.

adorable Sealyham dog. Luckily it was a fine day, though not hot, and it was all out in the garden, which was a mass of rambler roses. We had refreshments and the Queen came and shook hands with me. Everyone went away about eight. I had rather hoped that someone would ask me to dinner but no one did so I biked back, passing Frogmore and I went in. An awful melancholy fell over me – other people seemed to belong to each other whereas I am alone. I am always alone. In my mind I identify myself with other people's families, only to realise that I do not belong to them at all, that I am only an outsider, a looker-on, and must always return to my own solitude. Here in this blissful haven, where I have been happier than anywhere else on earth, it was soothing to wander for a little, quite alone. The evening was beautiful and peaceful and I looked at the graves by the Mausoleum,* then went over to the lake, and again I could think of no lovelier resting place than this.

Monday, 19 June

Last night was v. disturbing – warnings went ceaselessly and then one heard the eerie sound of these robot planes followed by the sharp gunfire and fearful ominous explosions that shook the house. But all the time one thought how far, far worse it must be for London. We heard that the Guards' Chapel was hit <u>during</u> the service yesterday and so <u>many</u> of one's friends go there – Mr and Mrs Marriott always do. Lord! What ghastly devastation! Apart from this the news is good – the Allies have <u>cut</u> the Cherbourg peninsula and we are within six miles of Saint-Lô to the south.

---

* The burial ground for members of the royal family since 1928.

Tuesday, 4 July

Returned just in time for tea and Mummy had already arrived. Before dinner I showed her my portrait and, to her own and my surprise, she greatly admired it, though she made out it was v. flattering, which I don't agree about. She said it gave me sex appeal, which I lack completely. The sad thing is I know this is true now. Mummy says it is living with old people and away from all contact with that sort of thing and that it is due to my attitude of indifference to young men in general – I realise that living here has influenced me more perhaps than I imagined. I do definitely prefer old people to young – firstly I think because they stand for something that I know is dead and lost, and secondly, because I invariably enjoy more success with them than with younger people.

Wednesday, 5 July

Just before I left work, I saw a flying bomb fly right over the house. It was the nearest one I'd seen. Mummy walked to meet me and we talked in her room till Rosary. She gave me a little box of powder that someone had brought her over from <u>Bayeux</u> – it was thrilling to have something from the midst of the fighting!

Friday, 7 July

A bomb had dropped to the left of the Copper Horse on our side of it this evening – it broke some windows at Royal Lodge and made a terrific explosion even at Queensmead. I biked round that way to see it on my way home – it fell, luckily, in an open field and hurt nobody.

Saturday, 8 July

I went to the film at the Castle. It was Noël Coward's *This Happy Breed* and v. good indeed. The K, Q and princesses came, and Prince Philip of Greece. I sat behind him and PE. Prince Philip laughed v. loudly during the film and the King made comments aloud during the film of his visit to Normandy, which was v. amusing. I guessed that PE was v. happy and I wished her success in my heart. Joan Philipps asked me to go back to dinner with her, which I did. She was alone and we cooked our own dinner and just before I left the siren went, so I waited a bit but then thought I must go. I felt rather nervous. I got safely to the drive when I saw one of these things with the whole of its tail lit up like fire flying across from the house – so I fled round by the road and then to my horror saw <u>another</u> coming straight at me. In a terror I dashed through the stables as hard as I could though actually it was quite safe, as they were flying fast with no sign of dropping and we never heard them explode, but it <u>was</u> frightening being out <u>alone</u> and seeing these flaming dragons charging through the sky and knowing no one was inside them.

Tuesday, 11 July

Glancing at *The Times* before breakfast I saw that Lady Mary Palmer* has been made lady-in-waiting to PE. The shock to my feelings was great, though I put on a forced cheerfulness all day. Life at the moment is indeed dreary

---

* Lady Mary Palmer, daughter of the Earl of Selbourne, was a lady-in-waiting till 1947, then an extra lady-in-waiting till 1949. She married the Hon. Thomas Strachey.

and disappointing. I've had to force myself lately to see things in their true light and I know that Lady MP is unfit for full-time war work, though only twenty-three and that the last thing they would do would be to take someone away from their job now; but how I should have loved it! That someone whom until ten days ago PE hardly knew by <u>sight</u> should take the place for which I have yearned for so many years. When I have known the princess so well ever since we were small children, is hard – though the fact that she <u>isn't</u> one of PE's own friends like me makes it bearable! The week before last at drawing PE said that MP was coming for the weekend, as the <u>King's</u> guest – she couldn't think why and the only thing they were sure about was that she was Lord Selborne's daughter and had a big nose – which makes me certain she knew nothing of the appointment. To make matters worse people talked to me about the new lady-in-waiting and I had to appear pleased and excited. I accept it as a trial from God, sent no doubt for my own good, and my implicit faith in Him helps me to bear it in a more sanguine manner; after all she will have to have more than one later on and meanwhile I can still remain her friend. I woke up in the night (still at QM) and thought at first it wasn't true, and I hoped Drusilla would not notice that I was unable to sleep.

Wednesday, 12 July

However reasonable an attitude I have made myself take, to have one's cherished ambition and dearest wish crushed, even temporarily, unawares by reading a line in a newspaper, is a blow from which it takes a good deal to recover and at the moment there are <u>no</u> consolations, no distractions to take my mind away. I believe Lady Mary Palmer is a very highly educated girl, efficient and hard-working and it did make me smile to realize that I suppose someone like that is more suitable, at first, at any rate, than a girl, frivolous, dreamy, and if not irresponsible, at least inexperienced like me.

Thursday, 13 July

Day off. Went to the Castle for drawing. After we'd finished the Queen came in and wanted to be shown all we'd done this term – she liked my cherries and was charming. I then waited in PE's sitting room and she called me through into her room while she got ready. I asked her if she'd enjoyed herself last weekend and she said 'he' had come unexpectedly and she was thrilled. We drove back to C. Lodge and had a delicious tea, then played racing demon and paper games with Aunt M, while Crawfie talked to Grandpa. PE asked me if I knew Mary Palmer and said she'd never seen her before last week but that she seems quite nice, though looks rather alarming. We were all friendly and gay and it was far easier than entertaining many other people I know. PM was amusing and v. sweet – once she said 'Aunt Magdalen' because I suppose she is used to hearing me calling her that!

Thursday, 20 July

It was the last drawing lesson unfortunately. Went out with the princesses and Crawfie for a walk – PE was rather moody today, silent and walking for the most part, some paces away by herself. She is like the King in this way, v. different from PM, who darts from one side to the other of those she's walking with, catching at their hands or slipping her arm through theirs, chattering and telling the latest jokes all the while. One guesses that PE does sometimes wish to be alone and there I do sympathise with her. She was better at tea, though, and afterwards she asked me to keep Thursday evening free, though she couldn't tell me why yet. I returned to QM feeling pleased – here at least is something to cheer the summer up. There was news tonight that an attempt was made on Hitler's life and injured him, which has caused great excitement.

Friday, 21 July

Officers of the German Army have revolted against Hitler! There is a general disturbance and drastic measures taken to quell it and <u>rumours</u> of civil war but no one <u>knows</u> anything and v. little news leaks out of the country. However, it gives one hope and is certainly exciting.

Tuesday, 25 July

The King is in Italy, reviewing the troops – he landed near Naples, having flown over, and stopped in North Africa on way. Princess Elizabeth now acts as a Counsellor of State* for the first time.

---

* Princess Elizabeth became eligible to be a Counsellor of State at the age of eighteen. Six are appointed when the Sovereign goes abroad and two act in tandem. They are usually the six senior in line of succession to the throne. On this occasion the others were Queen Elizabeth, the Duke of Gloucester, the Princess Royal and Princess Arthur of Connaught. Princess Elizabeth acted with her mother.

Thursday, 27 July

Worked till three then met the Philipps and the rest of the party at the Castle and waited at the Augusta door for the princesses. Crawfie was with them and we all drove to Maidenhead in the shooting brake. We got into our boats, two small electric canoes, at the Boat Club, and started up the river as far as Cliveden, where we landed and chose a grassy path hidden from the river by bushes to have tea – which they'd brought from the Castle. We lit a fire to boil the kettle and then all sat down on cushions. The weather had been most disappointing all the morning but now it suddenly turned out lovely, though not <u>quite</u> hot enough to make me regret not bringing my new straw hat! I wore my flowered linen dress for the first time and took my brown coat – PE had a v. ordinary flowered linen shirt frock and PM a not v. pretty pink cotton one. We got back into the boats and went on a little further past Cookham Lock and then we had to turn back, v. regretfully as this part of the river was lovely. There were v. few other boats but it was extraordinary how <u>no one</u> recognized the princesses although the latter often looked at them full in the face and quite near to, especially in the locks, obviously enjoying the rare experience of passing unnoticed. I suppose it was because they would never <u>expect</u> to see them there and we were quite an unobtrusive-looking party, none of the men being in uniform. Going back I sat with PM and Jackie P in the end of the boat, which I enjoyed as we talked and laughed a lot – in fact we were <u>all</u> rather rude and roared with laughter at the other people we saw. Sometimes we threw ropes to each other in the other boat and pulled each other along. We got back to the Boat Club and had delicious dinner and there were v. few people there, though this time the princesses were known and everyone stood up. We practised archery on the lawn afterwards and laughed a great deal, then drove back to the Castle, singing all the way and arriving after ten. It was a merry party and I enjoyed it immensely. Said goodbye to the princesses, whom I won't be seeing again for some time.

Wednesday, 2 August

My day off. Elizabeth Anne had breakfast with me in my bed but she was such a fidget that it wasn't much rest! After lunch she and I biked to Queensmead where we picked Christie up and went to Clewer – to some stables. I hadn't ridden for at least two years and it was great fun, though the horses were v. slow and lazy. I wore an awful old pair of grey trousers borrowed from the Barclays and really felt ashamed of myself.

Wednesday, 9 August

Breakfast with EA and then I had to say goodbye to her. I found a letter from her which she wrote before she left this morning, saying how much she loved me, etc., etc. – it was angelic and it went straight to my heart.

Thursday, 10 August

I bought such a delightful print of a girl at a spinning wheel in a very old gold frame at Sheldon's for PM's birthday. As usual I like it so much that I long to keep it for myself, but it is so difficult finding something else for her.

Monday, 14 August

Hugh Euston's brother, Oliver FitzRoy, has been killed in Normandy. He was such a nice boy, though I didn't know him well. Robert Cecil's younger brother was killed on Saturday in a motorbike accident.

Wednesday, 16 August

Wrote a note to go with PM's present, which Grandpa leaves at Buckingham Palace tomorrow. I do hope she will like the picture. It should suit her room.

Friday, 18 August

Letter from Mummy, with instructions as to how to behave at Blair Drummond.* I am to keep my voice low and not squeak as this spoils me; I am to be smiling, laughing and un-Howardy – to take an interest in Europe after the war and say I intend to go abroad to work, to say I am v. tired but <u>not</u> grumble about the drabness of life, several other things and all so that Lady Muir should think me 'vital and worthwhile'. Some of her advice is good and certainly well meant, but why <u>should</u> I say I intend to do things I <u>don't</u> and she is <u>too</u> uncomplimentary. As always, her letter caused me the profoundest depression, so that I even lost all pleasure in my visit. I should know by now that I ought to guard my words in writing to M – it was a mistake to let her see I was lonely and dreary, for she thinks I am growing like those whom I live with. The great consolation is the news, which continues to be

---

* Blair Drummond was the home of Sir Kay Muir, Alathea's godfather.

wonderful on all fronts and we are progressing well in the South of France.

Monday, 21 August

Princess Margaret 14 today

Wednesday, 23 August

It was a bad morning but at one we heard of the <u>LIBERATION OF PARIS,</u> which made us wild with excitement and is indeed a good day for me to begin my holiday on. I left Queensmead – how thankful I am – and had high tea at home. Got the first-class sleeper to Edinburgh which I had all to myself and, having never travelled by night in England, was fascinated! I spread my supper out and ate it and was in bed before the train left at quarter past ten. I was too excited to sleep well and it was v. hot and stuffy.

Blair Drummond, Scotland

Thursday, 24 August

Arrived at Edinburgh at eight fifteen. I met Nada Muir and we came out to Stirling together. Some charming Russians, Count and Countess Kleinmichel,* and their fourteen-year-old daughter Sonia, and we all drove to Blair Drummond and had tea. Sir Kay greeted us. The Kleinmichels have come up from Balmoral, where they have been staying with the Grand Duchess Xenia, sister of the Tsar, who has been given a house there. They have seen the Royal Family up there

---

* Count and Countess Vladimir Kleinmichel.

and the Duchess of Kent and her children are at Birkhall for the summer. They wear long dresses here and everything is v. comfortable and the food excellent. Afterwards we played backgammon – I played first with the countess and then with the count. I already adore the former and think she is too attractive for words. They have a son called Dimitri* and I would give anything to meet him – but that is the sad thing now: one <u>doesn't</u>. He is fighting in Normandy in an English regiment. I have a lovely room – v. large, with a double carved gilt bed, two blue sofas and a beautiful view. I can't say I take the friendly interest that I ought when I see the VADs in the house doing just the same as I was doing two days ago!

Friday, 25 August

Sonia Kleinmichel and I went out with her father and Sir K to shoot duck on the ponds here. She is a nice child. We all walked to the kitchen garden and ate fruit. It was really boiling and the air here is lovely. The moral atmosphere is so much more stimulating than any I've been used to for a long while. They talk French, Russian and English by turns, and they are concerned with the sort of world I long so much to become part of and am so starved of in my present life.

Saturday, 26 August

We set off in the van for the moor to shoot grouse. The <u>midges</u> in the butts were <u>terrible</u> – we were all driven nearly

---

* Dimitri Galitzine, who was in fact the countess's son from her first marriage.

demented and returned covered with scarlet spots, which are most unsightly and have ruined my complexion! After tea I wrote to Daddy, and to PE to tell her how much I am loving Scotland.

Sunday, 27 August

Nada, the countess and I went to Mass at Doune at ten. We sang hymns and I made my three great wishes that I do every time I enter a new RC church. I love Nada – she is one of the most charming women I know, so brilliant and interesting, yet so naively amusing and so kind. I do feel I am a different creature here, where my best is brought out, to what I am at Queensmead and even at Cumberland Lodge, where I have nothing to feed my senses on even though I never regret spending the war there.

Tuesday, 29 August

Sonia Kleinmichel and I biked to Doune Castle to explore it – it was exciting with battlements and countless dark stone spiral staircases. Mary, Queen of Scots was there once. It belonged to her brother, the Earl of Moray. Later when we were alone Nada talked about PE, quoting the opinion of a great many who consider it a great pity she is not encouraged to read more cultured books and that all their conversation should revolve round the dogs and the latest radio joke. I so agree but then, much as I love them, they are not an intellectual family in any way. N said could I not influence PE at all, though she approved when I said that that was a thing the princess allowed no one to do, outside those who have a right to do so. Her sense of royalty would resent it and her steady placidity of character would never allow her to leap in spirit after the various types and circles of society she comes in contact with.

Friday, 1 September

With v. great regret I left this morning. I was so happy there. On the one hand we were gay, on the other interested in the European situation, but nowhere did there break in the jangle of modern music, or the talk of modern nightclubs, drinking and jitter-bugging. In short, I was <u>myself </u>there. I arrived at <u>Houghton</u> in time for dinner.

Houghton

Saturday, 2 September

Talked to Ming-Ming after breakfast then went out for a short walk with Mummy. I received at last (owing to forwarding) a letter from PM – it was v. short but sweet, saying that she had the picture hung up at once in her room at Balmoral where 'it looks so nice'. The Allies are entering Belgium and Holland now – it surely cannot be v. much longer. They are moving at such a pace one can no longer keep up with it all. In France Dieppe has been taken and they are moving up the coast. In the south they are at Lyon.

Sunday, 3 September

Five years ago today war was declared – I was here then too. It seems <u>such </u>A LONG TIME AGO. The evening passed quietly, and I was sorry to be leaving.

Cumberland Lodge

Monday, 4 September

Returned by train. I was hungry and exhausted, and everything seemed unreal as it always does when I return here.

Tuesday, 5 September

Back in uniform again! I was quite glad to go to Queensmead before lunch to escape from Grandpa's fussing, for almost every ten minutes this morning he called me for something utterly trivial. I found it hard to settle down to work and the cold and the gloom enveloped me once more. Life seems suddenly to have stopped dead – as I knew it would, buried here for a fortnight with nowhere else to go. We took Brussels yesterday and are nearing Germany itself but one dare not hope too much.

Thursday, 7 September

Yesterday Russia declared war on Bulgaria and today Bulgaria asked for an armistice! What a crazy world it is!

Sunday, 10 September

At six this evening we heard distant heavy gunfire, which rattled all the windows and doors, and we afterwards heard it was a battle on the coast, between Calais and Dunkirk.

Friday, 15 September

Daddy rang up in the evening and is v. sorry about me staying at QM, as now he will hardly ever see me. I was glad he rang up. Early this morning we heard a loud explosion and apparently it is the new V2 – a rocket that we can't see coming. They say fifteen have already arrived in this country and one in Glasgow from Norway.

Sunday, 17 September

We heard that Holland has been invaded by us in great strength. The clocks put back an hour last night and the blackout officially ended and the 'dim-out' began! Though it does not really make a great deal of difference.

Monday, 18 September

Lord Hartington has been killed – I am so sorry for all the family [the Devonshires] who will be heartbroken. The gloom tonight is terrible – with the early blackout, discomfort, and I am quite deaf from having washed my ears today, which feels horrid!

Tuesday, 19 September

Work all day and then went up to London. It was a horrid damp misty evening and I tubed to Grosvenor Square where I found Mummy and Elizabeth Anne. We talked before going to the Connaught to have dinner with Grandpa – Daddy and Aunt Magdalen were also there so it was a real family party! Absence does make the heart grow fonder, for never have I looked forward to seeing them all as I did today.

Wednesday, 20 September

I slept with EA and in the morning, I asked if she had any gossip for me, and she told me that after I left Houghton Mummy had said, 'Poor A, she isn't at all attractive – I hope she will find a good husband.' I was deeply hurt by this and also v. angry, as I didn't think Mummy thought this of me, though it doesn't worry me, as I know other people think differently and also she does not see me at my best now, in the same way that in the midst of her new circle I cannot admire <u>her</u> at all – the trouble is, she is so completely enveloped by these odd new people, whose only claim on her attention is their originality, that she condemns me and everything to do with me, because I am so different from them and also from EA, whom she is ruining by bringing her up among them. She <u>expects</u> trouble with EA later on but still she prefers her, <u>always</u> has done, to me whom she tries nobly to do her best by but quickly loses all patience and interest. She said they've got to leave the flat at Christmas – I am glad as I <u>hate</u> it but she wants to move into another, larger, one in the same building, with Aunt Alathea for after the war. Will she <u>never</u> tear herself away from this woman? I wouldn't mind if Daddy had not got to pay more than half of it and reap <u>no</u> benefit himself from it, although if I do have to live there with them, it will be wretched. To go abroad would be such a good solution – or if only I could marry but perhaps it is God's will that I should do none of these things, but stay and learn to make my own life out of surroundings not of my choosing. We had lunch with the rest of the family at the Connaught then I went with M and D to see EA off at Waterloo (back to St Giles). I said goodbye to Mummy soon after this – she didn't kiss me but thanked me for 'being so sweet to EA'. I could see how much she longed to get away from us all and be with her own friends again.

Wednesday, 27 September

Heard on the news the whole story of our withdrawal at Arnhem, which was v. moving and tragic.

Sunday, 15 October

Yesterday brought the news of the liberation both of Athens and of Riga. I think great hopes may be attached to the Russian campaign, especially in the south, at the moment, which is making rapid and far-reaching strides, while <u>we</u> are <u>preparing</u> for another great offensive in the west.

Wednesday, 18 October

Worked till two. Arrived at Arundel with Grandpa and Rachel [Davidson]. I had a lovely room with a bathroom, and a huge log fire – wore my blue velvet frock. Dinner was excellent and afterwards we talked and did crossword puzzles. I went to bed feeling happy to be here and divinely comfortable in my large bed.

Thursday, 19 October

Breakfast was brought me in bed, and I ate it in ease and luxury!

Went to see the three Howard children. Anne and Mary are the plainest children that ever were seen – as <u>thick</u> as they're long, with square faces and square-cut hair and Sarah, is only a little better. I walked up to Rachel's at the House on the Hill. Saw her children who are sweet. Harriet is an <u>angel</u> – it seems strange to say R has a child who looks like an elf but she does, with a tiny pale face and pointed chin, blue eyes that gaze at you and v. fair fine hair. R and I walked to the Fitzalan Chapel where Grandpa joined us and we heard the Pontifical Mass in honour of Blessed Philip Howard.[*] It was very beautiful. After this I went with Grandpa to my grandmother's grave and then back for lunch. I got back to Queensmead at two – exactly four hours. A good journey but v. cold and dismal in the dark.

Thursday, 26 October

Drawing started again but only PM, Dawn Simpson and myself this term. This is nicer, though we all find DS v. irritating. She left at four. I went out with both the princesses and Toni. It was <u>lovely</u> to see them again and they told me all about their stay in Scotland. I gather Mary Palmer was up there most of the time with them. PE said she was sorry she never answered my letter, but it was one of the things she was v. bad at!

Friday, 27 October

We had a <u>rocket</u> at six thirty, quite close, which shook the whole house. I stayed in for the rest of the day sewing and writing.

---

[*] Philip Howard, Earl of Arundel, was confined in the Tower of London by Elizabeth I and died there. He was canonised in 1970.

Thursday, 2 November

Biked to the Castle for drawing. We did potato cuts, which were very amusing. I asked Crawfie when we were alone if PE. might come to my dinner party and she told me to ask her when we were out, which I did, when we were leading the foals but the awkward thing was that she mentioned it later and PM. said, 'Are <u>we</u> coming?' so now I am in a complete quandary as to whether they're both coming or only PE as I had intended. I didn't invite PM as Crawfie asked me not to last year and I do consider she is far too young to dine out, though I must leave it to them to decide and <u>hope</u> they will give me some indication later. I went to tidy in PE's room and she told me they <u>are</u> doing another pantomime. I <u>had</u> hoped PE would not be allowed to do it this year. I did not have tea with them today as they had a family party for Princess Beatrice's* funeral tomorrow and PE was talking about the black evening dress she would have to wear – her first, which had to have red bows taken off for the occasion.

Saturday, 4 November

I have just read in the paper that Countess Kleinmichel's son, Dimitri Galitzine, has died of wounds – the news shocked me profoundly as they talked of him so much at Blair Drummond and she <u>worshipped</u> him. Poor, poor thing – I pity and pray for her with all my heart. To lose <u>all</u> your worldly possessions, position, country, your husband in one war, and then, in exile and poverty to have <u>first</u> your sister

---

* Princess Beatrice was Queen Victoria's youngest daughter. She had died on 26 October 1944 and her funeral was at St George's Chapel.

and then your only son killed in another war. What some people are called upon to endure! I loved her in the one week I knew her and I shall write her a short note of sympathy.

Thursday, 9 November

Biked to the Castle for drawing. We did lino cuts, which I became deeply engrossed in. I spoke to Crawfie about PM and she said she would so much love to come, as last year she was having a battle trying to separate her from PE but that now she has learned, it would give her great pleasure to come. I am relieved that the situation, which I felt I had mismanaged, has been settled so simply and nicely and I am glad now that PM is coming, though I do think it strange her being allowed to. We went out for a walk and it was very cold but we were all in v. good spirits and talked a lot about my party. PE asked me what I would like her to wear. It is not certain yet whether Crawfie or Mary Palmer will come and, much as I should like Crawfie, I am v. anxious to see Mary P.

Monday, 13 November

Simon Worsthorne* is missing in Italy, but one may hope he's a prisoner.

---

* Simon Worsthorne was a cousin of Alathea. Their grandmothers were sisters, their maiden surname being Bertie. Simon was born with the name Koch de Gooreynd, as his father was a Belgian general, who took the name Worsthorne from a village near their Lancashire family estate, Townley, when he stood for Parliament. Later Simon took his great-grandmother's name and was made Sir Simon Townley while his younger brother, Peregrine (known as Perry, later knighted), kept Worsthorne.

Thursday, 16 November

Went to drawing in the afternoon. Mr and Mrs Tannar came to tea in order to discuss the pantomime – sitting there, <u>wallowing</u> in the royal favour, gushing at me and calling me Alathea. It went v. much against the grain to be <u>smiling</u> and nice to him. I came back to work at six. Letter from Mummy – she told me Grandpa Langdale's present to me would be the eggs and pheasants for my party. How typical! Really I think he is excessively mean!

Tuesday, 21 November

I worked all day, changed into my navy blue dress and taxied to the Castle. Went to the schoolroom, where the princesses were with Crawfie and Toni. The rest of the party then arrived, the Philipps and several Grenadiers – sixteen in all. We went along to the small dining room, overlooking the quadrangle for tea. Afterwards we played games in the Red Drawing Room – there were saucers and bottles laid out on tables and we had to taste and smell their contents and guess what they were! Then we passed bits of paper round on the end of a drinking straw and had races. We also played charades in which my side, including PM and Jackie, did an exact replica of the others' scenes only to a different word – we thought ours was better – but they didn't appreciate it and when we came in for the last scene we found them all hidden behind the curtains to pay us back!

Friday, 24 November

My Twenty-first Birthday.

Mass and Communion at nine, and after breakfast I opened all my presents and very touched at the number of people who remembered me with telegrams, etc. A lamp came from the princesses, in pale green and pink, which I love. Mummy arrived before lunch – she criticised many of my presents and it was all I could do all day not to let her spoil the happiness of this birthday for me. No one knows how much this habit of hers of crabbing my things annoys me – I wanted to remind her that <u>none</u> of <u>her</u> family had given me a <u>farthing</u> today and I was conscious again of a great longing to be right away from her after the war. The princesses arrived at eight fifteen with Crawfie and they brought with them a present from the Queen – a beautiful brooch in pale blue enamel and diamonds with E.R. in diamonds and a crown on top – it is in a pink leather case, also with E.R. on it, and there was a note enclosed from the Queen. No words can describe how thrilled I am with it, nor how I value her great kindness. We were sixteen for dinner. Afterwards we looked at my presents and then played paper games till the men returned, when we played clumps and charades – it was v. amusing and it all went <u>perfectly</u>. I think everyone enjoyed themselves, even Mummy fitted in and they did not leave till quarter past twelve. PE looked very nice – she wore her tartan gauze, though I don't really think it suits her as it enlarges her figure. PM had the cream gauze with the green bows that I love so much, though Mummy condemned it as 'cruel'. I went to bed at last, not in the least tired, but radiantly happy and delighted with every minute of my party – I could not believe it was at last <u>over,</u> after I had looked forward to it for so long.

List of Presents for my 21st Birthday

Pale blue enamel and diamond brooch	The Queen
Pale green lamp with pink shade	The Princesses
Pearl and diamond bracelet	Gpa. and Daddy
Opal brooch in shape of butterfly	Mummy
Large round diamond brooch, open design	Aunt Magdalen
Diamond and aquamarine brooch and pendant	Bernard
Large ornament brooch to wear in coat	Sir Kay Muir
Watercolour picture painted by herself	Elizabeth Anne
Tortoiseshell and silver box	Lady Shaftesbury
Cream-coloured box painted with flowers	All at Cumberland Lodge
Wastepaper basket with Victorian fashions	Sonia
A pair of flowered china vases (miniature)	Ursula
Book: *British Statesmen*	Miss Drummond
Jacqmar scarf	Mr Throckmorton
Embroidered evening bag	Rachel
Small shagreen leather jewel case	Katherine
Lipstick	Crawfie
Book in which to write lists of books	Toni de Bellaigue
Queen Anne tapestry chair cover (to work)	All at Queensmead

Ten shillings	Miss Dunham
Pink satin and net pincushion	Lady Serena James
Dark red leather powder case	Miss Sandbach
Necklace of green stones and crystal	Aunt Gwen
Chain bracelet of amethysts and crystals	Annabel
2 lace-edged handkerchiefs	Ming-Ming

Monday, 27 November

I had the most angelic letter from Countess Kleinmichel – she was sincerely pleased that I wrote to her and her letter made me almost weep with happiness. It was so sweet and so sad, though for <u>her</u> I feel the deepest sympathies and affection. Had to return after tea to Queensmead where I wrote a thank-you letter to Drusilla – the coldest, most formal note I could compose.

Tuesday, 28 November

Worked till four then biked home for the evening. Spent it arranging my presents and Lord knows what else, but I never sat down for a minute till dinner except for my bath.

Thursday, 30 November

Diana Bowes-Lyon rang up and asked me to a small party in London for her twenty-first birthday on Saturday. I am in a dilemma because I would love to go and <u>could</u> manage it, but Annabel is coming to stay.

Friday, 1 December

Rang Diana Bowes-Lyon up and she said I might bring Annabel too so we were delighted and arranged to stay at Claridges. I have been given an extra day off too, which is wonderful.

Saturday, 2 December

A and I wrote and talked in the morning and went down to Eton and lunched at the Cockpit with all her family and spent the afternoon watching – or rather <u>not</u> watching – the Field Game, which was v. cold but v. amusing as we saw so many people we knew. Then A and I got the train and went straight to Claridges where we changed – I wore my short black organdie – and then taxied round to Charles Street – the Bowes-Lyons' house. It began as a sort of cocktail party and went on as a dance upstairs to a radiogram. It was v. well done, with a buffet running all the time, about sixty people and plenty of men. PE was there, with the new lady-in-waiting, Mary Palmer. To my surprise I thought her <u>most</u> attractive, though not at all <u>pretty</u>. She is small and dark with an <u>interesting</u> face, a quiet voice and manner, but v. gay and laughing and is, I should think, most capable and efficient. I think I should like her if I knew her. Her husband was there, and looked v. dull, fat and unattractive, but as Mummy says, it's v. often those sort of people who turn out best. PE wore a bright red crêpe dress – the colour suited her though the shape was ugly, and her shoes were <u>terrible</u>. She enjoyed herself greatly and didn't leave till after twelve, when everyone began to. I am glad as she gets so little pleasure now and never alone like this. She said she was staying in London the night. I envied Mary with all my heart. A and I returned to Claridges having enjoyed the party immensely, but I could not sleep v. well as I had that aching, restless feeling that makes me wish so often that I was not always wanting and reaching for something I haven't got.

Thursday, 7 December

Went to drawing in the afternoon – the last lesson, which always makes me feel v. sad. PM and I talked alone in the schoolroom instead of going out, as it was so cold. PE came back for tea from having inspected the Household Cavalry at Aldershot – she said she loved Diana's party but we couldn't really discuss it because the Tannars were there again, much to my annoyance.

Sunday, 10 December

Went to Zelda's at three for her twenty-first birthday party. Several other people were there, including Drusilla. It annoyed me to find how I dreaded seeing her till I remembered how little worthy of notice she really is.

Monday, 11 December

Just before lunch an invitation arrived to a dinner dance at Buckingham Palace on 14 December, the King's birthday. My brain whirled round and round in circles and I was wild with excitement.

Thursday, 14 December

Grabbed some breakfast in the kitchen and the car took me home from Queensmead. Changed while Billy packed, all in a great hurry and confusion, and Grandpa and I went up to London. Had lunch with Lady Moray[*] and Mary-Anne at 1 Hans Place, which I enjoyed v. much, and we sat talking after till three. Came back to Mrs Wyndham's[†] at five and had tea. Bathed and changed into my painted net and wore the Queen's brooch, hung on a black velvet ribbon, and the pearl bracelet <u>over</u> my gloves. Car came seven fifteen and I called for Mary and Elizabeth Lumley on the way. We arrived at the Palace at quarter to eight and waited in the long passage before filing past the Royal Family and on into the Bow Room, where eight round tables of ten were arranged and our names written on the places. The Royal Family were divided between two or three tables – they were <u>all</u> there, the Gloucesters,[‡] Duchess of K and Princess Royal, who looked <u>awful</u> in salmon-pink velvet! We only shook hands with the King and Queen and the princesses, who all wore the same as at the dance on 5 May. The dinner was delicious and afterwards we danced in the middle of the same room and returned to any of the tables for refreshments in between whiles. Some people arrived after dinner, so there were about ninety or a hundred in all. There were v. few older people but I saw all my friends and enjoyed it wildly. It ended at

---

[*]   Barbara, Countess of Moray, was a widow and the mother of three girls, of whom the eldest Mary Anne was a contemporary and had been a childhood friend of Alathea in London.

[†]   Mrs Wyndham was a family friend who sometimes came to stay at Cumberland Lodge and had a London flat.

[‡]   The Duke and Duchess of Gloucester – the Duke of Gloucester, Prince Henry, was the King's brother.

three, and when I said goodbye to the Queen she remarked on my wearing her brooch, so I was delighted I had. PE was charming but PM looked very white and drawn all the evening.

Monday, 18 December

Stayed in this morning writing. Elizabeth Anne came at lunchtime and she has grown a lot and she's always in a very good humour when she first returns from school. We started out for a walk in the afternoon, but it rained so we came back.

Wednesday, 20 December

The news is bad at the moment – the Germans have launched a big <u>offensive</u> and have penetrated back twenty miles across Belgium in several places. One mercy was the fog preventing me going back to Queensmead so I enjoyed a fifth night in my own bed. It was a most uncomfortable one, though, as poor EA appeared in the passage as we went up, in tears saying she couldn't sleep and was frightened, so she came and slept with me and coughed all night. She isn't v. well, I don't think – she has this cough and is very overtired.

Thursday, 21 December

EA left at eight to go to Houghton with Aunt Alathea. Off in afternoon and Z biked home with me. Had a Christmas card from the princesses – a charming one with a photograph of them in summer frocks with a dog and quite plain on the outside with a gold E and M.

Saturday, 23 December

Went up to the Castle with Zelda and Major Loyd for the pantomime at two thirty. *Old Mother Red Riding Boots*. It was certainly the best they have ever done – the clothes and scenery were beautiful. The princesses were both girls this time – fictitious characters – and they sang and acted excellently. Mr Tannar was in it and he annoyed both Z and me considerably as usual! But we enjoyed it. The King and Queen were there.

Monday, 25 December

CHRISTMAS DAY

I biked to Mass in Windsor at eight and went to Communion, then returned to Queensmead for breakfast. It was icy cold and, though no snow, everywhere was white with frost. We did v. little work and had our turkey and plum pudding at one. We all listened to the King's Speech at three and to the wireless till tea at four. I biked home at five, gave the servants their presents, then the family, then opened mine. Mummy's was a brass bangle from Brussels, which she described as 'rather Heaven' but which I don't like at all and put on one side to give to somebody else. We had Rosary then I bathed and changed for dinner, which was a real Christmas one and we had sherry and Champagne to drink. I sat up reading over all the Christmases of the war in my diaries. None of them have been very cheerful – last year I was contented; this year I have hated. It is strange how life fluctuates back and forth, a mixture of joys and sorrows but more often than not a pattern of little varying sameness. My greatest pleasure I derived from the little Dresden vases Grandpa gave me, which I chose. I love them very much.

Wednesday, 27 December

The frost still continues – everywhere is white like snow and the cold intense.

Churchill and Eden are in Athens for conferences. The news from the Western Front is slightly improving.

Sunday, 31 December

I am now writing in this diary for the last time and I look forward tomorrow to fetching my new one from home and hope it may have something more of interest in it than this one has had.

1945

19 Worked till 5. Billy brought my clothes, & I had a bath & changed & d., Drusilla Moira & I went by bus t Farnham Common to Brenda's for her 20th birthday

19 party. Her family were there & four other girls & we played games, had a treasure hunt, & ate a delicious buffet supper all standing round the dining room table.

19 It was fun, & I think it made a happy day for Little Bren. I do hope so anyway as she has been rather upset lately by Mrs. P. & various happenings t do with

19 with the kitchen — Collins, the taxi, came for us at ten & we (the four of us) were driven back in his new American car wh. sails along & we had lovely music on the wireless t listen t! We had'nt known such luxury for years, except for Moira in America, & we all wished the drive cd. have gone on for ever!

A handwritten page from Alathea's diary.

Monday, 1 January

I worked from seven thirty till five and then came home. Only Grandpa and Aunt Magdalen there, as Daddy has gone to Houghton. We had a delicious dinner for New Year's Night and some Chablis, which did me good, as I felt so very ill – nothing in particular, only a dreadful lassitude, shivering and vague sickness, so that I somehow I felt immune to everything, unable to think or even care about anything, good or bad. I changed back into uniform at nine thirty and the car took me back, picking up Zelda on the way.

Monday, 8 January

Life which, for a few days, was wretched beyond words has now fallen back into the dull, apathetic state I know so well – only a little worse at the moment than it has been for a long while, with nothing to look forward to, and the cold and physical discomfort here now are torture to me.

Sunday, 14 January

Mummy and Daddy have decided on an allowance of £40 a year for me to buy odds and ends and all clothes except coats and dresses, etc. This with my pay makes about £90 per year, which I am delighted with.

Tuesday, 23 January

We all drove to London in spite of the snow. Grandpa and I chose a leather writing wallet for Elizabeth Anne's birthday. I then went to Park Lane where Mummy and Aunt Alathea are moving into a new flat – it is a much larger and nicer one, though of course the building is dreadful and <u>they</u> were fond of Grosvenor Square, which I detested. We lunched in the restaurant attached. Mummy said she never does give EA a present for her birthday – it is too soon after Christmas and she really can't be bothered. I do think it is mean and unkind and <u>unnatural</u>.

Thursday, 25 January

Aunt Magdalen rang me up to tell me that Lavinia has had a fourth daughter! What a terrible disappointment – everyone was so sure that this time it <u>would</u> be a boy.

St Giles, Dorset

Wednesday, 31 January

My leave started today. Arrived at St Giles at six. EA so very much happier here now than she was when I last came over a year ago.

Thursday, 1 February

Watch the dancing class. EA dances quite well and gracefully – they're doing the ballet exercises I used to do at the Castle.

Burloes, Hertfordshire

Saturday, 3 February

Had breakfast with EA and then left for the station. Annabel met me at Royston. It was lovely to see them all again and I am so very happy to be here. After dinner, three Americans whom A knows at her canteen came. We talked and at intervals went into the dining room to drink sherry – they are extraordinary: they do not want to spend an ordinary evening in the presence of older people, playing cards for instance, but just like hanging about with their arms round a girl, talking utter drivel and <u>never</u> know when to leave. One of them, Dreiling, offered to buy my golf clubs and on the pretext of discussing it he bore me off into the drawing room and we sat on the sofa and I waited for what I knew was coming – he held my hand, then pawed my arms and finally kissed me, which he went on doing for about five minutes, till the others came in. This was my first experience of being kissed and quite frankly I thought it revolting but the whole thing amused me so much that I couldn't help smiling, even while it was going on and I wanted to see what it was like. They didn't leave till nearly twelve and then how A and I laughed!

Cumberland Lodge

Thursday, 8 February

Churchill, Roosevelt and Stalin are now conferring some-where in the Black Sea. We have once more taken the offensive on the Western Front though progress is slow and the mud appalling. The Russian advance has slowed. I am reading my 1944 diary and I notice that throughout almost all the year I seemed to feel I was destined to be lonely and almost unwanted all my life, that, try as I would, the world held no real place for me. Now I feel quite differently, perhaps because the birds are singing outside, which reminds me of approaching spring but I believe I have indeed a place in the world to fill, that it is coming to me, slowly, through difficulties and disappointments it is true, but nevertheless coming.

Thursday, 15 February

Biked up to the Castle for drawing. Only PM and me today and we continued with our lino cuts. Went out with Crawfie and groomed the foals and came in for tea. PM. caught mumps at Sandringham but is now recovered and PE. developed it here last Saturday and has it slightly worse than her sister. When I was going away, PM opened the door and tried to pull me in and I just caught a glimpse of PE sitting in an arm chair by the fire and spoke to her through the door. PM told me Prince Philip sent PE a photograph of himself for Christmas and she danced round the room with it for joy! She then said: 'I wonder who Lilibet will marry?' Prince Philip certainly seems to consider the possibility and PE would welcome it, I am sure.

Thursday, 22 February

Biked to the Castle for drawing. I saw PE to talk to with 'a room in between us' as she is up but still infectious.

Tuesday, 27 February

Although my cold was rather heavy I had quite regained my cheerfulness. James Denny[*] dined. I taught him to play backgammon after dinner – he is so nice.

Thursday, 1 March

Worked till two, changed and then biked up to the Castle for drawing. PE asked me to a party on Wednesday – of a new kind, beginning at six and including dinner and dancing. I am thrilled.

Monday, 5 March

It was officially announced today that PE has been given a commission in the ATS and is taking a driving course. It all sounds rather odd, but I can't believe she will give up all her time to it. She always liked the WRNS, but I suppose for practical purposes the ATS is more suitable, since they have HQ in Windsor. I shouldn't have thought it necessary but no doubt it is a good gesture for the last few months of the war. Tonight, they report fighting in Cologne and our advance on all the Western Front making excellent progress.

---

[*] James Denny was yet another young Grenadier officer.

Wednesday, 7 March

Worked till five – not too hard – and changed into my blue velvet frock and bussed up to the Castle. Everyone had to go along to the Red Drawing Room in small groups because the Duchess of Kent doesn't like meeting a great many strangers at once. We shook hands with her and the princesses and then drank and talked before doing the treasure hunt, which was arranged by the princesses and very cleverly done. My partner was J. Denny and we won the first prize! There were twenty-four people altogether – the ladies were Anne Anson and Diana [Bowes-Lyon], Mrs Townsend [wife of Peter Townsend], whom I don't care for much – she is a nondescript little thing – Joan P, Toni, Crawfie and Madame Poklewska (Zoia), who was with the duchess [of Kent] and made us all roar with laughter as usual. I knew a few of the men only – mostly Grenadiers. We played clumps – I was in the duchess's group and she was the greatest fun and charming. Then we played sardines and PM and I hid in an attic above the organ loft that contained rows and rows of odd-shaped tin boxes in which were the cocked hats the footmen used to wear in the old days! After this we had supper in the private dining room above the Sovereign's Entrance, at three tables. I was at PE's and we ate cold chicken and pastry things and delicious ice cream and cakes. We then played charades in the same groups as we sat at supper – the Duchess of K acted well and really seemed to enjoy herself and enter into everything with a good spirit. The dance began and I had one lovely waltz with J. Denny and we ended up with the Dashing White Sergeant, which I enjoyed most of all. This was about midnight and then we said goodnight to the princesses in the corridor. It was a perfect party and I think even those who don't enjoy playing games – and I know there are many – must feel themselves affected by the natural gaiety of the princesses and their unrestrained enjoyment of their own party.

Thursday, 8 March

Biked to the Castle for drawing. Both the princesses were in London at the dentist, so after the lesson Crawfie and I took the dogs for a walk in Frogmore and then had tea in her sitting room. We had long discussions on everything and everybody. She said she regretted PE had no taste at all but she wanted them to be so perfect so she was inclined to be disappointed, that there were so few people she could be critical with, it was a relief sometimes. She told me that PE is now driving about here in the ATS and soon goes to Camberley for a course every day for three weeks and after that she ceases it – thank Heaven! But they think the experience will do her good.

Thursday, 15 March

Biked to the Castle for drawing. Went out with the princesses and Crawfie – PE was wearing her ATS battle dress, which consists of trousers and I thought she looked awful and that it is shockingly bad for her to be seen about in them. She now drives all over the place, even halfway to London – I really cannot understand them allowing her to do it and everyone I've met says the same, though I say as little as possible about it. It may be a good thing for the post-war world, but in my opinion to preserve her dignity should be the first consideration. We came into tea and two ATS officers

285

were there, the one who goes driving with her and the other who had come to give her a lesson in map reading. They came from Camberley and were quite nice, but we were all very polite and quiet at tea! PE begins her course at Camberley next Friday. She has had her hair done shorter, which does not suit her as it broadens her face so.

Thursday, 22 March

At four went out with the princesses and Toni. They asked me to fix a date for my picnic, which they seemed v. anxious to bring about and we decided Saturday 7th. The K and Q are back but I didn't see them. We had tea in the school-room, a much gayer one than last week and we were all in the best of spirits.

Saturday, 24 March

Elizabeth Cavendish arrived. She is very entertaining, as she chatters ceaselessly to anybody and everybody she happens to be with and with equal ease to Grandpa or to the taxi driver. She knows more people than anyone I've ever met, and she dines out about three times a week in London. But I do not envy her life at present – too hurried, too much of the sordid rush from club, to office, to nightclub. I should hate never being alone when I got back in the evening and I suspect if I <u>were</u> in London I would have very few nights out.

Wednesday, 28 March

I biked to the Philipps at Frogmore to dine afterwards. Played rummy, which was very amusing, and Jackie was killing. He too disapproves greatly of PE joining the ATS and crawling under cars.

Thursday, 29 March

Walked to the Castle for drawing and began a new lino cut. It was much colder today and windy but PM and I went out with Crawfie too. We walked to the slopes and picked primroses, for me to take back, though I wish it had been <u>home</u> and not to Queensmead. We came in for tea and just as we'd finished the K and Q came along and we had a long discussion in the passage as to how I was going to boil thirty eggs at once for breakfast tomorrow! PE appeared at the same time, having just returned from Camberley – she looked quite nice in her uniform but rather like the Princess Royal. She asked me to go with them to a party at Coppins on Monday week, which thrilled me beyond words. I walked back and found several letters and my spirits were so high that I just danced through my work all the evening! The news is so good too – we are <u>far</u> into Germany on a two-hundred-mile front and the Russians have reached the Austrian frontier.

Thursday, 5 April

Last drawing lesson today. PE appeared, just as we were finishing and appears to be enjoying her course at Camberley v. much – I can quite understand it as passing her whole day in such new and utterly unaccustomed surroundings, quite on her own as it were, must be an exciting and not unpleasant experience, for a little while, though I do not think she would care for it always.

Friday, 6 April

Elizabeth Anne came in at about three and had tea with us. I had a bath and changed early and went along to talk to her.

Saturday, 7 April

EA came and had breakfast in bed with me and then we went out to pick flowers for the house. It was so cold and dull outside. Crawfie rang up and we settled to have it [tea] indoors. The party came together at five – PM, Crawfie, the Philipps, Zelda and James Denny. We played Consequences while we were waiting for PE, who had gone to watch a football match at Wembley. We all had tea once PE had arrived and then played poetic Consequences, followed by clumps in the dining room and then the whispering game. It all went off very well and I was pleased. Both the princesses were in high spirits and quite informal and at ease.

Monday, 9 April

I changed after tea and drove to the Castle. The princesses came and we all drove over to Coppins – I went in the brake with PM, Mary Palmer, who is now Mary Strachey (she got married in November) and several of the men. MS is perfectly charming and has a lovely soft voice, which I think is her greatest attraction, as she is not pretty. The princesses wore the same as at their own party but PE didn't look at all her best, for which I was very sorry. We were greeted by the duchess [of Kent], who wore a classic dress of aquamarine silk. There were thirty people altogether including the whole Luxembourg royal family.* The girls are all very shy and quiet and terribly dowdy but nice. We began by playing games, and then we went upstairs to tidy for dinner, which we had at several little tables in the dining room. We ate curried eggs and lobster, chicken in aspic and salad, and chocolate soufflé, orange salad and pastry cornets, filled with real cream and we drank Champagne and coffee. I sat next to Freddy Shaughnessy,† who took a violent fancy to me, though I don't think <u>him</u> attractive. We danced all the rest of the evening, except for playing one or two rather amusing games and we had one turn of forfeit dancing in which J. Lascelles‡ and I had to do an Arab dance and PE and Lord Herbert§ a ballet! Lord, how I enjoyed myself!

Thursday, 12 April

Off in the afternoon and I biked to Eton to buy a book to give PE for her birthday and I chose an old volume, bound in white vellum, of fancy dresses – beautifully illustrated – and then with my own uniform allowance I bought the most lovely volume of fairytales illustrated by Edmund Dulac and bound in brown leather and gold. It will be a lovely thing to keep for one's children to look at.

---

* The Luxembourg royal family were in exile in London during the war.
† Freddy Shaughnessy's mother had married Piers Legh, Master of the Household.
‡ John Lascelles was the son of the courtier Tommy Lascelles.
§ Lord Herbert was Private Secretary to Princess Marina.

Friday, 13 April

Heard that <u>President Roosevelt</u> is dead. He died suddenly but quietly yesterday – it is indeed a great blow to our cause and to the world in general and a supreme misfortune at this hour, when he would have been so essential and valuable a figure in the difficult days of peace after the war. Vienna has been liberated, though after much fighting I believe.

Monday, 16 April

I worked till four, then went straight to Claridges, where I met Joe Dormer and we had a drink. We saw *The Gayeties* which I didn't care for greatly, then we dined at Quaglino's, which I loved. We danced once – he was just as dull as I'd expected and utterly devoid of charm, but it was nice of him to take me out on his leave and he ordered a most expensive red wine! He also had a car to take me back to Paddington and he came and sat in the train until it went, then he whispered something to me which I didn't hear, so he had to repeat it, which must have been very embarrassing for him! He said, 'Do you think we might manage a quick kiss?' There were some soldiers in the carriage and I had wondered if he were asking me if I would be all right with them and nearly said, 'Oh, yes, quite all right,' then, realising, I said, 'Do you think we really want to?' and then I covered up <u>the</u> confusion by thanking him for the evening and shaking hands openly as he stood up to go. But this, coming from slow, heavy Joe, surprised me so much that I couldn't help laughing. I think if I encouraged Joe, he would marry me – he is determined to get a suitable Roman Catholic girl, pushed on by his mother.

Friday, 20 April

Grandpa rang me up in the evening to remind me that it's the anniversary of Granny's death tomorrow. It is also PE's birthday – her nineteenth tomorrow and it is a combined date, which I never forget.

Friday, 27 April

I had a charming letter from PE, who I think is really pleased with the book of fancy dresses. She said she would see me on Saturday.

Saturday, 28 April

Worked till four and I almost fainted in the kitchen after lunch, we had such a strenuous morning! Changed and got the train up to London. I had a bath and put on my painted net dress and taxied to Claridges at seven fifteen, where I joined the Philipps and their party, including John Stanley.* The princess arrived with Anne Anson, as lady-in-waiting, and I wondered whether she may be temporarily taking the place of Mary Strachey, who must soon be unable to do any more. [She was pregnant.]

We had an <u>excellent</u> dinner and drank claret and afterwards we drove to a house in Grosvenor Place, which one may hire for dances. It must once have been quite fine but now it has rather a sordid air, with one or two windows boarded up, no furniture, dirty entrance hall and the rain dripping through the dome on to the landing. PE wore a v. ugly dress of shiny white satin. It made her figure look its

---

* John Stanley was the future Earl of Derby and the elder brother of Richard Stanley.

worst and her hair being now short and tight accentuates the impression of great solidarity she gives. It _is_ such a pity, as she _can_ look so nice and she has such pretty things about her, if only she would show them off with more graceful and more original clothes. John Stanley danced with me quite a lot – I can't help rather liking him though he _is_ supercilious and superior to an uncommon degree, but he has a certain, almost sullen charm. The princess left at one thirty and took me with her – we said good night to her at the Palace and then the car took us home in turns, which was very kind of PE as it was a terrible night.

Sunday, 29 April

The papers yesterday were full of peace reports, which were however contradicted on the wireless. Himmler is supposed to have made an offer of surrender but not an official one to the Three Great Powers. Meanwhile Mussolini has been executed in Milan and Hitler reported dying. The K and Q have returned to London and the war is now officially expected over any day.

Wednesday, 2 May

Hitler is declared to be dead, though the details are all so mythical that one is inclined to believe either that he died some time ago or else that he is still alive and hidden away somewhere. Admiral Doenitz has been appointed his successor.

Thursday, 3 May

I can't believe that I'm going up to Yorkshire tomorrow for the dance at St Nicholas – I'm looking forward to it greatly. The whole of Berlin has now surrendered to the Russians and yesterday fighting ceased officially in Italy.

St Nicholas Abbey

Saturday, 5 May

I have a delicious room this time, with a high four-poster bed in green and pink. Stayed in this afternoon because it rained and read in *The Times* of the appointment of the Hon. Mrs Gibbs* as Extra L-in-W to PE. It only cast a slight film of depression over my day, worrying me mostly whenever I was alone. I felt mostly <u>annoyance</u> that another quite unknown person, who is herself not even of noble family, should step in but I must accept now the fact they wish for married women, who perhaps are more experienced in the world, and <u>not</u> for her to choose her own friends. We dined at eight, sixteen in all and then we began to dance. I wore my blue and gold brocade. About sixty people came and it was a very gay party. The men weren't interesting or amusing but then they are so seldom these days. All the same nearly all the other girls seem to have a success with <u>someone</u> – why is it I never do? It is true that no man ever looks at me twice, never dreams of dancing hotly with me as they seem to want to do with others – for which however I am heartily thankful, as I detest it, but occasionally I do get depressed

---

*   The Hon. Mrs Gibbs, formerly Jean Hambro, had married Captain Vicary Gibbs, who was in the Grenadiers and killed at Nijmegen in 1944. She went on to marry Queen Elizabeth's nephew Andrew Elphinstone after the war.

as year after year I continue in icy seclusion. Ursula admits she has the greatest difficulty in keeping herself <u>out</u> of love – I often think it quite impossible to fall <u>in</u> love!

Monday, 7 May

Got back to Queensmead last night. Off in afternoon so went out into the garden and lay on a rug and slept. Suddenly I was woken up by Moira,* who came to tell me that the war was over! We all rushed to the wireless. It wasn't yet official, but they gave out that Churchill would officially announce the end tomorrow at three and that the King would speak at nine. Somehow it is impossible to believe or realise or even to be excited, and oddly enough my depression increased instead of lessened – it is so long since I <u>have</u> felt depressed that I suppose I noticed it more.

Tuesday, 8 May

THE DAY OF VICTORY IN EUROPE.
The great day dawned at last and yet how exactly like any other it seemed! We all walked to Victoria Barracks for the Drum Service on Castle Hill – we had to march up there and it was v. hot but it was funny too, as all the Red Cross officers were throwing their weight about and sporting their medals! There were hundreds of other people taking part too. It was quite a nice service and we sang hymns; we got back at seven and worked till nine when Mrs Bathurst kindly asked us all to come in and listen to the King's Speech and drink Champagne. The King spoke for ten minutes, better

---

* Moira (surname unknown) was a local Windsor girl, who had been evacuated to America and who came to Queensmead in 1944.

and stronger than ever before. After this four Grenadier officers came round – Moira knew one of them and the others were his friends. The four of us went with them down to the Old House, where we talked and had a drink and then we went out and paraded down Eton High Street – it was by this time quite dark and there were <u>hundreds</u> of people all shouting and singing and waving flags. All the windows were hung with red, white and blue and we tore down two enormous flags to carry round ourselves. All the Eton boys were out in force, running in one dense procession, though in no particular direction! Our party got separated in the dark and I found myself with two officers whom I still don't know the names of! But they were v. nice and we spent most of the time getting rides on the running boards of cars, which was great fun and by now I was really excited and enjoyed myself madly. In spite of all the merry-making it was an extraordinarily quiet, <u>friendly</u> crowd, almost like some <u>village</u> festival, with all the guardsmen calling out cheerful greetings to their officers and constantly meeting people one knew.

Wednesday, 9 May

We worked again – unfortunately there could be no two-day holiday for us – and I came by bus to Cumberland Lodge. We had more Champagne at dinner in honour of the peace. The Royal Family are, of course, in London and they appeared several times on the balcony of Buckingham Palace, where thousands of people were waiting for them and their reception in the East End today, where they drove, was wonderful to hear (we listened on the wireless). I slept at home tonight.

Friday, 11 May

Some news, which has given me a great shock for his poor parents' sake, is that Miles Marriott has died of wounds in Germany. Somehow, I never believed he would be killed, and I hate to think of the grief of his parents, who <u>idolised</u> him, being their only child.

Wednesday, 16 May

Crawfie had rung up yesterday to say drawing would begin again on Thursday but that PM would not be there this week. She is going to the House of Lords where the King is to receive addresses from both Houses of Parliament. Grandpa tried to get seats for Aunt Magdalen and me but, unfortunately, they will not allow any ladies in on account of room.

Thursday, 17 May

I had lunch alone then biked to the Castle. There were only Dawn and me, but I loved my lesson. Then Toni asked me to stay to tea with her, and we took the dogs for a walk in Frogmore. I believe she thinks I am lonely, and over-serious, as when I told her I would probably live up in Yorkshire, she seemed sincerely perturbed and exclaimed loudly against me, 'burying yourself'! I biked home slowly because of the heat and trying to convince myself that it is needless to worry – my life will work itself out well in the end, that I must have courage and face these moments of lowness and fear of the future.

Wednesday, 23 May

The Coalition Government has resigned today – Churchill went twice to see the King and it gives one a strange, insecure feeling to realise he is no longer Prime Minister. They were gloomy at home and the whole world seems gloomy.

Saturday, 26 May

The Caretaker Government has been formed and appears rather satisfactory. Elizabeth* and I went out for quite a long walk before lunch. After lunch we drove to the Home Park for the horse show with Grandpa. All the Royal Family were at the show. PE and PM drove again in the phaeton and won the cup, which they really deserved. PE drove all the time with a v. set, anxious expression on her face.

Tuesday, 29 May

Off in the afternoon and accompanied the PoWs† on a tour round the Castle. We did see PM with the Girl Guides over the terrace wall and she told me later she saw me but at the time no one else recognised her and I moved away quickly.

Thursday, 31 May

Biked to the Castle for drawing. We gossiped till five, when PE and Toni came in and we had tea. Mrs Gibbs was there too as PE was going to Slough in the evening. She is attractive

---

* Elizabeth Cavendish, who was staying.
† Queensmead provided provisional accommodation for soldiers from countries in the British Empire who had been liberated as prisoners of war in Nazi-occupied Europe.

and seems v. nice. I still think I could fulfil the position equally well, which I did not think when I first saw Mary Strachey. Both the princesses were sweet today and with them I feel happy and at home so that my fears and doubts for the future fade.

Friday, 1 June

Grandpa's ninetieth birthday. A luncheon party for him at Claridges was supposed to take place with all his <u>men</u> friends but, owing to him being ill, it had to be put off. I rang Mummy up and she advised me to stay at Queensmead till it closes and then find some sort of a job in London for the winter.

Wednesday, 6 June

Grandpa now comes down to dinner, but he is so changed that one wonders whether he will ever resume all his old activities, which is strange when the only <u>illness</u> he had was a cold from which he has now recovered. He does have fits of coughing at dinner, which are very unpleasant for everyone – Aunt M gets up and leaves the room, but we can't all do that, so Daddy and I sit there and pretend not to notice. I cannot say I <u>like</u> it at home now, except for the comfort of my own room and of Billy, and yet I feel I must come as often as possible as in case my remaining time here is short. I suppose I could almost count the nights on my fingers, and this gives me an odd, sad feeling.

Thursday, 7 June

After lunch I biked to the Castle for drawing. Afterwards PE told me they are having a dance at BP on the 20th, which is too thrilling for words. PM took me to see the pictures, which have just been put back in the Grand Corridor – one has got so used to seeing it bare for five years that it looks quite overcrowded now, though they are extremely beautiful and we spent over half an hour looking at these and other objects of interest.

Tuesday, 12 June

Simon Worsthorne arrived and Mrs P* allowed me the night off, which was a great treat. Simon is very well and not much thinner, though of course he was only a prisoner of war from October to May. Grandpa is now v. much better and was pleased to see Simon.

Wednesday, 13 June

I went up to London for the Cavans' cocktail party. PE was there, looking extremely nice in navy blue, and spent most of the time talking to older people and had little chance to talk to her friends but, apart from this, she said she enjoyed it.

Wednesday, 20 June

Went up to London by train and Tim Barclay happened to come by that train too so we travelled together and he gave me a lift in a taxi to Park Street [where his mother had a

---

* Mrs Pearson had taken over from Mrs Hovell at Queensmead.

flat]. Tim returned at eight and we dined at the Coq d'Or – he is nice but he bores me. We got a taxi to the Palace. We all waited in a small room off the corridor till ten past ten, when the doors into the Bow Room opened and we filed past the K and Q, the Duchess of K and the two princesses. The Q had a beautiful dress of pale-coloured gauze, v. full, with bands of gold sequins, and both the princesses looked quite delightful in pale pink. We began dancing and the windows on the terrace were kept open all night and chairs put out there so that one could go and sit there in the moonlight and hear the music from within. There were about a hundred and forty people there and, though I didn't dance with anyone who particularly pleased one, I had a good time and was not <u>stuck</u> with anyone boring. I had supper at PE's table, in a room with marble pillars that I had not been in before. PE's dress was easily the prettiest in the room, though there were a great many v. well-dressed people there. It ended at about four and we went in to have another supper and then the Royal Family returned to the Bow Room to say goodbye to all the guests by which time it was already getting light.

Thursday, 21 June

Got up at ten and had breakfast with Mummy, who wants me to take a secretarial course in the winter – the whole outlook is so <u>new</u> that unless one has any real interest or ability, it is difficult to do anything but <u>drift</u>. The one role for which I believed myself fitted God has denied me the happiness of fulfilling. Both PE and Crawfie must be aware that the possibility crossed my mind and I cannot decide whether it was my youth, my religion, my lack of title or merely lack of worldly experience which was against me.

Thursday, 28 June

Mummy's newest idea, which she takes quite seriously, is to buy a property in the Bahamas where we may all go in case of trouble. Her conviction that England will not only be unbearable but <u>unsafe</u> is so deep-rooted now that it is useless to argue with her. Got to Queensmead at eight and began work – everyone was either upset or bad-tempered over something and I found the tension almost unbearable. I changed and went to drawing, and afterwards went for a walk with PM and Toni in the rain. PE was there at tea and she told me she has also been invited to Arundel for the weekend of the 28th, though she is not quite certain if she is able to go yet or not. I begged her to do her best to go. It would be such a good thing for her as she never goes away, except with her family, because there are now so few places able to put her up and entertain her in a proper manner. In this sane, calm atmosphere, my confidence returned and it was a profound relief to be with people who have no wild fears for the future but who face it with a gracious tranquillity, determined to do their duty and win affection and respect by the simplicity and dignity of their conduct. It is because there is nothing extravagant about them, that they give the impression of solidarity and endurance, qualities beloved and innate in the British people.

Thursday, 5 July

I went on to the Castle in the car for drawing. I then went out with the two princesses and Crawfie – it was hot again and we sat on the grass but PE was rather silent and serious.

Thursday, 12 July

Biked to drawing. PM and I drew an old Staffordshire figure of a shepherdess. Afterwards I tidied in PE's room today and noticed a large photograph of Prince Philip on her mantelpiece, though it was unsigned.

Monday, 16 July

Had another letter from Joe Dormer asking me to dine with him on his leave. Why must it always be him?

Tuesday, 24 July

Worked till three fifteen, then biked up to the Castle. Waited in the quadrangle with the Philipps. The princesses and Crawfie came out and we drove in the horse brake up to Royal Lodge. It was the most perfect day and we were all v. happy. We walked about the garden until tea was ready – laid out on a table on the lawn with an enormous umbrella to shade us from the sun. After tea we launched a rubber dinghy on the swimming pool and I rashly said I would get into it with Jackie P, the result being that the water came over the edge and <u>soaked</u> the back of my dress! Crawfie had to <u>wring</u> it out for me and then just let it dry on me! But it made everyone laugh and then two of the men sailed in it with more success! The evening passed very pleasantly and peacefully. We went into the house to tidy for dinner, which we again had out in the garden – salmon mayonnaise, cold chicken and salad and a great variety of delicious fruit. After this we danced to the gramophone in the Saloon, among others Strip the Willow and the Dashing White Sergeant. PE was at her gayest and sweetest today, and really enjoyed herself. She asked me if I would like to go down to Arundel on Saturday with her, which is most kind and will be much nicer for me. We left in the motor brake this time and they dropped me at Queensmead.

Thursday, 26 July

<u>The Labour Party have won the election with a vast majority of 153 seats.</u>

Churchill and Eden have kept their seats. I went up to drawing and afterwards walked down to Frogmore with the princesses and returned for tea and talked of the election. We listened to the news and to Attlee's mean accusations against Mr Churchill. How sad a day it must be for him! Outside it was cold and wet, and inside was mournful spec-ulation and a feeling that everything one had known would change, that a dark, difficult era had passed to give place to a blacker, more abysmal one yet. I could not sleep well and I thought of the many men who have slaved for their country's good who now, defeated, join the sombre ranks of the opposition and of the countless ignorant people who voted Labour without knowing why or how they voted and of those who believe by doing so things will fall into their laps that would otherwise be kept from them.

Saturday, 28 July

PE rang up early to say that Jean Gibbs was ill, so there would only be her and me going down,* which meant that I would really act as her lady-in-waiting! I bussed to the Castle at five. PE appeared and we set off. We arrived at Arundel and were met by Bernard and Lavinia and the rest of the party. L took us up to our rooms – PE had the first bedroom in the Red Passage, and I was next to her. We dressed for dinner – she wore her white satin and I wore the blue lace. After dinner we set off in different cars for Amberley.† Lavinia went with the princess and two men. I went with John Stanley. The dance was admirably organised and the setting was beautiful – they floodlit the ruins and we danced in a huge marquee in the garden, entered by a little wooden bridge over the lily pond and then one walked into the house for refreshments, which were excellent – but the whole thing lacked spirit and spontaneity, like the hostess herself, Mrs Emmet. Lavinia Emmet,‡ whose 21st birthday it was, looked <u>awful,</u> in a pink <u>woollen</u> frock like a dressing-gown. However, we all enjoyed it up to a point though were not sorry when it ended. We returned and raided the kitchen for some cake, which greatly amused PE. Then we talked for a little in the drawing room before going to bed. I went in to see PE and we gossiped some more. I told her we had no paper in our WC so she produced a roll from hers and we unrolled reams of it across the room!

---

* To Arundel for the Emmets' party at nearby Amberley.
† A romantic medieval castle fairly near Arundel in Sussex, once owned by the Dukes of Norfolk and bought by the Emmet family in 1926.
‡ Baroness Emmet lived at Amberley Castle and, unusually for the time, she was an Oxford graduate. The Hon. (Gloria) Lavinia was her daughter and a contemporary of Alathea.

Sunday, 29 July

Mass in the chapel at nine. We had breakfast after – the princess had hers in her room and went to church with Lavinia later. In the afternoon the whole party drove to Angmering Park to see the stud, though I could not be as interested in it naturally, as most of the others, whose very lives are devoted to racing. PE is v. keen about it now too. We got back for tea after, and we played a priceless game called Ladida, which consists of sitting in a ring on the floor and passing ash-trays round in a certain manner. Then we went down to the smoking room, which they are now using as a dining room, and played a v. amusing game, called Freda,* on the billiard table with two balls. We went up to dress for dinner – PE had the most lovely black dress of stiff transparent stuff with red velvet bows on the sleeves and waist. I wore black too. The men spent three-quarters of an hour over their port while we gossiped upstairs and when they did join us, we played more games. Certainly, the weekend was the v. greatest success – the first the princess had ever spent away on her own on a private visit – she adored it, and everyone was pleased. I, too, am pleased to think that her first dinner and her first dinner party should have been with our family.

Monday, 30 July

We breakfasted downstairs, the princess too, and she and I left the Castle at about ten. I felt violently sick in the car and in the end I <u>had</u> to ask PE if I might lean out of the

---

* The game was named after Freda Dudley Ward, the girlfriend of Edward VIII before he met Mrs Simpson.

window by me, so there we sat, she shivering in the howling draught and me with my face glued to the window until near Windsor I managed to sit back and look a little more dignified – I felt terribly ashamed but what could I do when the alternative was much worse!

Wednesday, 1 August

The BBC gave a wonderful description of the scene in the House of Commons when the new Parliament met for the first time. When Churchill entered the opposition all rose to their feet, cheered and sang 'For He's A Jolly Good Fellow' with such spirit and energy that, at first, the Labour members, although in such gigantic force, were quite taken aback and silenced, until one of the back-benchers began singing 'The Red Flag' and they all took it up, each side <u>roaring</u> their own song across the chamber. Then finally they began business by congratulating each other on the heartiness of their singing! That <u>could</u> only happen in England and it is still the same old country, for all the changes wrought in it.

Thursday, 2 August

Biked to the Castle for drawing. Crawfie had rung me up to say no one would be there for tea as the princesses had to go out. PM left early and I didn't see PE at all. It was the last lesson, which is very sad, as next term they will no longer be at Windsor and who knows what will happen then? And yet I cannot look upon it as the definite end of a chapter, a wartime interlude – as I once feared it would be. The curious thing about life is its continuity – it rarely stops dead at a given moment and begins afresh; the old threads do snap, some still carry on intermingling with the new ones, and ties between <u>people</u> persist, despite outward changes in one's existence, and it is the <u>people</u> one is surrounded by who constitute one's life. And so I left at four, wondering whether I really had been in these rooms, which I have grown so familiar with these last five years, for the last time.

Saturday, 4 August

I worked till five and at seven I walked to the Crichtons', where I had a bath and dressed – wore my lace again. Brian Gething,* J. Denny and another came. After dinner Barbara, Anne and I put on our gloves, helped by Nannie, and then we all drove to the Castle. We waited as usual in the Green Drawing Room and then filed through into the Red, where the Royal Family received us. The King was in naval uniform, the Queen in grey tulle, the Duchess of Kent looking divine in a Greek net frock, and the two princesses wore pink lace and pink organdie respectively. The first person I talked to after this was Lady Hyde† – she asked me if I'd enjoyed Arundel and said, 'You were lady-in-waiting.' This pleased me, for though naturally I had regarded myself as such, I thought perhaps <u>they</u> had merely considered it all right for PE to go down alone, since I would be in the car anyway. There were only about 120 people. There was a piper who

---

* Brian Gething was the nephew of Lady Joan Philipps, née Fitzwilliam, and was Alathea's age. The families threw them together regularly but to no avail.

† Lady Hyde, née the Hon. Marion Glyn, was Woman of the Bedchamber to Queen Elizabeth.

played Scottish reels for us, which I <u>adored,</u> and we were able to walk out on to the terrace all night, it was so warm. John Stanley asked me to dance twice, quite of his own accord – he seems to rather like me and I cannot deny I am flattered by this, as he is a man who pays little attention to any woman outside his own set, and I am v. far from being his type. Many people dislike him because he is so superior, but I prefer him infinitely to his brother Richard – in fact, he is the only gentleman of my acquaintance whom I can find it in my heart to admire. The dance ended in a different manner from all the preceding ones – the band went away at four without playing 'God Save The King' and then Andrew Elphinstone played the piano and we had the gramophone. The K and Q had gone and so had a great many people, though a great many others did not <u>like</u> to leave and so stayed on till the princesses said goodbye at <u>five</u>. Everyone seemed to prefer the <u>other</u> way, as it had <u>dragged</u> on <u>too</u> long and all were <u>wanting</u> to go away and wondering whether they could. It was broad daylight outside, which gave rather a sordid ending to an otherwise lovely evening.

Saturday, 11 August

Mrs Woolcombe wants me to return to Queensmead for a couple of weeks after my holiday – I asked if it would <u>really</u> only be for that time and they said I could leave on 17 September. I was <u>miserable</u> at having to return to this wretched place after having set my heart on going and terrified at the prospect of coming back into their clutches again. Had to Tube to the flat and dressed very hurriedly. (Wore my painted net.) I walked along to the Dorchester where I was dining with Sir Algar Howard,[*] Lady Howard and their two daughters. PE. was dining there too with the Leghs in quite a large party. We went through to the ballroom and did not remain in our own parties so I saw everyone I knew and enjoyed it enormously. PE told me that should peace be declared with Japan, which is imminent, they will naturally have to be up in London for VJ Day and therefore unable to dine on Tuesday. She is tremendously energetic at dances, hardly <u>ever</u> sitting down at all, and this is as much due to her fear of disappointing the many young men who come up in rows to ask her.

Tuesday, 14 August

PE rang up at ten to say they were able to dine as the official reply from Japan is still delayed. I went home at five and wrote two letters before Rosary. Grandpa told me that poor Aunt Gwen is very ill and, though she is not in <u>bed</u>, Bernard does not think she will last very long. I am very sad about it. Zelda arrived at eight and also John Ashley-Cooper,[†] who is charming. The princesses came at eight fifteen alone. PE looked lovely in her black dress and PM wore her yellow muslin, with the green velvet bows. She was in high spirits and quite adorable. I wore my lime green crêpe dress, which PE had not seen before, and she admired it. Dinner went v. well and afterwards we played games. Daddy was so hopeless at them, poor darling, that it was terribly funny, only I was rather embarrassed! John A-C made all the difference to the evening, as he gave that added stimulant and joviality that only a man can on such occasions.

---

[*] Sir Algar Howard was a distant Howard cousin and Garter King of Arms.
[†] John Ashley-Cooper was the son of the Earl of Shaftesbury.

Wednesday, 15 August

<u>Victory over Japan</u> was proclaimed at midnight and these two days as holidays. So our dinner party was <u>just</u> in time, though my hair appointment today was naturally doomed! Mrs Loyd very kindly fetched Z and me in the car and drove us to Queensmead, where we had to work as usual. On duty till eight thirty, when I went down to the town and I stopped in the doorway of a pub to listen to the King's speech. Everyone was making such a clatter with their drinks and talking and not paying the slightest attention. In the end I walked right inside to hear better and when they played 'God Save The King' at the end not <u>one</u> person got up, not even soldiers in uniform. Boiling with rage, I stood as stiff and erect as I could and then walked quickly out. The rest of the evening we walked about, watched the fireworks. Although there were crowds there was not so much gaiety or noise as on VE night and I myself felt extremely dispassionate and thought it a deadly day. The first enthusiasm that one felt over the German defeat is passed and the people have had a taste of the difficulties of the peace.

Blair Drummond, Scotland

Saturday, 18 August

The train journey to Scotland seemed endless and we arrived at Blair Drummond in time for lunch. I have the same lovely room I had last year. We walked to the garden before tea. It was so warm that we all wore cotton frocks, so I was glad I'd brought one.

Sunday, 19 August

Went to Doune to Mass: the church was filled with Polish soldiers, who sang lustily in Polish! I did my tapestry and wrote my diary and then we all went for a walk by the river until tea, and after this Mrs McGrath,* who is also staying there, took me up to her room to show me photographs of the Bahamas, where she has built a house – in fact she is responsible for Mummy's craze to buy land out there. I like her very much – she is intense, vivid, dramatic, fearfully affected but very kind. I enjoy meeting varied and opposite types of people – it makes life so much more interesting and also develops one's own character. Why is it that I have so much success here, whereas at dances and with my own generation I have none at all? I know their admiration is sincere and that they understand me, while with so many young people I feel there is an insurmountable barrier between us, which they are incapable and, in any case, unwilling to surmount, and if I do make an effort or attempt to do so, I am miserable and out of place.

Friday, 24 August

We talked a lot today of the European situation, the Balkans and the Russian menace to England. I wondered whether individual happiness can count any more – sorrows connected with marriage and personal griefs seem so utterly dwarfed and inconsequent besides the enormity of the despair of tormented Europe and the future of our own poor genera-

---

* Mrs McGrath was born Rosita Torr. She was a travel writer and novelist. She married Robert Forbes in 1911. They divorced and she married Colonel Arthur McGrath in 1921.

tion too vast and insecure to allow for any concrete hopes
or plans.

Houghton

Monday, 27 August

With great sorrow I left Blair Drummond. They are all so
angelic to me there and though I am less than half their age
I feel so happy and almost like one of them. Ate sandwiches,
read and slept in the train then changed for Market Weighton.
I met Ursula James and we arrived at Houghton together.
Saw my darling Ming-Ming who is v. well and delighted to
see me again.

Tuesday, 28 August

Letter from PM thanking me for the pink shell I sent her
for her birthday. It was short but v. sweet.

Wednesday, 29 August

Elizabeth Anne is going to the Assumption convent at
Aldenham in Shropshire next term and I think it will be a
success and, again, small and very <u>unschooly.</u>

Saturday, 1 September

Went out blackberrying with EA in the morning, and in the
afternoon we went for a walk with Ming-Ming. We played
bridge after dinner, which I enjoyed. The entire conversation
still revolves round the Poles and the Bahamas but I'm glad
to see that other people do not <u>altogether</u> share Mummy's

gloomy view of the future and quite reprove her when she talks of England as a sinking ship.

Sunday, 2 September

Mass at ten fifteen. I always love the chapel here.* Afterwards I went to talk to Ming-Ming in the nursery and she advises me strongly to try and make my own life, as otherwise she foresees only greater friction and unhappiness. She told me that Mummy said that I am old-maidish and governessy and <u>far</u> worse than I used to be, and that I make <u>her</u> feel like a schoolgirl. I know she is all the time comparing me with EA, who is so much more like her than I am, and now she will not, or cannot, see that my genre does appeal to some people. The result is that, with her, I lose <u>all</u> confidence and feel my whole individuality being sapped as well. It is a hopeless situation and I can see no remedy for it.

Cumberland Lodge

Monday, 3 September

I arrived in time for tea. I had a bath and changed into uniform before dinner and the car took me to Queensmead at ten. I didn't mind returning much this time, as it is only for a fortnight. I was still sleeping with Zelda and we had lots to talk about.

---

* Alathea's mother later had the chapel pulled down.

Wednesday, 5 September

We all had a perfectly foul day with this enormous Red Cross fête in the garden for which we had to cut sandwiches, serve teas and be generally run off our feet from seven thirty in the morning till nine at night. I got appalling indigestion from so much bready food, as we fed on the remains for supper too.

Friday, 7 September

We had a very gloomy argument at dinner about the future of England. I said very little actually as it was hopeless to even <u>try</u> and counterbalance Daddy's ideas. I am desperately sorry for Daddy – he is the saddest man I ever met.

Sunday, 16 September

The long-awaited last day at Queensmead has come and gone! I worked from eight till five and said all my goodbyes. Dear old Mrs Hambrook's farewells and those of the Bathurst staff were quite sad. Mrs Bathurst's maid, Miss Watkins, and Fanny* were truly sorry to see Z and me go, as they always said we were their favourites!

Monday, 17 September

Daddy had a letter this morning from Lady Winterton† to whom he had written about a flat and she offered to take

---

* Fanny also worked for Mrs Bathurst.
† Lady Winterton, born the Hon. Cecilia Wilson, was married to Earl Winterton, who as an Irish peer, could be a member of the House of Commons and later a cabinet minister.

me in her house in Eccleston Square. It is most kind and a wonderful relief to feel really settled, even temporarily, and I like Lady W very much.

Sunday, 30 September

I arrived at Dyneley yesterday.* Aunt Joey has made her little sitting room into a chapel, which is too sweet. I went to Confession and Communion and afterwards had breakfast with the priest. Then I did my tapestry and talked to Aunt J. In the afternoon I read the Sunday papers aloud and later took myself for a long walk up the hills. I <u>love</u> the country up here, which reminds me of dear Derwent.† It also reminds me of my last, very happy visit here just before the war with the boys‡ and it makes me a little sad to think of it as we were all so young and irresponsible then, and though we were on the edge of the world war, are we any better off today? There is great trouble brewing between the Jews and the Arabs in Palestine now.

Monday, 1 October

Perry [Worsthorne] arrived and we spent the evening gossiping. Simon has already sailed for Palestine.

---

* Dyneley was in Lancashire, where her great-aunt Aunt Joey, Lady Alice Bertie, lived. Lady Alice was the sister of Alathea's late grandmother, Lady Fitzalan.

† Derwent in Derbyshire had been the family estate of the Fitzalans but was compulsorily purchased and drowned by a reservoir, which must have added to her father's gloom.

‡ Simon and Peregrine Worsthorne, Aunt Joey's grandsons.

Wednesday, 3 October

Perry left which was sad but I liked seeing him again – he is v. good looking and has great charm now. Aunt Joey tells me P is a great admirer of Catherine Macmillan.[*] I personally think she is revolting to look at and her behaviour worse.

Monday, 8 October

I arrived at Houghton at five and had tea. Just Mummy, Grandpa and Aunt Alathea here. Mummy has been <u>much</u> pleasanter to me this time – she told Ming-Ming I am a different person with my hair parted on the side and that I'm greatly improved and less governessy since I've been away from the atmosphere of Cumberland Lodge – this is nonsense but I think it's the effect of my hair, as it did irritate her the other way.

Cumberland Lodge

Friday, 12 October

Went to Queensmead. It seemed very strange to be there as a stranger! But I am <u>thankful</u> I have left as now, with all their new staff, they have rotas typed out and pinned on to our door and I could not bear this! Bussed and walked home and read till Rosary. Changed for dinner. The dullness and futility of the conversation here makes me tremble.

---

[*] Catherine Macmillan was the daughter of Harold Macmillan, later prime minister. She married the Conservative politician Julian Amery.

Saturday, 13 October

I set off for London by train and I felt that curious, sick feeling of excitement because this day really marked the beginning of a new life for me and somehow I knew it would be a success. It is a complete break from the old routine and surely new opportunities must offer themselves. I arrived at Mrs Wyndham's flat in Sloane Square at six. Mollie Wyndham-Quin* was sharing a room with me – I hadn't met her before and found her sweet. She has beautiful hair and skin. We had a buffet dinner for about eighteen people, very few of whom I knew and then we went on to a dance at 23 Knightsbridge. We went by <u>bus,</u> which amused me greatly, and luckily the other passengers were good-humoured and kindly. One of our party was Robert Cecil – he danced with me, and soon after that Mollie asked me to go on to the 400 with them. We stayed there till four and as we were leaving Mollie asked me if I'd mind her dropping me home and then leaving me (because we had to share the key) because she'd <u>just got engaged</u> to Robert Cecil! Life works itself out in strange ways – I never thought, five years ago, when my heart was stirred for the first time by Robert Cecil that I would be in the same party with him when he proposed to another and be the first to know their secret. I can imagine no greater happiness than being engaged to RC. I still think he's the most attractive man I've ever met, and I consider Mollie the luckiest girl in England in <u>every</u> respect.

---

* Marjorie (Mollie) Wyndham-Quin was the daughter of Captain the Hon. Valentine Wyndham-Quin and was brought up mainly in Ireland. She was a famous beauty and became a well-known gardener.

61 Eccleston Square

Monday, 15 October

I went off by bus at nine to Wimborne House, Foreign Relations Department of the Red Cross. I was put in the German-Austrian Section, which I liked, and my work consisted of carding – writing cards out for all the people who have either enquired after, or have been enquired after by, their relations in Germany and Austria. It was muddling at first, but everyone was v. kind and helpful, though there are a great many people working in the room, so they don't take much notice of one. I had lunch in the canteen in the basement. The house is lovely – or must once have been – with endless richly decorated reception rooms in the style of the eighteenth century. The room I work in looks over the Green Park and has walls of red silk and a magnificent ceiling of red, blue and gold mosaic. I left at five thirty and went on to Lady Winterton's at 61 Eccleston Square, where I am to live for the next two months. She showed me my room and after I'd unpacked, she took me round to a little Italian restaurant where we had dinner. She was very kind but slightly alarming and, of course, one does miss the comforts of home and the absence of the ordinary dinner and evening in company made me feel a little friendless and alone. I came up to bed early and then sat and wrote my diary in my fur coat over a chiffon nightgown because my dressing-gown has not yet come! My room is large and comfortable with a telephone and writing-table.

Wednesday, 17 October

I was put on the Czech table today, which I did not like so much as there were only deportation forms to card and no letters to read. My cold was so bad that it was a great struggle to get through the day at all. I came back and went straight to bed with just an apple to eat and the evening paper, feeling more ill than words can say. Lady W came up and was so kind – she insisted on giving me a hot whisky and some tablets.

Friday, 19 October

I worked till six. Lunched with Daddy at Pruniers. He seems to have lost all patience with life now and even a civilised control – this is very painful to me and I cannot see how he will overcome it. I hope gradually my life will get into its stride – I would not admit it to anyone, but I am finding London terribly lonely so far. Other people seem to have hundreds of friends to ask them out, but I always seem so desperately alone. I cannot see how it is possible to find a husband for myself – I would so much prefer to have a suitable one produced for me and then make the best of life. I have always believed one has as good a chance of happiness that way and often better, than through a marriage of one's own choice.

Monday, 22 October

I saw a message from Crawfie, so I had to ring her up and she asked me to come to drawing again as usual on Thursday. I had resolutely made my mind a blank concerning this, determined not to speculate, nor to be either surprised or disappointed in the result. I met Joe Dormer at the Berkeley and we went to see *Private Lives* by Noël Coward, which I loved, then we dined at the Bagatelle, then went on to the 400 where we drank J's own Champagne from Germany. He brought me back at three thirty. Exactly nine hours alone with Joe is certainly a strain – he <u>is</u> an unattractive, dull creature – but it makes an evening out and I extracted some more coupons out of him! He suggested going out again the next night, but I said no, though I agreed to next week.

Tuesday, 23 October

I overslept and had an awful rush to get to work! Worked till six then bussed to Westminster to Grandpa's new flat, 61 Westminster Gardens. He and Aunt Magdalen now spend two nights each week there. I was agreeably surprised with it all and we had a delicious dinner – sent up from Cumberland Lodge.

Thursday, 25 October

I taxied to the Palace at two thirty and drew still life with P. Margaret in the <u>passage,</u> because they haven't yet got proper windows back in their rooms[*] and it was too dark! I talked to her afterwards in the nursery and heard all about Scotland, but I didn't stay to tea as they were engaged and PE was out.

---

[*] During the war, on account of the bombing, the windows had been boarded up.

Friday, 26 October

I am now installed on the Czech table, which also deals with Russians, Latvians, Estonians and Lithuanians and I like it very much.

Saturday, 27 October

Worked till one, then rushed off to Windsor for Diana Legh's wedding. Went straight to the Crichtons' where I changed. I wore my green dress, brown coat and my new hat of brown net and ribbon and autumn-coloured flowers, which looked rather pretty. We had places in the front row, which <u>faced</u> the aisle in the outer part of the chapel. Diana Legh arrived in a royal carriage and looked very pale and small, and <u>alluring,</u> without being pretty, in a dress of oyster-coloured satin and a beautiful lace veil, held in place by a band of pearls. The bridegroom, Johnny Kimberley[*] looked awful, so like a fish. The King and Queen and the princesses were in the front part of the church, but they came out down the aisle after the bride and before the family, and everyone curtsied. We walked up to the Castle and the reception was held in the Red, Green and White Drawing Rooms, with a buffet in the dining room beyond. The King proposed the toast and the bridegroom replied to it in quite a good and dignified speech, but he has no charm. I spoke to PE and saw lots of friends.

---

[*] John Wodehouse, Earl of Kimberley, left her after a year and went on to marry five more times.

Thursday, 1 November

Zelda came for the first time and works in the same room. I didn't take my lunch hour today as I left at two to go to the Palace. Drawing went well and I saw PE after, in v. good spirits, having just returned from three days at Newmarket. I gather I shall not stay to tea now, as they have it with the K and Q, and today, for instance, Queen Mary was there. This is sad, as I used to enjoy it so much – we were so gay and happy – but perhaps occasionally the K and Q will be away and surely too there will be a few parties which I shall be asked to?

Monday, 5 November

Went to the Berkeley to meet Joe Dormer. I wore my long black dress. He had ordered a Rolls to drive us from place to place and we dined at the Savoy. He had to catch the train to Dover, as he was returning to Germany and he kept saying what a maddening curse it was we couldn't stay at the Savoy till twelve and then go on to the 400 – I was heartily thankful and enjoyed my evening because it was so short! It is unfortunate that Joe is the only man who ever takes me out and I still see no possibility of meeting any more. He gave me twelve coupons, which was something, and I said goodbye to him at Victoria station. I felt rather sorry for the little man, as I believe he is fond of me and I suppose not many women bother about him.

Thursday, 8 November

Walked to the Palace. We drew Crawfie but Princess M left early and I didn't see PE today. I used to look forward so much to Thursdays but now, though I wouldn't give it up for all the world, it is rather a sad and depressing day. On the way back I had to go to Caxton Hall about my ration book and the woman was so rude that it somehow increased my deep sense of loneliness and I had to force back my tears all the way home.

Saturday, 17 November

I rang up PE. at Royal Lodge to ask them to tea on Sunday week. She was so sweet and I'm really glad to be coming down here on my own for my birthday and having them to tea.

Thursday, 22 November

Today was rather an exciting day – I arrived at Wimborne House [where she was working] at nine to hear burglars had come into our room and ransacked all the papers, etc., and burned some of them for light! Luckily no one had left anything of value in the drawers. We weren't allowed to touch anything because of fingerprints until the police had been. Later on, all our filing had to be moved to another room because the floor of our present one is in danger of collapsing due to dry rot! PE rang up to say that poor PM had her appendix out today – in the nursery! So, they won't be able to come to tea on Sunday, as PE will probably be remaining in London. Apparently, it wasn't sudden, and she is going on v. well. It is sad about Sunday, but they are coming some other time. I got a taxi to Quaglino's, where

I met Annabel, Charles Stourton* and John Wiggin for A's party – she is twenty-three today. We dined and danced and then went along to the 400. It really was a great success and we all enjoyed it.

Friday, 23 November

At six I went to the Wigmore Hall for my birthday concert – Elizabeth Lumley came and Anne Anson and Rosemary Lyttelton.† It was all Mozart and I <u>adored</u> it – I could have sat there all night listening to it. We had supper afterwards at Manetta's, which was v. good, and then Skip [Elizabeth Lumley] and I bussed back together. I was v. pleased with my little party and I think they all liked it.

Saturday, 24 November

<u>My 22nd Birthday.</u>
I went to work as usual but I met E. Lumley and we lunched at the Berkeley Buttery. I returned home and found a lovely box of white handkerchiefs from Zelda. I wrote letters and read and went out later to have some tea, as I was cold and hungry. I began dressing at six thirty, under the utmost difficulties, as the lights had fused; the geyser wouldn't work owing to a gas strike, so I had to wash in a saucepan full of boiling water! Wore my blue lace. Charles Stourton fetched me and we drove to Quaglino's where we

---

* The Hon. Charles Stourton, later Baron Mowbray, Segrave and Stourton, premier baron of England, was a cousin of Alathea's mother.
† The Hon. Rosemary Lyttelton was a daughter of Viscount Chandos and the sister of Alathea's friend Julian, who was killed in 1944.

dined – had oysters – and went on to Lady Somers's[*] dance at 23 Knightsbridge. I enjoyed it enormously – it was one of the best I've been to. PE was there in a new dress of flowered taffeta, very pretty; she wished me many happy returns of the day.

BIRTHDAY PRESENTS

2 small silver boxes, one plain, the other embossed	Aunt Magdalen
Pale green and white striped ninon skirt, and white lawn shirt with narrow panels of lace let in	Mummy and Daddy
Pale blue flared skirt	Gpa
Lipstick and blue beret	Sonia
4 white handkerchiefs	Zelda
Safety pins on a stand	Billy
Green leather belt	Annabel

Sunday, 25 November

I caught the twelve o'clock train to Egham and got home to Cumberland Lodge for lunch. I had a letter from Mummy, saying I must remain here for Christmas, which <u>greatly</u> disappoints me, as I had so wanted to go to Houghton! Changed for dinner and we drank Champagne but Daddy began one of his gloomy discourses, this time on the futility of buying

---

[*] Lady Somers was widowed in 1944. Her only daughter, Elizabeth, for whom the party was given, was the heiress of Eastnor Castle in Herefordshire and went on to marry Major Benjamin Hervey-Bathurst.

any Christmas presents because 'life isn't worth it'; Aunt Magdalen was ill-humoured because she had no cigarettes to smoke and she said something that hurt me too and quite suddenly I could bear it no longer and burst into tears – Aunt M was immediately sorry but Daddy only said, 'Shut up!' He is so kind in some ways and yet <u>never</u> was there a person so lacking in <u>understanding</u>. Lord, I am miserable in this family – why has it suddenly got so much worse? My mother asked in her letter if none of these young men were flirting with me and then said she was sure something nice would happen to me one day because I am so kind and good. Anyone would think I had <u>no</u> other attractions whatever and it isn't even true – I see myself sometimes as bad-tempered, scheming and greedy.

Thursday, 29 November

Walked to the Palace at two thirty for drawing. I took PM a book and she asked me to go in and see her. She looked v. sweet in bed surrounded by flowers and presents.

Friday, 30 November

The whole world is dark, socialistic and hopeless. I worked till six and then went home but I walked in the opposite direction in the dark, which was most annoying!

Tuesday, 4 December

The papers were full of PE's first visit to the Bagatelle and photographs of her there and in the theatre. It was the Wills's party, I believe, and I had heard of it beforehand from Sonia, whom Myra Wernher had told. I dislike hearing things of this kind from Sonia, I don't know why.

Monday, 10 December

Went home to Cumberland Lodge for the night. Had an invitation to a dance at Buck House on Friday, also to Robert Cecil's wedding on 18 December. I was exhausted but it was nice to spend a night at home.

Tuesday, 11 December

Daddy and I drove up to London and I went straight to Wimborne House. Had a letter from Mummy. She annoys me in almost every line and somehow since I have been in London I have felt more strongly against her than usual, for no real reason, but perhaps because I now really am on my own, I feel more hurt and embittered by her, whereas I used to just ignore it. She said: 'Why don't those princesses ask you to a theatre?' I hate her referring to them like that and also it wounds me in a sore spot, especially as the next morning the papers had more glaring headlines of the princesses' night out in a small party. Naturally they cannot always ask me, but I always fear PE will forget me and what I mind most is the fact that other people expect one to go and I suppose because I am proud and jealous I suffer intensely inwardly. *C'est quelquefois terrible d'être l'amie d'une princesse.* [It is sometimes terrible to be the friend of a princess.]

Friday, 14 December

Had a bath and then rested on my bed till eight thirty. Wore the painted net with the black velvet bands and my crystal locket hung round my neck on a black ribbon. The Lumleys called for me and we drove to the Palace. We all waited in the corridor and the Royal Family received us in the Bow Room. The Queen and PE were in black because Lady Southesk* died today. PM was not there as she is not yet well enough to dance. The King wore naval uniform. Everybody noticed how long he danced with Vi de Trafford† and as a rule he v. rarely chooses girls as his partners! He did this last time at Windsor too – it is a singular triumph for Vi and I must say she deserves it, as she was by far the most beautiful girl in the room – she wore plain black velvet with a white flower. There were fewer people than usual which left the floor wonderfully clear – many familiar ones were absent, Anne Anson, Joan Philipps (because of divorce?), Sonia, Diana Legh, Sarah Dashwood. There were a lot of new young girls, who have just come out, which I think is quite right. The men were all very young – it is odd how even there I meet none of the men I would like to. There were two pipers and we danced reels and, on the whole, I enjoyed it greatly, though I cannot say wildly. A person that I like very much better than I used to is Peter Townsend – he danced with me and we got on very well.

Jean Gibbs was there and, try as I would, I could not rid myself of a deep, painful envy of her. It still seems to me

---

* Princess Maud, Countess of Southesk, was a daughter of Princess Louise, Duchess of Fife, and thus a first cousin of King George V.
† Vi de Trafford was the daughter of Sir Humphrey de Trafford.

unfair that what I longed so passionately for should have been granted to one who never gave it a thought before and who never even knew any of the Royal Family. I have come now to believe that I have never really got over this death blow to the first of my two dearest wishes – the hope of it kept me alive and buoyed me up for so many years and now that I have finally admitted defeat it has left a dark blank, which I am seeking desperately and so far vainly to fill by a successful marriage.

Sunday, 16 December

Went to Claridges Causerie to lunch. Brita joined us (I had seen her last night) and we saw several other people we knew. B came home with me and we talked in my room for a bit. It was fun seeing her again. She said there really is a plan for her to go to Sweden next winter and I <u>might</u> be able to go with her. I hardly dare to hope but it would be quite wonderful.

Tuesday, 18 December

Put on my wide brown hat and new red shoes and drove with Grandpa and Aunt M to the Abbey for Robert Cecil and Mollie Wyndham-Quin's wedding. We had v. good places and it was the loveliest wedding I've been to, I think. Mollie looked beautiful in ivory satin and lace and Robert was <u>not</u> in uniform. There were hundreds of people there and everyone was frightfully smart – there were a great many hats with ostrich plumes, which were v. pretty. Grandpa was quite intolerable – he is far too old to go about now.

Saturday, 22 December

Arrived at Cumberland Lodge in time for tea. Elizabeth Anne there but somehow I wish she <u>wasn't</u>, because I know she doesn't like it here and she will hardly let me out of her sight. I had an enormous pile of Christmas cards to open, including a lovely one from the princesses, with a photograph of them both in evening dress on a staircase and their initials and coronets on the outside.

Sunday, 23 December

EA is sweet really and I do love her but being with her all the time I find her extremely tiresome and she has grown up so much lately and she reminds me so much of Mummy. We are terribly different and as she grows older, I am afraid this is going to cause a breach between us.

Tuesday, 25 December

We all had breakfast in bed – EA came along to me and we opened our presents in bed. Unfortunately, her stocking etc is all up at Houghton. I had a lovely <u>dark red</u> Wedgwood jar from Daddy. Mummy gave me a vanity case, which I <u>don't</u> like. EA and I went for a long walk before lunch and in the afternoon we stayed in and listened to the King's Speech, which was v. good and gave the servants their presents. At four we had Benediction and then tea after which EA and I did her jigsaw puzzle till time to dress for dinner. We had turkey and plum pudding and sherry and port to drink but I do long for a gay Christmas again, with lots of young people and lots of children. It is so long since I have known this. I have almost forgotten what it is like.

Saturday, 29 December

Zelda and I lunched at the Green Park snack bar and then we went to her house. We wrote in the nursery till tea and at six we had our baths and dressed. I wore my lime green crêpe. Had supper together and afterwards a taxi took us to Farnham Common, for the dance got up in the hall by the village families. There were one or two nice people there, including a charming boy in the Life Guards called Dunlop[*], who took a violent fancy to Zelda and thanked her afterwards for such an enjoyable evening and hoped to see her again! Z was undoubtedly the highlight of the evening – she looked so fresh and young and happy, whereas I felt jaded and ill as I had another cold beginning and I have lost all my illusions, while Zelda still cherishes many and there is a certain naivety about her which is wholly charming.

---

[*] Malcolm Dunlop, whom she later married in 1954.

Afterword

In May 1945 Alathea reflected on what the end of the war meant for her life:

I am wondering whether the Royal Family will remain at Windsor this summer and whether Princess Elizabeth will now spend most of the week in London. I hope drawing may begin next week and I should <u>think</u> they would keep Windsor open till they go to Scotland and then return permanently to the Palace in the autumn. My own horizon at the moment is clouded and unsettled – for so long now, all one's grown-up life. One's vision has been bounded by the end of the war and now that it has come, I feel rather lost and insecure. That it spells changes, I cannot doubt – indeed I <u>want</u> them – but in what shape and form my life will carry on I cannot foresee – it is as if one had woken from a long dream and found oneself in an epoch far distant from one's own, which one knew so well, so that a sea of bewilderment engulfed one and one could not even be sure of one's most immediate footsteps. And that dark interval, the dream itself, though past and in no way forming part of one's life, was too real to be forgotten, and in fact it stretched its long, cold fingers over the span of decades and generations, shrivelling and freezing all that had once bloomed in a fairer garden, the conscious and the unconscious alike.

Alathea's life was not easy after 1945. Her wish for a grand marriage eluded her and she married a younger son in 1953 – in a register office, as her husband had been married before. Her greatest wish in life was to have children but, sadly, none arrived. She once intimated to me that had we met earlier in her child-bearing years (I am the mother of six children) she could never have been my friend. Her marriage was not a happy one, as her husband was a tricky man, but they stayed together and she cared for him until he died.

She never became a lady-in-waiting. Whether it was because she was Catholic, impractical or not quite robust enough, I just don't know. Perhaps it was always a false hope, though I'd have thought she'd have been very good in some sort of position at Court. In her own way she regretted this. 'It occurs to me sometimes that my diary would make very dull reading these days,' she wrote in 1982, 'and had I been made lady-in-waiting to The Queen, as at one time seemed to me and to others not only possible but probable, it would one day be really worth reading. Well, *tant pis*, it's a need I can't give up.'

She was invited to Princess Elizabeth's wedding in 1947 and in her diary there are descriptions of the dress and the service. She writes that 'The solemn beauty of the ceremonial and quiet pageantry were impressive but over and above all shone the sublime happiness of the Princess.' She also described the other guests and the response of the crowds in the streets: 'I noticed Don Juan's [the Count of Barcelona] wife who is very royal-looking with her huge Bourbon nose . . . as soon as I got home I rushed to the balcony to cheer them. The excitement and crowds were terrific and people were wild with enthusiasm and affection. How good it was to see and what a wonderful day for Lilibet.' At the end of the day, she concludes, 'My thoughts are still very much with PE, her wish of so many years ago at last fulfilled. Yet it is hard to realise that she is married, when once she seemed so much younger than me, and even at Windsor, for all her dignity and self-possession, she was so very immature.'

When Alathea was told of the King's death on 6 February 1952 it was a great shock to her even though she knew he had been ill:

She is now Queen and returns from Kenya by plane immediately . . . I pity her with all my heart, the horror of this news when she was happily relaxing at the hunting lodge . . . with all she has to face the moment she steps out of the plane. When she wrote to me after her engagement, she said, 'It is also a great comfort to me to know that in times that are not so easy, there will be someone to whom I can turn.' I only hope that he will be a help to her now, no man could have a better wife, nor the Queen a better daughter, and nor England a better Queen.

The following day Alathea wrote to the new Queen: 'I began Your Majesty and I can no longer put with love from,' she confided to her diary, 'but I wrote the rest of it as simply as possible, for I write to her as a friend, who constantly saw how much she loved her father.' On 8 February: 'The Queen was proclaimed this morning as Elizabeth II. Poor thing, how tired and harrowed she must be.'

Alathea watched The King's funeral procession on 15 February from the second floor of Scott's restaurant in Piccadilly:

The whole thing was very sad and moving, I thought all the time of the strain and sorrow of the poor little Queen and her mother.

There is something so much sadder about it than a normal passing of an elderly monarch – he was only 56 and he died because the life of a King was too hard for his constitution. His family adored him and lived to serve him and his daughter is a young and lonely figure who commands the admiration, respect and affection of the whole world.

She went to the memorial service later that afternoon in Westminster Abbey, The King having been buried at Windsor. She described the service as 'simple and fine'.

Alathea wasn't asked to the Coronation and writes, as her mother leaves, all dressed up: 'Once upon a time I too would have been invited but my star waned a long time ago.' Instead she watched the service on television and went to see the balcony appearance, recalling that 'despite the rain the crowd was dense and the people mad with joy'.

Alathea's friendship with The Queen persisted to the end of her life. In 1999 she gave a small cocktail party for The Queen in a family flat in Ennismore Gardens. I asked her if I could help in any way, perhaps with the canapés. She said she had everything organised with Marks & Spencer – frozen canapés, which would have been perfectly all right had she thawed them. When The Queen arrived, Alathea gave rather a feeble curtsy, as she had twisted her leg skiing. The Queen suggested arnica. When The Queen departed and Alathea curtsied again, The Queen said, 'That was much better than the last one!'

Her last entry in the diaries was on 25 January 2001 and she died thirty-nine days later, aged seventy-seven.

The other day, I went to Alathea's Grove. It is a little plantation of six oak saplings planted in her memory a year or two after she died, with the help of our children. They are arranged in the lee of a wood here at Milton and have grown well. I told her about the diaries and how I thought she had been the greatest of aunts and great-aunts.

Alathea, in 1983, with Tom and Violet,
her great nephew and niece.

Acknowledgements

I would like to thank the following people, without whom this book would never have got off the ground:

Richard James for transcribing the diaries, starting in 2010. He completed fourteen of them over five years and I'm very grateful that he took on the task.

Charlotte Mosley for giving me invaluable advice and pointing me in the direction of Zuleika.

Tom Perrin for his enthusiasm and just being the kindest and most diplomatic. Rowena Webb, Karen Geary and Ian Wong at Hodder and Stoughton who have been nothing but encouraging.

Lesley Hodgson for her help with the pictures and Mouse Vickers for reproduction work. Hannah Gates for completely getting Alathea and believing in her as a writer. She was so obliging and never missed a trick. Eleo Carson for her good company and solid and tireless advice on everything publishing. Sarah Molloy for her helpful time and trouble. Florence Houston for her wonderful map.

Philip for his wisdom, good English, technical support and putting up with me and my malapropisms. And my children for all their interest and support.

I would finally like to thank Celestria Noel, who despite being a friend, has been so professional and delightful to work with, endlessly open minded and a shoulder to lean on and share many decisions with.

Isabella Naylor-Leyland
July 2020

Picture Acknowledgements

Insets

Courtesy of *Country Life*, 1947: 4, above. © Lisa Sheridan/ Studio Lisa/Getty Images: 4, middle; 5, below; 7, below. Courtesy of Hulton-Deutsch Collection/CORBIS/Corbis via Getty Images: 4, below. © Royal Collection Trust / All Rights Reserved: 5, middle; 7, below. © Granger Historical Picture Archive/Alamy Stock Photo: 6, below. © William Hustler and Georgina Hustler/National Portrait Gallery, London: 8.

All other images are from the author's collection.

Chapter images

Author's collection:

viii: portrait of Alathea from her 19th birthday, 1942. 112: Invitation to the inspection of the Foot Guards by Princess Elizabeth, 1942. 174: group picture at Queensmead, 1943. 220: Invitation to a dance at Windsor Castle, 1944. 278: handwritten page from Alathea's diary, 1945. 337: Alathea with her great nephew and niece, 1983.

Additional sources:

2: Thank-you letter from Princess Elizabeth to Alathea, 1940, © Royal Collection Trust / All Rights Reserved. 60: Cast of characters for pantomime *Cinderella*, 1941, © Royal Collection Trust / All Rights Reserved.

—————— This book was created by ——————

Hodder & Stoughton

Founded in 1868 by two young men who saw that the rise in literacy would break cultural barriers, the Hodder story is one of visionary publishing and globe-trotting talent-spotting, campaigning journalism and popular understanding, men of influence and pioneering women.

For over 150 years, we have been publishing household names and undiscovered gems, and today we continue to give our readers books that sweep you away or leave you looking at the world with new eyes.

Follow us on our adventures in books . . .
🐦 @HodderBooks 📘 /HodderBooks 📷 @HodderBooks

HODDER &
STOUGHTON

Errolston
School

The Royal School

Royal Lodge

All Saints Chapel

Cumberland Lodge

Smith's Lawn

Beaumont
School

ENGLEFIELD GREEN